By the same author:

Ancient but Modern
An anthology from Country Life
(out of print)

Living Stones
Reflections from the Holy Lands (1988)
100pp. Ilustrated. £3.00

First World, Last World
A Journey in the Third World (1989)
200pp. Illustrated. £4.95

Windows on The Sudan
A Story of Pain and Pride (1991)
164pp. Illustrated. £5.99

Wandering Like a Madman
Faith around the World (1992)
(out of print)

Su 'n Dan
A human saga of The Sudan (1993)
64pp. Illustrated. £2.99

Letters to God
A priest tells God all about it (1995)
115pp. Illustrated. £5.00

Available from
Sarum College Bookshop, 19 The Close, Salisbury SP1 2EE
or
the author at
36 Hound Street, Sherborne, Dorset DT9 3AA

CHURCH WARDENS I HAVE BURIED

The Journal of a Country Vicar
1998-99

TIMOTHY BILES

First published October 1999
Reprinted January 2000
Reprinted December 2000

© Timothy Biles

ISBN No. 0 9517915 4 0

Printed by Creeds the Printers, Broadoak, Bridport, Dorset. DT6 5NL

Acknowledgements

The author is grateful to

MYRTLE GILDERSLEVE
who typed the original manuscript

JOHN ANDERSON
*who drew all but one of
the illustrations*

CAROL BISS
for the drawing on page 135

COLIN CUFF
for the photograph used on the cover

JOAN BILES
for designing the cover

VIVIEN PRIESTLEY-SMITH
for her care and advice as proof reader

and all the parishioners who have helped tell the story by allowing their names to be used. Each one has been shown the text to ensure that there is no breach of confidence.

Cover picture: The church wardens' staves were given to Beaminster Church by Mrs. Brenda Travers in gratitude for the years she, and her husband Bob before her, served as church warden. They were made by Ron Emett of Beaminster.

With gratitude this book is dedicated to the memory of

Arthur Broughton
Bill Strawbridge
Bob Fry
Bob Travers
David Pearson
Dorothy Wallbridge
Eddie Hansford
Geoff Gale
Godfrey French
Harold Curtis
Harold Harris
Harry Hardwill
Herbert Yates
Jesse Davis
Jim Hardman
Kathleen Dyson
Ken Hackett
Kitty Grinter
Leonard Giles
Leonard Studley
Pierse Hayes
Reg Johnson
Ronald Johnston
Ronnie Wallbridge
Sid Bailey
Tom Best
Victor Thompson

the Church Wardens I have buried

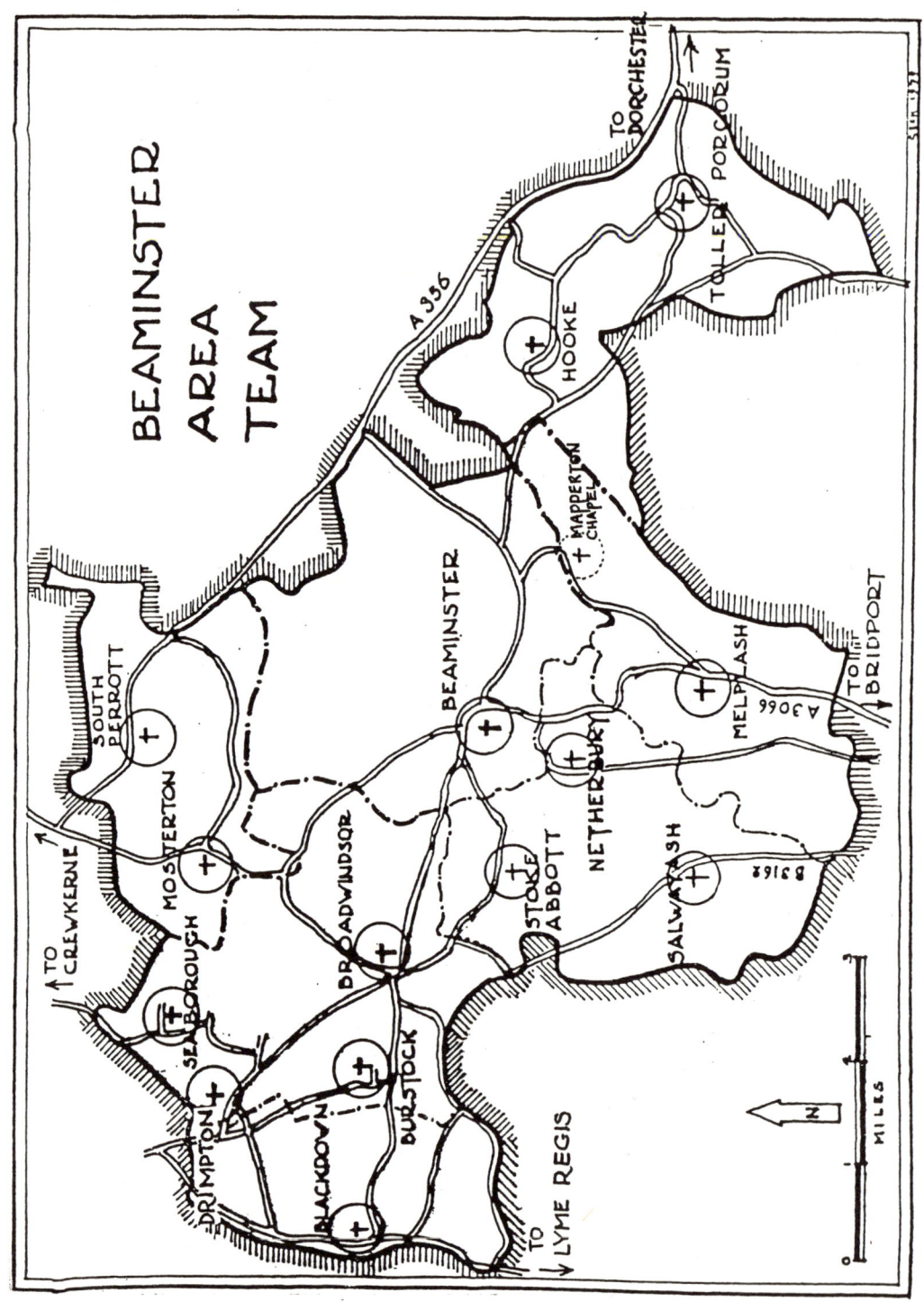

The Journal of a Country Vicar 1998-99

Tuesday, 13th October

This may not be the best day to start recording the life of a parish priest – it was not typical. Meetings of the Cathedral Canons are seldom exciting and today's meeting threatened to be more tedious than most. The agenda was the new Statutes which govern Cathedral constitutions. Sounded awful. But I was duty bound to be there.

The day began well enough with a visit to Creeds the Printers, at Broadoak. How lucky I am with Creeds! Not only have they printed our parish magazine each month for the last eighteen years but they have also produced six of my seven books, and an untold number of leaflets, guides and posters, and they have done it all with unfailing good humour.

If I was not doing the work I am doing, I would like to work at Creeds. They have retained a rare sense of family. Half the staff are blood relations and the other half always seem to be. No-one has bothered to update their building, which could revert to the chicken house it once was without any bother. It would never surprise me to see hens laying eggs in the litter of filing boxes all over the place. On the other hand, the technology has not only been updated, John Creed seems to have kept ahead of the game – and he does all the repairs and maintenance himself. He must be some sort of a technical genius. As he was first a farmer, it's all the more puzzling where he gets such skills from. Anyway, he hasn't only got them, he's passed them down the line and the next generation seem just as capable and just as good humoured. Sadly, I would never get a job there, even as an office boy. The technology has raced ahead and I am among the clergy who have been left behind.

Sometimes I think the clergy should have been pressed into training in computer technology. It is so evidently valuable and it is a major influence in shaping our day and age. But I am not a part of it. Years ago, my computer-clever nephew told me I was a 'hopeless case' and I realised that no matter how well I knew the New Testament in Greek, I was among the new illiterates. But in other ways I am pleased not to have been re-trained. I still hold a pen, write in longhand and scrunch the page up when I make an error or the words can be improved. The written repetition takes time but it clarifies thoughts and, by the time the Sunday sermon comes, I know every line by heart and I not only believe it, but I have an affection for it. I wouldn't want to sit in front of a screen and see all the words dancing around at the press of a button. I wouldn't love the product in the same way.

As usual, the visit to Creeds was cheering. I had asked for the magazine centre pages to be in full colour, for the first time. They had enjoyed the challenge and produced the proofs with pride. They had taken such care, adjusting the size of the photographs to balance the text in a way well beyond the call of duty. I imagine this is the sort of service which businesses used to provide and which has been overtaken by the supermarket self-service syndrome. Creeds are the perfect antidote. Long may they prosper!

By then, the time had passed and the train had gone so I had to drive the 66 miles to Salisbury, and arrive late.

It was embarrassing to walk in an hour after the meeting had begun when three bishops, four archdeacons, the dean and another 20 canons had all got there on time. I had missed the 'keynote' address (as they are called these days) and so I decided to stay silent as a penance. Besides, listening is under-practised. We clergy love to do the talking, and there were plenty there to do it. In fact the discussion about statutes was above my head and I wouldn't have spoken anyway. I recognise that rules and regulations have to be reviewed and reformed or we would become outdated. The Church (or cathedral in this case) would be left behind, in the same way that I am left behind by the computer revolution. So there have to be 'talking shops'. But sometimes I wonder if there is much else. There was something sad about the whole of the Diocesan 'top brass' debating their own roles. No doubt it was a necessary 'consultation' but I wondered whether we were complicating the simple. Anyway the lunch was excellent and it was was good to see familiar faces. I wouldn't want to miss these occasions twice a year but neither would I want them increased to four times a year, as someone proposed. We would only talk and talk and then talk some more. My African Godson Kilele, when he was 5, said "Uncle, you don't work. You just stand up and say things." It looked a little like that today among the College of Canons.

I gave Cathedral Evensong a miss because the mists were swirling around the spire and the long drive lay ahead. But on the way back I regretted it. Cathedral Evensong somehow symbolises Anglican tradition and our distinctive culture – the mysterious combination of music and liturgy so carefully prepared and beautifully offered. I was a fool to have missed it. How easily we take treasures for granted and overlook the blessings which surround us. Instead I tuned in to the News and heard about the vicious and almost unbelievable cruelty by Police to their dogs. Not at all edifying. In fact, plain disgusting! I wished I was in the Cathedral with the choir's prayers floating around me, instead of hearing such bestial stuff. Worship and escapism are near neighbours.

A little domestic disturbance awaited my return. "You didn't wear that jacket did you?" Joan reproached. "Why not?" I asked. "It's awful, and it doesn't go with those trousers," she continued. I couldn't see anything wrong with the jacket or the trousers. "Looks all right to me," I said. "It looks dreadful," she said. "Thank goodness I wasn't there." So she is going to take the jacket to Oxfam in the morning.

9

It was a mirror image of an incident with the Canons a little earlier. There had been a suggestion that all the Canons should be clothed in new robes with distinctive colour so that they look more distinguished in the processions. What nonsense!

Wednesday, 14th October

Today wasn't typical either! London trips for the Sudan Church Association meetings are but twice a year, and this was one of them.

I look forward to them – it's the train I enjoy. Two hours, uninterrupted, twice in the day! A good book to read; no telephone to ring, no visitors to call and no guilt about it. At home I would not settle – there would always be a letter to write, a visit to make, a sermon to think about, a meeting to prepare and the abiding sense of not having done the things I ought to have done. All these feelings fade as soon as the train takes the strain. It's bliss. Once, when pressure had built up I got into the train and went to Waterloo and back just because I knew I would not be got at. It had cost £19 and was worth every penny.

The meeting ran true to form. The Sudan Church Association is the only organisation which makes me feel young. The Chairman recently referred to me as the "virile young editor" of their magazine. As I am within a year of retirement, the remark said more about them than about me. Most of the membership knew The Sudan in the days before Independence, now forty-two years ago, which means they must be eighty or thereabouts. The marvel is that the years have not dimmed their affection for the land and the people they served. The sadness is that as they look at the present tragedy, the chaos and corruption on every side, they see their own life's work in ruins. Yet still they come, with here a crutch and there a hearing aid. There is a dignity about their bearing and an integrity in their speech which only emphasises that they are of another age. The regular list of Obituaries and the fall in the number of Covenantors relentlessly remind them that their day is done. The Chairman tells us of the decisions he has made between meetings. This time he has doubled the membership fee – from £5 to

£10. Those who heard, nod their assent. The present situation is reported – tribal wars in the South, on top of the official Civil War against the Islamists of the North. Atrocities and slavery, famine and disease, all commonplace. The old stalwarts who cleansed the country of such ills shake their heads. Brian Carlisle, the Chairman, is to retire. His has been a benevolent dictatorship. It's hard to tell how the Association will shape without him. He presented to us his heir. The mantle had fallen upon the Archdeacon of Warwick, the Venerable Michael Paget-Wilkes, who has known Sudan for many years and who is constantly advising on the financial affairs of the troubled relief agency in Khartoum. He seemed a good choice and the nomination was made and agreed within a minute and without dissent. He looked a little younger than me; I would no longer be the Committee's 'young hopeful'. I wonder how he will attempt to reshape the Association and I wonder if he feels, as I do, that although he was among dinosaurs who had survived, the foundations laid are good and true.

Alan Gibson's book "A Mingled Yarn" was today's train choice. It was a delight and, with the coffee coming at intervals, all was at peace. The train was snaking through the countryside, a slither of light in the gloom. I took it as a sign of what the Sudan Church Association tries to be for the suffering people it serves.

Back at home, the jacket destined for Oxfam was still where I had left it. Joan said it looked fine with my suit trousers, so it had been reprieved. Most odd. If a thing is bad, it's bad. But then I thought of myself – I get on fine with some people and not at all with others. Perhaps my jacket had the same problems. Anyway, one thing led to another until she asked what jacket I had worn to London. When I told her I hadn't worn one at all, she pronounced me 'impossible'. And I thought I was being co-operative!

Thursday, 15th October

It was cheering to visit Mary Cross this morning. I had picked up on the grapevine that she was ill. Cancer had been suspected and she had been to the Royal Marsden for treatment. That is usually an ominous sign; people don't go to the Marsden unless it is beyond local help. So I didn't know quite what to expect. In fact she answered the door and welcomed me with good cheer. She had been well treated, the prognosis was good, the neighbours and friends had been marvellous, her son was there, her daughter was coming, 'Get Well' cards covered every surface and I was warmly thanked for troubling to call.

This was a welcome antidote following a very different sort of visit. Another widow, not as ill as Mary Cross, had complained most bitterly, especially about 'the Church' which had let her down and forgotten her. I knew that she received 'Meals on Wheels' and it was one of our congregation who brought them, but that didn't seem to count. Nobody ever called, she said; the neighbours were too busy, the Church wasn't interested. I offered to do some shopping but it turned out the neighbours had done it. I offered to bring Communion but there wouldn't be time because the hairdresser was coming one day, the chiropodist another day and the home help every day. Old age can be very cruel and I don't blame people for transferring their unhappiness on to others, and the Church is always the easiest target. I don't blame them – but the attacks still hurt. I couldn't help noticing there were no 'Get Well' cards in sight.

Behind the moans and the groans lies a powerful and painful pastoral point. When people say 'the Church' they actually mean 'the Vicar'. It wouldn't matter how many of the congregation visited. It wouldn't matter if they cleaned, shopped, cooked and weeded the garden. If the Vicar hadn't called, the Church would be neglecting her. How long will it be before people grow out of such thinking, or non-thinking? At least a generation. And as long as the Clergy run around trying to meet the impossible expectation, so they will run themselves into nervous breakdowns and fuel the false expectation. The idea that Ministry is a shared enterprise has no root. We have failed to use Lay Pastoral Assistants for this reason. We have failed to develop a Non-Stipendiary Priesthood for this reason. The people don't want it. They want the Vicar and none other. And this leaves every member of the congregation

congregation useless as a eunuch and the Vicar hounded to exhaustion. My daily prayer is for forgiveness for all those things I have not done that I ought to have done. And the chief thing I have not done is that, after twenty years, I have not conveyed the simple truth that the Church is the people. They still think it's the priest.

Friday, 16th October

When Mary arrived at the Office this morning she gave me a shock. I let her in as usual and a few moments later Mary Hooper arrived – to help her fold the weekly leaflet, I expect. The two Marys are both Clergy widows and both have served the Church faithfully for more years than I have lived. Both of them know the pressures of a clergy household and neither of them ever miss church. In short, they are "backbone" people and I am lucky to have them – and others of their ilk – as partners in these parishes. All this made what happened next, the more surprising. Mary H. suddenly said of Mary M. "You know she fell through her greenhouse and was badly hurt, don't you?" I didn't know. I had let her into the Office every morning and I had never noticed a thing. And then Mary M. added "And I'm losing my sight". This is terrible. A catalogue of misfortunes is befalling a most dedicated helper. The truth is she is ageing. We all do. The process spares none of us. The shame is that I made matters worse. I have been telling her for a long while that she should stop driving and when she said "And I'm losing my sight," I took the opportunity to make the point again. "Then you should give up driving," I said, quite forcefully. No doubt my remark was well short of the gentle sympathy expected of a priest. Sometimes, the pastoral, like the truth, can be painful.

The irony of all this is that Mary is one of our Lay Pastoral Assistants. She is meant to be helping the elderly of the parish. Clearly she now needs the help. In this predicament I see a larger issue. We are all being encouraged to choose suitable people to be ordained 'Local Priests'. I have supported the idea and encouraged the search – but there is one big snag. Most of those chosen will be in retirement years and what will happen when the ageing process does not spare them? "We won't renew their licence" says officialdom. But in our intimate country life that is easier said than done. It would be unkind to take Mary's 'pastoral' licence away from her at this moment, and if I tried to do so she would hold on tenaciously. As she is a 'visitor' it doesn't matter too much. But a sick or ageing 'local priest' could hold a parish back for months or even years.

The day's task was to call on all the retired clergy and show them their part in the November rota of services. These priests are, one and all, God's gift – not only to the parishes, but especially to me. If I counted all the blessings of my Ministry and arranged them in order, surely the retired clergy would head every list. Every one of them has brought gifts, different and distinctive. Three of them have been bishops; Douglas Wilson, once of Trinidad and Tobago, Geoffrey Tiarks, once chaplain to the Archbishop of Canterbury, John Waller, once Central Chaplain to the Mothers' Union.

Bishop Douglas was a father figure to me in the early days; we made each other laugh. I enjoyed his stories and he came to love me; when he died, I was like a little boy lost, but I gave him the best funeral possible, with eight bishops surrounding the coffin in Beaminster Church.

And then came Geoffrey Tiarks, his giant figure dwarfing us all and his acerbic wit controlling us all. His illness and immobility became such a pain, but the parishes brought the altar forward, so that he could celebrate while sitting, and continue his ministry to the end. I would like someone to do that for me when the time comes. And at his funeral the snow lay deep and crisp and we tramped across the fields to Netherbury because the lanes were dangerous, and the Archbishop's representative couldn't get through and it fell to me to preach in his place and lay the great man to rest.

And then there was Derek Eastman, chaplain to the Queen, Canon of Windsor, Archdeacon of Buckingham and the humblest soul in the place. Steeped in the best Anglican tradition, with a pastoral heart open to all – and especially, it seemed, to me. He died in the doctor's surgery on the day I was robbed and beaten and left for dead in a Nairobi ditch.

I arrived home in time for the memorial service in Windsor Castle but, at the time of the funeral, I was in South Sudan and knew nothing about it.

And there was Murdoch Dahl, the Canon Theologian from St. Alban's Abbey, so learned and so erudite that he lived in a scholarly world possibly inhabited by the saints but certainly not by us. His sermons, like his books, took us beyond this plane and beyond ourselves, which is perhaps where the faith should lead us. How he struggled with modern Anglicanism, and how he railed against it! With all these theological traumas he heated our pulpits until he took the path to Rome, and cooled down.

Then there was Christopher Donaldson, priest, poet and prophet from St. Martin's, Canterbury, who trod a pilgrim path all over Europe, wrote the life of St. Martin with vision and passion and used our Team as the model for his "Rising from the Root" prophecy. His blue eyes flashed, the honeyed words poured forth, his black cassock billowed as if he was Batman. And I felt I was Robin, learning great lessons, in his wake.

Then there was Father Pat, about whom a book should be written, not a diary note. He came into my life at an Archdeacon's party, when he recognised my M.C.C. tie. His father, Stacy Waddy, had played against W. G. Grace's M.C.C. in Australia and had hit a famous century. He had become the world leader of S.P.G. and Father Pat had also travelled the world, becoming Dean of Bombay Cathedral before he, amazingly, arrived in our midst. A life of devotion to Our Lord, coupled with classical scholarship and a love of cricket made him a friend for life. How fitting that we should celebrate the diamond jubilee of his priesthood in the presence of the Bishop of Salisbury, John Baker, who received the sacrament at Father Pat's hands. All that, ten years ago, and the holy man is still with us, now 94. God bless our plans for the 70th anniversary of his priesthood, coming next month.

And until his second retirement recently there was always Norman Sutcliffe. It's so hard to believe he had a career in the Army. Who can imagine this peaceable pastor carrying a gun? When his daughter-in-law was savagely murdered, there was the usual cry for the death penalty, but Norman put revenge aside and in a Team News' article he pleaded otherwise. It drew an appreciative letter from the Bishop of Salisbury, John Baker, who admired such faith in adversity, as did we all. When his voice and hearing weakened, Norman had the further grace to hand in his licence. Now he encourages us from the pew, not the pulpit.

And then there was Percy Nichols, for so many years the pastor at West Chinnock, who would never talk about his war heroism but became the master pastor because he trusted God, loved people and kept it simple.

All these men have brought the riches of wisdom gathered from years, long years, in the deeps of our great Anglican tradition. They have lived among us and brought untold blessings. And it has all been given for love – free gratis and for nothing, never a penny charged. It has been a gift of grace, a blessing on me, a blessing on us all. Sadly, there are still people who like to see one vicar all the time (very boring) and so not everyone has enjoyed the blessings.

Today's duties turned into a joy because we now have yet another wave of blessings, from the newly retired clergy.

"Come in," said David Shearlock, formerly Dean of Truro, once President of the Three Spires Music Festival and author of works on preaching, music and liturgy. He will happily do all the November duties we have asked. He will happily chair the Beaminster Arts Festival Committee. He will be happy with whatever we wish him to do at Christmas, and he doesn't mind how small the village or the congregation. Signs of grace.

"Come in," said Edgar Hornsby, so we sat in the sun lounge, in sight of my favourite of all the beautiful gardens of the area. Forty-six years he has been a priest, a life's experience in education and chaplaincy work. Now his commitment and licence is to Bath & Wells Diocese, but he is still happy to help us when holidays deplete our numbers or festivals overwhelm us. "The people are so welcoming," he said, "and you always say thank you," he added.

"Come in," said Keith Yates at the door of his new home in Broadwindsor. They have recently moved across the Redlands road, but it was so homely they could have been there for years. The November programme pleased him, he would gladly go wherever he was sent. He also found the people welcoming, the churches in good order and well prepared. He seemed to compare it favourably with all his years in Sloane Square. I wish I was free to hear him preach because in his years as a lecturer in ethics at the theological college in Salisbury he was known as a scholar and a communicator, a rare combination, and another sign of grace.

"Come in," said John Whettem, formerly rector of the Swanborough Team, a canon of Salisbury Cathedral, the diocesan wicket keeper, who took up marathon running and boxing at the age of sixty, and has not only lived to tell the tale but is supremely fit. He will fulfil all the November duties with pleasure, after which he and Mary take off for a winter chaplaincy in Cyprus and won't be back for a while. Wherever he goes, people recognise the pastor with the counselling skills and Mary who is a counsellor in her own right and has published volumes of reflective poems and meditations; gifts of grace in abundance.

"Come in," said Jack Broadhurst, now in the 65th year of his priesthood and soon to celebrate his ninetieth birthday. "Yes, I will go anywhere you send me," he said, as he looked at the November programme. "And never forget, if ever you're stuck with someone falling ill, call on me. I only need ten minutes' notice," and he smiled as he spoke. In fact, I have never known him without a smile. When I visited him in hospital after a major op. he was sitting up in bed, first day, smiling. When he was nursing Connie through all sorts of difficulties, he was smiling. And now that he is alone, he tends the roses which have won him national awards, smiling the smile of the just and the peaceful. Oh! If I live to be ninety – let me be like him.

One thing puzzles me. So many parish priests complain about the clergy who have retired to their parish. I hear all sorts of horror stories which amount to the fact that the retired priests are an 'awkward lot'. Today, ours have given me a lovely day, as they always do. They are so appreciative and so understanding. They compare the churches they find here with the churches they have served elsewhere and they find the comparison favourable, which is very encouraging.

If only more people appreciated the blessings which abound!

Saturday, 17th October

Someone rang up early this morning, asked for an immediate meeting and apologised if they were interrupting my 'day off'.

Days off! They are a waste of time and I don't believe in them! How can a priest have a day off? If I walk down the road or go into the Square, do I say "Not talking to you, I'm having a day off"? It's nonsense. A priest is always a priest and can't have a day when he is not a priest. Of course he will be wise enough to take time away when duties allow, but a regular day off seems absurd. On a day off, do I refuse to answer the phone? Of course not. It might be Andrew calling from Sudan. Do I refuse to think about Sunday's sermon? I am the loser. Being a priest is a way of life which I can't shed one day a week, and don't want to shed, any day of the week.

These views are now 'incorrect'. Bishops expect clergy to state their day off, and keep it. Theological colleges insist that curates' hours should be limited. It's all meant to protect families, ensure quality time with children and guarantee time for creative leisure. Exactly! Why should those things be confined to one fixed day? Suppose the 'day off' is Wednesday but the boy's school sports is Tuesday? How does that give quality time with the children? Suppose the 'day off' is Tuesday but the annual golf tournament is Wednesday, what does that do for creative leisure? Once we start partitioning life, we are on a slippery slope. My nightmare is that clergy will gradually become clock watchers, only on duty at certain times of the day. Then they will want the protection of a trades union, then they will want a contract, then their duties will be defined so that someone else will have to lock the church (not in the contract!), someone else will have to type the letters (not in the contract). Where will it end? It will end when these clergy triumphantly declare themselves more professional. This means they will become managers instead of pastors. They will become overseers instead of participants. They will assess flow charts instead of listening to people. Professionalism is the wolf in sheep's clothing. Priesthood is a vocation. And 'vocation' is in danger of becoming a forgotten word. Trades unions, contracts, 'days off', will not protect the priest's family, but they will end priesthood as a way of life and a vocation.

So I agreed to the unexpected and unscheduled meeting. It was a 'happy couple' eagerly making the date. It was good to share their faith, hope and love. We don't want to take a day off from such things. They are the very things we are meant to proclaim. And anyway, they fed good ideas into tomorrow's sermon which was a help, not a hindrance.

Sunday, 18th October

There is enough time between Sunday services not to rush, and that was proved today in an unusual way. The timing allows for coffee in church, if it is available, or to come home if it is not, and light the fire, which is exactly what I was doing after the 9.30 service when the phone rang. It was Clive Chamberlain, the policeman. "Sad news," he said, and then he told me Annie Froggatt had been found dead in bed; the doctor had been, but could I go and say prayers before her body was removed? We are lucky with our policeman. He truly cares about people and has a sensitivity which springs from some deep well of his own making. He knew Annie's faith and tradition, but not many policemen would have thought to call the vicar. I abandoned the fire and was at her bedside within minutes. An historical novel was open on the pillow. She had gone to sleep reading, and had not woken up. I said the Prayers of the Dead, made the sign of the cross on her forehead and commended her to God's mercy. She had been one of the Lord's more exciting servants all her life. As a nun, it must have taken intelligence and devotion to have become so senior in her Order. It must have taken a matching amount of faith and courage to leave her Order and make her way in the world; and then to become a highly regarded 'Dame' at Eton, a calligrapher to Royalty and a constant support to the Community at Pilsdon. On my way to the next service, I remembered that the last time Annie and I talked, she said she hoped she would go quickly and not cause trouble. She wanted to be like her near neighbour, Joan McMasters, who was waving goodbye to her family when she fell down a step and died. Annie had spent the day at her spiritual home, Pilsdon, where she celebrated their fortieth anniversary at a Requiem. She had prayed for all the Community members now gathered to glory and had come home – and joined them. It all seemed so right for her, but as I arrived at Hooke for the 11 o'clock service, I was annoyed with myself for not thanking Clive for being a very special sort of policeman.

House communion with Betty Tiarks followed the Hooke service. I am sure Sunday is the right day for house communions – it means that the congregation in church is called to remember the sick in prayers and the sick person is reminded that the congregation still cares for them and that they are still part of the church, even if absent. It isn't a convenient day for the priest but I am certain it means more to the sick person than turning up in midweek between chiropodist and hairdresser. Sunday is the Lord's day in a unique way and that is the day that the housebound should be included in the worship. They suffer enough exclusion, without being relegated by the church to midweek.

Betty always has something which needs to be done before we pray. Last time, it was preparing the veg. for her Sunday lunch; today, it was putting ointment in the cat's eyes. Barnabas is a very important part of the scene and I took it as a sign of trust to be involved. However, it may not happen again. Catching him was chaotic. Betty called, but he didn't come. That showed more spirit than most of us when Betty calls. No doubt he took fright because of my presence. With some cunning, he went under the trolley which was to be our altar. I poked him on the backside with my prayer book and he shot out and leapt for the sideboard. I flung my arms up and grabbed two legs as they flew by. I once saw Richie Benaud make a similar catch to dismiss Colin Cowdrey at Lord's. It was pure instinct, the sort of thing you do once in a lifetime. I took the cat to Betty who was propped in her chair. "Don't hurt him," she said. "He is very precious." I had other thoughts about the cat at that moment but I remembered I was still in my priest's robes and that I do believe and teach that the secular and the sacred are both holy in the sight of God. "I'll hold it," said Betty. "You put the drops in." Barnabas shut his

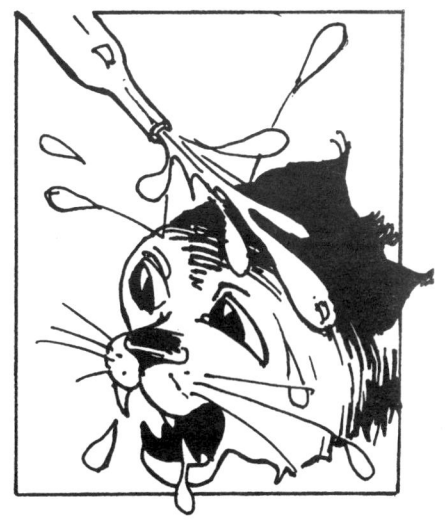

eyes, tightly, but I pressed the tube nonetheless. The ointment went on the eyelids and down its nose and on my fingers which I wiped on the thing's tail. I didn't see any go in its eyes. I thought this, like the catch, was something I would only do once.

Betty is truly remarkable. The widow of Bishop Geoffrey, she was once used to palace life at Lambeth. She was with the Royal Family when Bishop Geoffrey christened Peter, the son of Princess Anne and Mark Phillips. It must be hard after such a life not to be in control and command any longer. Instead, she now depends on people whose goodwill has to be earned. She knew the whole service by heart and said every word with devotion, eyes closed and hands extended in prayer and praise. Beaminster has certainly drawn to itself an amazing collection of characters and the priest is the privileged person, to know and serve them all.

The afternoon and evening had to be at Pilsdon, sharing the celebrations – and beginning the funeral arrangements for Annie.

I first came across Pilsdon's work in 1966, when it was in its infancy. There was a sort of connection with St. Francis School at Hooke, where I was chaplain among 'maladjusted' boys – as they were then called.

Canon Percy Smith, the Pilsdon founder, lived among 'maladjusted' adults, though he would have rejected such a term, even then. "We all live in a maladjusted society," was all he would say. He simply kept an 'open door' for anyone troubled in heart or mind. Visitors come, join the family, share the work until they are ready to leave. The problems may have involved prison, or drugs, or alcohol or the depression which comes from a hundred other sources. No questions would be asked. This was Percy's policy and, in forty years under three leaders, it hasn't changed much. Percy once said to me that I should eventually succeed him. I must have looked like a young hope, thirty-two years ago! So today, on the 40th anniversary, the least I can do is attend – even if I now look more like an old has-been than a young hopeful.

It was good to see Percy again, looking as fit as ever with the same shock of shiny black hair, the same urgent actions, the same intense eyes, dancing and demanding attention. His sermon was sharp as stiletto, cutting through all life's protective verbiage – exposing wounds, yet opening the way to healing. This always was his genius. No one would think he had been away for fifteen years. On his return, he fitted as if the place was still his home. I spoke to him over supper, but he didn't recognise me – so much for the young hopeful of yesteryear!

The crowds were so big that the marquee was soon filling with overflow from the church. I counted a dozen people from our parishes and thought Pilsdon's efforts and achievements were worth more. Perhaps one of the many failures of my time is not to have made much closer ties with such a significant neighbour.

Among 'ours' were Mary Moorhead and Elizabeth Busfeild who arrived together. So Mary is still driving at night, against my advice. Mary is a Scot, a Highlander, of strong and sturdy stock. She qualified as a medical doctor in days when young ladies didn't do such things, which means she must have a brain to match her determination. And she has worked in our Team office with a dedication, second to none. But none of these qualities make her a good driver – ask her clutch! Mary's progress will never be silent; the clutch revving sends advance warning from miles away. Her garage must keep a stock of clutches handy. I was not surprised when Elizabeth Busfeild, looking more than usually white, asked if she could return with me. I agreed and later we saw Mary off, travelling alone. "I ought to be with her," said Elizabeth, who is herself nearly eighty and prevented by a heart condition from driving. "What help could you be?" I queried, as Mary revved off into the night. "I have a torch," said Elizabeth. "I could read the road signs when she is lost." I thought it was best that I had separated the pair. On the way back, Elizabeth was unusually agitated. "What's the matter?" I asked. "Can't you relax?" She was shining her torch out of the window, up and down the hedgerow. "Slowly," she kept saying. "Go slowly. Mary could be in any of these ditches."

Monday, 19th October

There are only 24 hours to collect 'Team News' proofs from Creeds, correct them, fit them into columns, fill the odd spaces with illustrations and give the magazine a professional look.

Vivien Priestley-Smith promised to set about proof reading, which includes some copy editing, without delay. She would rather have two days because she likes to phone contributors directly to check every query. Not so much as a comma will escape her scrutiny – which is right because a comma in the wrong place can change the meaning completely. A lot of the sentence construction sends her into decline but she recovers, and the red pen does it correcting work. No school child ever had a more demanding task master, but an excellent result is guaranteed. The magazine will be an easy read with none of the irritating errors others are prone to. Meanwhile, I have my problems too. If there is a space I must write a quick filler, if there is too much I will cut out something of mine because I learnt in the early days that it is more than my life is worth to cut someone else's effort.

John Anderson came to the rescue today, as ever. The space to fill was a column width and an inch and a half deep. His illustration would be ready by 9.00 p.m. if I cared to call and collect it. I have never known him fail. Whether it is an animal cartoon or an ancient building, a scene of conflict in the Arab/Israeli war, or in the Mothers' Union, he will produce the goods, and in time to meet the deadline, fill the vacant space and make the readers smile. There seems no end to this talent. When my book on Sudan needed an illustrator, there was no doubt whom to choose. And, though he had never been to Africa, the images were so true to the culture that Africans have valued the book, more than the English. But he is more than an artist; he has repaired our broken furniture, made all the cupboards and display boards for the Team office and most of my bookshelves. Don Bradman was once described as having "the skill of an artist with the temperament of a scientist, which makes for genius." I would say the same of John, though he wouldn't appreciate the cricket analogy. I once asked him to do a cricket drawing. In his American way, he said "Is that the one they play with a paddle?" And then he did a perfect drawing. The strange thing is that, although his cartoons have been enjoyed and admired in every parish, hardly anyone knows him. Everyone knows Ena, his wife, but John remains quiet and retiring – not the way we imagine Americans to be! Whatever brought them to the tiny village of Hooke I neither know nor care. What I do know is that there have been many journeys to Hooke, at all hours, to collect the vital parts which complete the magazine jigsaw – every journey has been worthwhile and I have more than two hundred of his original drawings to prove it. Tonight, I arrived at 9.00 p.m. and of course it was ready, as promised.

Only the magazine cover remains to be done and Joan will have it ready by the morning. I wonder how many covers she has done. We must be well past two hundred issues and she has probably done half of them. In the twelve years before we turned to Creeds' computer technology, she did not only the cover but also the whole lay-out, by scissors and paste. Every month the traumatic magazine week would come and she would moan and groan deep into the night, so that even the dogs shivered and retreated to my side. A hundred and fifty issues came out of that process and I can safely say that the marriage which survives that will survive anything.

If the morning brings the cover, all will be well for another month, unless ... the business manager has other thoughts. For twenty-one years, Brenda Travers has handled the advertisements and every penny of the annual £10,000 budget, and balanced the books. We have made only one price increase in the past ten years, yet we still break even. The secret of success is Brenda's relationship with the advertisers, who sometimes need late changes or additions and Brenda always pleads their case. I can't refuse her wishes because she works so hard for no reward or payment (like everyone else). She can't refuse the advertisers because they keep us in profitable business. So if she comes with a last minute change, I will be back to the drawing board. John's cartoon may have to go, in spite of all his efforts. When the magazine finally drops on the doormat, a hundred parishioners will have had a part in it. And that is its real value. It uses local skills, it unites the villages and keeps me in pastoral touch with a hundred people every month.

Tuesday, 20th October

The day started well. Joan produced the cover on time, Vivien had corrected the manuscript, Brenda did not put a spanner in the works and I had juggled the text until it all fitted and was ready for the press. Another issue could go to bed. Then the phone rang. It was Robin Musson, Secretary of the Salisbury Diocese Sudan Committee.

"Tim, there is bad news from Sudan," he said. I braced myself. There has been so much bad news from Sudan for so long that I am used to it, but there was something in his voice ... "Yes," I said, inviting him to continue, but he was faltering. "Daniel Zindo has been killed," he said, mincing no words. I don't think I spoke. "It was a car crash," he continued. I still don't think I spoke. And I still can't take it in. Daniel Zindo is dead. It has taken the Sudanese Church a long while to choose its new leader and now the Archbishop-elect is dead and the tragic Church deprived and leaderless again. Daniel was with us two months ago, under our roof, planning the future. He told us how his wife had been murdered and a daughter with her. His brother had died and two nieces as well, all in six weeks. He was left with twenty-one traumatised dependents and now he is dead and they are bereaved again. It is too much. He was such good company. In spite of all his sufferings, he was full of hope and purpose. His smile had dazzled us, his shining eyes had sparkled. How could such trauma and such trouble produce such a face? And now he is no more. When the father-figure is removed in a patriarchal church, everyone is bereft. The remaining bishops will not know which way to turn. All the old feuds of tribal tensions and political power games will come to the surface again. They have just been through all that, and so have we, with them. It is too  much. I thought I ought to feel emotion, for his twenty-one dependents, for the loss of his great beaming presence, for the sheer tragedy and trauma of it all, but my emotions had dried up. Anyway tears would be useless, pointless and no help to anyone. It was all too late. I could not forget my last words to him as he began the journey back to Sudan from Salisbury. The Americans had bombed a factory in Khartoum. The Sudanese Government had expelled our Ambassador. Our government had told British nationals to leave the country. It was evidently the wrong moment for him to go to Khartoum, so my parting words as I shook his hand had been "You'll be safer in Kampala." How wrong can I be? What irony! None of it makes sense. I rang Andrew, in Sherborne.

On his phone, the silence was broken only by an awed and disbelieving "No!" "No!" "Not Zindo!" There was nothing we could say. There is nothing we can do. It was Andrew who had greeted Zindo and his 'platoon' of dependents when they left their Yambio home and arrived in Kampala. It was Andrew who had got them entry permits to Kenya. It was Andrew who had driven them across the border, thinking Nairobi would be safer. It was Andrew, with me, who had met him and all the other Bishops at Gatwick when they arrived for the Lambeth Conference. Zindo had been wearing an ill-fitting jacket which threatened to burst its buttons. It was Andrew who had given him his own suit so that he could look smart at the Salisbury Garden Party and the Lambeth Conference. "Now," said Zindo, "I shall look like a leader instead of a beggar" and he had laughed in the huge, irresistible African way that made everyone else laugh too. Dead. No more of those great laughs. And for the 'platoon', the twenty-one innocents, more emotional trauma. And for the Church and its remaining bishops – also twenty-one, but not so innocent, more political trauma.

Meanwhile, I took the magazine to Creeds the Printers on time. They would not have known anything out of the ordinary had happened.

Back at home, Ansaphone was at work. The Bishop of Salisbury had been asked for an obituary by the Church Times; could I help? The former Bishop of Salisbury had been asked for an obituary by The Telegraph; could I help? A message from Brian Carlisle, head of the Sudan Church Association, said the body would be flown from Nairobi to Yambio for burial; would Salisbury help pay? The Archbishop of Canterbury wanted to be represented at the funeral; who could go? Salisbury Cathedral would have a memorial service; when should it be?

This evening was one of those awkward times which are all-too-common, when interests clash. Beaminster Church Council was due to meet, with significant issues on the agenda – the pattern of services in 1999, the review of our children's work, preparations for an appeal to raise quarter of a million pounds for tower restoration. I was certainly expected. Beaminster School governors were due to meet, also with major issues on their agenda – access road, sports hall, learning resource centre, staff stress, to mention a few. And Stoke Abbott Church Council was also meeting, and hoping for a priest to be present. My colleagues had agreed that I should go to the governors, Rose should go to Beaminster Church Council and Stoke would miss out this time, and that's how it was. It was right because I had missed the last few governors' meetings. But it isn't satisfactory.

My concern is that the 1999 service rota will go through, and I will not have had a say in it. But when the complaints and criticisms come in, they will all be directed at me. This happens again and again. Others make decisions, quite often decisions I would not have made, but the poisoned arrows which follow are aimed at me. Some would say that a system which allows such things is fundamentally flawed. I see it as the painful cost of becoming democratic, a style the church is not used to. I understand why so many clergy prefer the old autocratic ways. There is less pain that way, and it's clearer; everyone knows who is in charge. Just like it used to be. But the bold experiment we have made would be ended. The elected councils would revert to their puppet status. The future cannot be down that path. That is yesterday's way. So we continue to feel our way to democracy, with all its pains and problems.

The governors' meeting put my mind in a spin. Three hours we were talking and, at the end, most of the problems remained because they are intractable. But one decision we did make was to proceed with building the Learning Resource Centre, even though we are a little short of the £482,000 target. I voted to get on with it. It's been on our agendas for at least ten years, first as a library, now as a Learning Resource Centre. It was good to get one thing on its way, but sports hall, access road, the £3 million budget and staff stress will have to be 're-visited', to use the chairman's phrase.

It was 10 p.m. when I returned home, and not a word of the Daniel Zindo obituary is written. It will have to be a night job.

Wednesday, 21st October

The Daniel Zindo obituary was faxed off at 7.00 a.m. I was strong on the later years, but weak on the early years. I hope they find someone else to help with that.

The Wednesday communion service, and the Team meeting which follows, have become fixed points in the pattern of every week – and very good it is to have some fixed points. Otherwise the week could become a ceaseless and chaotic run-around. Judging by the numbers who come to the Wednesday communion, others feel the same. There are seldom fewer than twenty people, sometimes a good many more. This is as many as a lot of churches have on a Sunday. I remember when the service was said with no sermon, and the congregation was about six. I introduced the music and the sermon and was roundly told it would 'kill it off'. The numbers grew, though the late Mrs. Gibson stopped coming. I went to ask her why. "I like my communion to be private," she said, "but now someone comes and sits next to me." She was over eighty and had been a devout church attender all her life so I took communion to her at home after that. But it does show how pious people can prevent progress, and they often do.

I spoke about Zindo in the sermon; how could I do anything else? And we used the prayers for the Mission of the Church and we sang

> *He who would valiant be*
> *'Gainst all disaster*
> *Let him in constancy*
> *Follow the Master ...*

Nothing could express Zindo better than that. At last my emotions began to emerge but, on the whole, emotion is best left out of worship. We have a great Liturgy to carry our feelings and in our culture emotion is kept within bounds. Charismatics and happy-clappies and the 'Hallelujah People' may have their place but that place is not within the austere dignity of the English country church. Whether the congregation saw the significance of Zindo's death, the conflict and confusion which will arise from it and the trauma for those dependents, I do not know. But it is good for people to be confronted with the fact that the comforts and securities we know in Beaminster are not typical. The Gospel was not written with West Dorset in mind. Some people criticise the time I give to the Sudan but it is necessary to be stirred from our complacency. It widens our view of the Church, the World and the Gospel, and that is necessary, and not only here. So I have nothing to apologise for, I am proud of the Sudan involvement.

When we returned to the Rectory after church, the November issue of "Sarum Link" was on the doorstep, eight hundred copies for distribution. And there on the front page was the article I wrote three weeks ago "Introducing Daniel Zindo" and there was his smiling face, photographed in our garden. What an irony! Readers will receive my 'Introduction' on the very day The Telegraph receives my 'Obituary'. It is all too much. I can only hope the 'Introduction' will now be read as a tribute, prayerfully.

Team meetings are usually wonderful fun. It is amazing how much there is to laugh about. I suppose it is the variety of characters that make up our congregations. Thank the good Lord for colleagues who have always seen the funny side of things. But today was different. The phone kept ringing and it was always about Zindo. One call was from a bishop who said "It's hard to see what the Lord has in mind, when He does such things." I replied politely but I didn't feel polite. How can anybody, let alone a bishop, believe this is the hand of God, and that He goes about killing people?

This facile theology has to be faced and corrected. If God is a great dictator organising events from on high, then he is making a horrible and cruel mess of it, and doesn't deserve our worship at all. And if He is directing and controlling things, what does that make us? Mere puppets on a string? It is too simplistic to lay everything at God's door. It makes Him into a master monster and reduces us to wretched robots. This view has been put forward by church and preachers for generations but it will no longer do. If churches are emptying it is not because of the old language of worship; it is because of the old theology. If Daniel Zindo's death in a car crash is God's plan and God's way, then I see no difference between that sort of God and the Devil. I had the same feelings when I had to bury a family friend who had died of cancer aged 34, leaving two young daughters. The vicar of her London parish had visited her when she was dying and had said to her "You must have done something very wicked for God to be punishing you like this."

No wonder they didn't want him to do the funeral. A lot of the stuff which we have put out from the pulpit has been devilish. It's my purpose to expose this false theology. And to show in the face of Jesus, a truer image of the divine. All my teaching, preaching and writing has been to that end and, if it fails, it won't be for want of trying. Sadly, the prevailing wind is in the other direction. All the world's religions are retreating from the modern world and modern thought and hiding in fundamentalism. Better to face the modern world, however frightening, than to cling to primitive notions about God more suited to the Dark Ages. I should have said that to the bishop who implied that Daniel's death was all part of some super plan. But I didn't. It's easier, and politer, to accept the traditional platitudes. Shame on me for being such a wimp.

One interesting thing cropped up at the Team meeting and, as it is for about the hundredth time, it is obviously an issue unresolved. There was a thoughtful letter from Drimpton Church asking for a family service each month – and continuity in the person taking it, so the children would know whom and what to expect. There was also last night's decision of Beaminster Church Council to increase the 'family services' from one to two a month, which means alternate weeks. Similar moves are going on all over the country. There is a clamour for 'family services' to replace the traditional forms of the old and new prayer books. And I can understand it. With fewer and fewer people being confirmed, the sacramental worship belongs less and less to the whole nation and more and more to a diminishing elite. That is the problem. Our Church of England is meant to be the church of the whole nation, but the over-emphasis on the sacramental worship has left people feeling excluded and the congregation looking like an exclusive club – the confirmed. A generation or two ago when Mattins was the order of the day, this was not the case. The occasional 'Give us back our Mattins' cry is not so much a love of Mattins as a searching for a 'popular' service the nation can be comfortable with. Hence the hope pinned on 'family services'. But are they the answer? My experience is that they make a brave effort but that they are not the answer. Too often they are ephemeral, forgotten in a week. They fail to engrave indelibly in the mind and on the heart, as the old traditions did. Too often they reduce the minister to some sort of entertainer who has to think up ever new ways of holding attention. This will not create a sense of the holy, as the old tradition did. The effort to make family services user-friendly and suitable for beginners can reduce the worship to something and nothing. The idea of this twice a month as Beaminster's main morning service dismays me. But I can not deny the need to reach out beyond the sacramental club. So what should be done?

The first thing is that the church should recognise the error of making a hurdle between baptism and communion, namely confirmation. Baptism is the mark of membership and no one who is baptised should be barred from communion. This would throw the club open, as it should be. The best of our music, the beauty of liturgy and language and the sense of the holy would be restored to the people.

The second thing is that the church should recognise all that has been happening in education. Children no longer sit in rows, being talked at. The church model is out-dated. Schools expect children to participate; the church expects them to be passive. The church needs to take on board the educational dictum:

> "What I hear, I forget;
> What I see, I remember;
> What I do, I believe."

Where there are special children's events, they must be allowed to *do*, if they are to believe. And that takes so much skill, so much planning, so much material and so much time. David and Jill are achieving it once a quarter on 'Fun and Learning Days', but there is no way it can be achieved every alternate week in Beaminster, by people without the skills, the time or the material.

The Team meeting decided I should write to Drimpton and offer Rose and Lilian to share the family service. They will do it as well and as carefully as anyone could do. Lilian has a lifetime's experience in education, Rose has a sensitivity to people, both know that we are aiming for holiness, not entertainment, and everyone at Drimpton will work with them. My pessimism is not about them. It comes from my uneasy feeling that 'family services' are the wrong answer to a very important question.

I cannot imagine how awful it must be to be a priest, without a team of colleagues. It is the opportunity to discuss all these issues, the interest of sharing different views, the value of listening to each other's experiences, the safety-net of exploding when something or someone has been annoying, the refreshment of laughing, that keeps me going.

Thursday, 22nd October

In 24 hours' time, Joan and I will be in Jerusalem, for her half term.

It seemed a good idea when I suggested it, a long while ago. And it may be worth it when we get there. But at this minute I would give anything not to be going. It would be so much easier to stay here and get on with things instead of running around trying to do all the things I have not done.

Karl Dixon's drawing of a statue of St. Francis, to be sculpted for Netherbury Church, needed to be returned to the donor, so I shot over to Strode Manor. The statue will be in memory of local farmer, Dacres Symes, and I like it and I hope it will go ahead. His widow, Diana, was at work in her greenhouse which her loving tender care was making into a nursery. "This is where I relax," she said. "Plants are wonderful therapy." She invited me in for coffee and I returned the drawing with the archdeacon's cautious comments and I promised to get a faculty application posted to her before I went to Jerusalem. This project has taken three years already. "Oh! We know, it always does," she said, and she went on to recount the arguments and delays which surrounded her family's first gift of a statue. It had been of the Virgin Mary, in memory of her father. There had been strong opposition to the faculty, in the village and in the diocese. Statues, especially of Mary, were considered to set us on the deadly path to the 'Scarlet Woman', the Church of Rome. It was considered by others to put us on the edge of idolatry. Three hundred years ago, the Reformers had removed all the Netherbury statues (four) from their niches for those reasons, so why should we restore them? Were we abandoning our Reformation heritage? Were we no longer Protestants? How thankful I am that I wasn't Vicar then! I don't believe that those statues had been destroyed for profound theological reasons. It was wanton vandalism by rampaging soldiers. And if the reasons were theological, they were a false theology anyway. The Symes family is merely making reparation for past wrongs. It took several years for a compromise to be reached, which stated that Mary should have Jesus in her arms and the statue had to be the smallest possible. "It's always difficult to make any change in a church," she said "even if it is for the better," so she was quite expecting the latest application to take several years as well. I am not! I want to dedicate it! I reminded her that her family had also given the Saint John statue which took only four years to plan and that I had dedicated it and preached. I still have the sermon. I gave my heart and mind to it because I believe any effort to restore the old tradition of the church as patron of the arts should be encouraged and given full support. The people who are willing to give should be thanked and valued, not made to feel a nuisance. So many hurdles are put in front of them, followed by so many delays that it is a wonder anybody ever gives anything. I phoned the Registrar in Salisbury and asked for the forms to be put in the post today. I want to see that St. Francis statue up, before I retire. Get ready for form filling, nit picking and rebuttals. God give me strength, and Diana Symes a long life!

While in Netherbury, I called on Kate and Gordon Brown, hidden away up a lane in their farm cottage. They are the sort who are easily forgotten. They never make any fuss, never call for help because they have always been used to giving help. Kate was 89 last week and all her long life she has dutifully attended church, served the church and loved doing it. Now she is stricken with cancer. Gordon let me in. "Not too good," he said, when I asked after her. The fire was blazing cheerfully and Kate's smile – she was in bed in the living room – was just as cheerful. And so was her brain, cheerful and active. She remembered old days with happiness. She knew she had been the centre of her family, holding it together in the old way. A priest who had seen her in hospital had corrected her. He had said "No, it's not you at the centre, it's God." I said that I thought she was the centre of her family, but that God had always been her centre. She nodded her agreement and Gordon said "They've been a good team!" I thought that was as wise and gentle and true a summary of Kate, of God, and of a lot of country folk, as ever could be made. It was the right moment to say prayers, thank her for all those years of work and sign her with the sign of the cross. At the door, Gordon said she hadn't eaten for three days and she didn't want any more treatment, and he didn't think it would be too long. "Thank you for calling," he said. "It will do her the world of good." I think he is right. The Vicar's visits do more good than we imagine – among the generation who hold that simple dutiful old faith. The sad thing is, it wouldn't have been the same to her if a lay pastoral assistant had called, or a church warden. It's still the vicar she wants – but she would never have made a fuss, which is why we often forget faithful old servants who quietly hide themselves away. Meanwhile we rush on with £480,000 to raise for the school learning resource, £250,000 appeal due for the church tower, new service rotas to produce for 14 churches (14 different controversies assured!) the magazine running off the presses – while in quiet corners hidden people are hoping to see the vicar, and that he will care.

Back at home, just time to get travellers' cheques from the bank, phone for travel insurance, root out my passport and put a film in the camera. Sunny began to read the signs, his tail disappeared right under his body, his ears and dewlaps suddenly lengthened in a long forlorn look which confirmed my wish that I was not going anywhere. Within a minute he was in a corner, shivering. It was time to harden the heart and deliver him to the kennels for his seven-day sentence. Can any seven days away be worth this? No. Andrew arrived to drive us to the airport. "I haven't got my bag out of the loft yet," Joan said. She had only finished teaching half an hour earlier. She was further behind than I was, which was a relief and made me feel better. In fact while she went into the loft and made an awful fuss, Andrew made a cup of tea and calmed her down while I telephoned everyone who I knew to be sick to wish them well and say I would be back in seven days. Sadly, I am sure there are still a whole lot of 'Mrs. Browns', faithful and true, hidden away, making no fuss but feeling forgotten.

On the way to the airport, I stopped to phone David Wakely and let him know my whereabouts. I have never been away without telling him, but this time I had forgotten. He and his family are the most professional funeral directors anyone could wish for. After working with them for more than twenty-five years, I have never known a lack of courtesy or a word out of place. They often do our pastoral work better than we do because of their long knowledge of every local family. David has a gift for cheering grieving people and turning tears to laughter. If there was a competition for the world's most cheerful undertaker, he would win it. But if there was a similar competition for the most dignified, he might win that too. This interests me because as a priest I have always believed humour and dignity can be partners. David is a perfect example of this and his son, Simon, is not far behind. No doubt it was Grandad Jack Wakely who began the tradition and deserves the credit. I shall always be grateful to him because the second funeral I ever conducted was a very difficult one at Toller. A young mother was to be buried and her mother was following the coffin with two young sons whom I was teaching at Colfox School. I was overcome and wondered how I would get the words out, as we brought the coffin in. Jack saw my discomfort. "Steady on," he said. "You got to encourage them." Of course he was right. I gathered myself together, and the service did encourage them. Jack taught me something in that minute which three years at theological college had failed to do. He said the right thing because he was being a true pastor to me, and to the mourners. That pastoral care has passed down the family line, which is why I didn't want to let them down and thought I should phone to let them know. "Have a good break," said David. "You need it." It was true that

I hadn't had a break since February, and I should be looking forward to it, but I am not.

As we approached Gatwick, Andrew told me that the memorial service for Bishop Zindo would be in Salisbury Cathedral on Saturday. I would miss it. "I didn't tell you before, in case you wanted to turn back," he said. He knew me very well. I would have wanted to turn back; back to Sunny and all the things I have not done that I ought to have done; back to pay my deep respects to the memory of Bishop Daniel Zindo.

Instead, we are now in mid-air and we will soon be stuck in Jerusalem, away from it all for a week.

Seven days later ...

Sunday, 1st November All Saints' Day

It was tippling with rain when Andrew met us at the airport. It had been pouring all day. Roads were flooded. Football matches had been postponed and Andrew had driven through gale winds with the rain sheeting this way and that. It didn't seem possible that we had lunch in the open air under the Jerusalem sky. We hadn't seen the feather of a cloud in the whole of the sun-soaked week, but all the way home the windscreen wipers worked overtime as we splashed our way through the night.

Andrew had come straight from Salisbury, from the Daniel Zindo Memorial Service in the cathedral. He was so impressed by the numbers who had attended, by the way it had been conducted, by all the bishops, archdeacons, dean and canons who had paid their respects. "Only one missing," he said. He had made sure they all knew why I wasn't there. The surprise was that the Bishop of Salisbury had flown to Nairobi during the week, had chartered a flight to Yambio and had attended the funeral on behalf of the Archbishop of Canterbury and had taken several Sudanese bishops from Nairobi with him. And he was back for the Salisbury service. It seemed our diocese had made a great effort. The disappointment was that Andrew had been the only person from Sudan at the cathedral service. Thank goodness there was one!

Back at home, the week's post had piled up. Sixty-six envelopes and a few packages – about par for the course. Ten a day is the average. I had planned to go to bed because it was 3 a.m. when we arrived, and the post would wait until after the morning services. But it didn't work that way. I couldn't sleep with all those letters holding their secrets. Curiosity overcame me. They had to be opened. I put them in three piles – parish business, Sudan affairs and personal matters. They looked about equal size, to be answered later. It was a good job I did open them. Kate Brown of Netherbury had died, on the very evening we had flown to Jerusalem. The funeral had been delayed for my return, and would be Tuesday. Suppose I had not read the post, and had gone to church on All Saints' Day, without knowing she was now among them? It paid to read it through; though it meant going to bed at 5 a.m. and getting up two hours later. The body clock will be confused for a few days, that's for sure.

The morning service at Hooke disposed of any tiredness. It is impossible to be tired at Hooke. The service was sung to the old Merbeck setting, unaccompanied. It was wonderfully refreshing to allow the whole liturgy to wash over me. Is there any other village church which sings the whole of Merbeck unaccompanied? Who would have thought that a tiny village deep in the Dorset countryside, total population under a hundred, would be the place for such an achievement? Lucy Crocker was there today which gave us all a boost. As an amateur operatic singer, she started Hooke's tradition of unaccompanied singing. She trained us so well, and gave us such confidence that we can now do it even when she is not there. The Merbeck rhythms seem timeless and their genius is that everyone seems able to take part, even me. If my original ambition for this Team had been fulfilled, each church would have developed its own distinctive contribution to give to the whole. One would have a healing ministry, one a children's resource centre, one a theological library, one would reserve the sacrament, one would develop inter-faith dialogue, another would co-ordinate the pastoral care. It's a disappointment that it hasn't happened. It is too much for each small community to do all these things. Each should develop one thoroughly, for the sake of them all. The sum of all the parts would be tremendous. That must be the ideal, the way forward for village churches. In my time, they have learnt to share the priests' ministry which is a step in the right direction but the real advance will be when each village has developed its own ministry and shares it. Hooke's special offering would be its unique musical tradition and the singing of Merbeck.

I wasn't on top form today. Maybe it was my streaming cold. Maybe it was lack of sleep. Maybe I hadn't prepared as thoroughly as usual. It didn't matter. That is the marvellous thing about a good liturgy. It covers the faults and foibles of the priest. It has a strength of its own. Some priests seem to think they have to make their own mark on the service, press their own personality on the people. God forbid! Let the liturgy speak. All the priest has to do is keep it moving, let it flow. So often the priest interrupts it with page numbers or other directions, or (at worst) with jokes! That is assassination! So today the liturgy was strong enough to carry me through and at the end I felt better and so did everyone else, as far as I could tell. People who make up their own liturgies find themselves exhausted at the end. It has depended too much on their presentation. Today's experience was the opposite. I began exhausted and ended refreshed, which is the right way round. I am sorry for people who don't understand the repetitive nature of the liturgy and want 'simple' services which are 'user-friendly'. They don't know what they are missing. I have the uncomfortable feeling that my generation will be the last to treasure the tradition. But if the tradition is abandoned in favour of concoctions depending upon the personality of the performers – God help us all!

Monday, 2nd November

Five things pressed today and I knew only three had a chance of getting done. The three piles of post had to be answered; Gordon Brown had to be visited because Kate's funeral is tomorrow, and Andrew had to be driven to Heathrow for the next of his commissions in Sudan.

Arrangements for Remembrance services at Beaminster, Toller and South Perrott would have to wait another day. Brenda Travers came to the rescue on the fifth issue which was putting together a list of people to receive Christmas hampers. Nobody knows Beaminster better than Brenda and nobody is a more tactful pastor. I can't count the number of people she has befriended at time of need. So she was the right person to draw up the list; she was sure to have it ready in time for the Beaminster Charities on Wednesday. It only needed a phone call to get that going. The other things weren't so simple.

Irene Hansford, Kate's daughter, was determined to read at the funeral. She practised on the telephone, and it sounded fine. It wouldn't be so easy on the day and I told her to give me a signal if she didn't feel she could do it when the time came. When I read at my mother's funeral, I was helped by the vicar who told me he would be ready if I shook my head at the time. Having a 'safety net' is a help. I have made the offer twenty or more times to grieving relatives and they have all appreciated it, but none has ever taken it up. It's amazing where strength comes from, but it does. Irene and her father were both convinced that my visit and the prayers had opened the way for Kate. She had died in her sleep a few hours later. This is an area of mystery; who can say they are not right?

The piles of unanswered post agitated me. They stood there like a judgement on my holiday and they made me wish I had never gone away. I wouldn't be able to sleep while they were there. So I gathered up the Sudan pile and decided to read them in the car while Andrew drove to the airport. It would give him the chance to comment, and advise on the replies. The parish letters were my problem so I sorted them into smaller piles – some were Minutes of meetings I had missed; some were agendas of meetings to come; others were reports from Cathedral Chapter, village worship groups, school headteacher, County Education Officer, Deanery Finance working party and the new Chancellor of the Diocese who had written a much-needed booklet of advice on faculty application. I could read the whole lot in one good evening session. When the pile was broken down, only a couple of letters needed written replies. It did wonders for morale to move the pile from one place to another.

The idea of reading the Sudan letters on the way to the airport didn't work because Andrew had decided that Kilele and Timothy should come and see him off. It was a good idea. It would help them so much if they felt a part of the venture and if they shared the excitement of seeing the plane and being with all the adults. On all the previous journeys, I had taken Andrew on my own, so the two boys looked upon it as a promotion to come with us. Instead of being long faced and worried and a bit tearful, they were laughing and excited and packing the car with Daddy's cameras and technical equipment. "Be careful," said Kilele, several times. "This is delicate" – and his four-year-old brother carried each piece as if his life depended upon it.

It was a shame to leave Anna at the house, but maybe she would welcome a time of peace and quiet and the chance to get the flat 'ship-shape' and think about her college course. It must be difficult for her with Andrew away so much. She has to provide for the boys, packed lunch every day, get them off to school looking clean and smart which they always do; then she gets herself off to college to study all day, in a language not her own, shopping on the way back and cooking as soon as she returns to two lively boys needing attention and food. Day after day after day – and she never fails. How she sticks at it, I do not know. But she does, and all credit to her. It must have been sad to wave Andrew off yet again, but I should think a few hours to herself would be more than welcome.

All the way to Heathrow the boys chattered on, ceaselessly. Kilele was counting the cars Daddy overtook, Tim was counting the lorries

41

and I was left to count the vans. The cars were winning easily until we pulled in for petrol. Then cars passed us at a great rate and for each one that passed a point was deducted. Kilele urged his dad to hurry, but by the time we got on the road again his score was 'minus ten' and I was suddenly in the lead. When we neared Heathrow, Timothy changed from lorries to planes and scored an incredible twenty-two in a few minutes, which said a lot about the busy-ness of Heathrow and the amazing organisation at that airport, but Kilele with his cars ran out the winner.

It was a long goodbye at Heathrow. I wondered how much the boys understood of their father's work. I knew that the latest commission would take him into the furthest part of Bahr-el-Ghazal, deep in the war zone. He would be at the front line where Arab North meets African South, where militant Islam meets infant Christianity. His work, for the Church Mission Society, was to report on the alleged raids by Arabs from the North, and to assess ways in which non-Government organisations could bring relief to the famine-stricken areas. The Northern part was under the Government control, the Southern part under control of the 'Rebels' or 'Liberation Army'. And the whole district was mined. It was a terrible commission, the most difficult yet. In spite of this, Andrew made the boys laugh and the farewell hugs were long and happy, with a lot of 'see you at Christmas' talk. "Bring me a nice present," said Tim. The only present I wanted was his dad's presence. That would be the only present that mattered.

I wondered how much of all the dangers was within the boys' understanding. Not much, I hoped. I took their hands after the farewells and I noticed they were both holding very tightly. "Uncle," said Kilele, as we left the airport and went out into the night, "if Daddy dies, will you look after us?"

It was a long dark journey home. The boys slept all the way, cuddled together.

Tuesday, 3rd November

There were three 'musts' today, all very different, and they all got done. It was essential to check that all the planning for my three Remembrance services on Sunday was in good hands; there was the Netherbury funeral in the afternoon and there was Colin Cuff's study group in the evening.

The Remembrance preparations were all different. South Perrott would have the ordinary communion service of the day, though Desmond Meadows would read the names for S. Perrott and Peter Coles for Chedington and Fred Cox had chosen hymns on a Remembrance theme. Toller, on the other hand, was hosting the Maiden Newton branch of the British Legion; and it would be a full Remembrance order of service, with five or six standards and similar number of wreaths to be laid. I explained there was not a memorial, but they thought the altar step would serve. I explained we only had fifty service sheets, but they said people could share. They asked if the service could be over in twenty minutes 'for the sake of the children' but I said it would be at least half an hour, even without a sermon. I am not happy that it will work well. The Legion comes to Toller every third year and there is a lot of difference between that and an annual event which builds its own tradition. The Beaminster plans were easier. That is an annual event. It has its own tradition and its own work force, who all know what to do. The only difference this year is that the Catholics have a new priest who doesn't know the routine but he has the adaptability of youth and inspires confidence. It would be nice if he also answered the telephone or put in an Ansaphone. I've made at least ten efforts to contact him since Sunday, without success. I have heard two conflicting theories over 'Ansaphones', and I can see the point of both. One is that an Ansaphone enables the recipient to filter the calls. He can deal with the ones he

43

wants and leave the awkward ones until he chooses. That's my method. The other is not to have an Ansaphone at all which keeps all predators at a distance; it also prevents problems piling up. This seems to be Father Jonathan's style. I don't blame him. It can't be funny to return home at the end of the day and find eight or nine problems waiting to greet you, instead of a wife.

The afternoon funeral was good. The people turned up and they sang, which lifted the whole occasion from gloom to gratitude. So often when someone has lived as long as Kate – 89 – the contemporaries have died and the funeral has an abandoned sort of feel to it. That wasn't the case today. Her country qualities may be out of fashion but proper respect was paid in a well-filled church. I knew what I wanted to say and I said it with conviction because I knew it was true. At any funeral I am in a strange position. It is probable that everyone present will have known the deceased better and longer than me – and yet I am the one who has to speak about her. In many cases, there has been some family rift or dispute and this means that the words spoken could favour one side or the other and make matters worse. This is the way Earl Spencer abused the privilege of the pulpit when the Dean of Westminster evaded his own responsibility at Diana's funeral. This is something I will not do. On the other hand, if I play safe with generalities and platitudes, it means nothing to anybody and the people will cough and shuffle their feet until it's over and I will feel a fraud and not sleep at night. The only way I can rest at night and sleep well is to have said something which the people know is the truth and is worth saying. I have known priests who have said what the people wanted to hear, rather than what was known to be true. I have also known priests who have three funeral addresses on file, and use whichever one seems most suitable. Whatever failings I have that is not one of them. If I do not believe a thing to be true, I do not say it. The integrity of the pulpit is not to be treated lightly. Today, the simple faithful life we were celebrating made preaching easy. Besides, her own husband had described Kate and God as 'making a good team'. That was complete, in itself.

I was not happy with my evening effort. I had prepared thoroughly and I was keen to do it well, but I didn't.

Colin Cuff's study group is important. Every parish needs a 'think tank' – a group of people who will wrestle with issues and problems. In an ideal world, this is what Church Councils would do. But this is not an ideal world and Church Councils are invariably confronted with long agendas which bog them down in the minutiae of parish life. They seldom have time to delve into theology.

Church Councils are important and I defy anybody to show me a more effective set of Councils than we have in this Team. They have raised sums of money which would have seemed unbelievable a few years ago. They have restored their church buildings and now they maintain them to a high standard, lovingly. They have chosen how to worship, and in what form. And they have – with the occasional exception – done it all with great good humour. But intellectual, ethical and spiritual fare has not been on their agenda; yet someone should engage the clergy in these issues, otherwise they will not be extended, they will live in their own world and their preaching will become removed from the way the people are thinking. It happens all the time.

So I recognised the value of Colin's group and I know that their present study book, "Bishops on the Bible", was opening a vital subject. In fact, I had taken the book to Jerusalem, read it thoroughly and highlighted key themes, of which there were many. How we understand the Bible and the sort of authority it has, are the crucial questions which lie behind every religious debate that arises. This became evident at the Lambeth Conference when all the world could see the huge differences between African and European understanding of the Scriptures and the utterly divergent views which followed. So I had prepared carefully, thought deeply and was looking forward to it. In spite of all this, the opportunity came and went, and I failed to deliver. The trouble was, I was over-prepared! I had used those long, dark evenings in Jerusalem to prepare a lecture, an academic response to an academic book. But when I sat down in a cosy living room, it seemed out of place, so I folded it up. Instead, I asked each of the group in turn to say how they responded to the book and how they used the Bible. The variety of replies made the evening worthwhile. They ranged from not using the Bible at all because its sayings seemed negative and unhelpful to using the Bible all the time as a comfort in all problems and even for ideas when letter writing. Some said their attitude to the Bible had been through many changes and was still changing; one said the Bible was the unchanging fixed point in a changing world. It was a good sharing of views and a good building of confidence in each other because we disagreed without being disagreeable. My lecture remained undelivered, and I was left nursing a problem. How do I communicate a sound and modern understanding of the Bible? And if I don't, will the false literalism of an earlier age continue, unchallenged and uncorrected? Those attitudes keep the Church locked in the theology and the attitudes of the Dark Ages. So the evening did not go according to plan and I was disappointed in myself. In fact I came home, put the lecture on the back burner and poured a vodka.

Wednesday, 4th November

The Wednesday Communion never ceases to surprise me – twenty-eight people were there this morning. It's all part of the Mothers' Union revival. They make the first Wednesday their own. They read the Epistle, they choose the hymns, one of them administers the Chalice and soon they will offer the Intercessions, I hope. Then they go off and enjoy coffee and chat and by 2 p.m. some of them are back to lead the small children in "First Steps", an introduction to church and to worship.

This amounts to a revival, and long may it continue. The M.U. has been written off by too many people, especially by parish priests. Its "sell-by" date is considered to be past. In many places it has become not so much a Mothers' Union as a Grandmothers' Union and here, a Great Grandmothers' Union. It has got into a generation gap which has fixed a great gulf between it and everyone else. This shouldn't be, and it needn't be. Grandmothers have a key role in any family. They are often the wise elders whose experience holds things together and whose warmth bestows understanding and sympathy all round. As individuals, most of them will have done this for their own family at some stage. It is a puzzle and a disappointment that, collectively, the M.U. doesn't achieve as much together as the individuals do, separately. Perhaps the tide is beginning to turn in Beaminster. There is such a store of good things in all these M.U. groups. If the store was liberated and poured out, the young mums, who have so much to cope with, would be hugely supported and encouraged. But there is that great gulf, fixed.

However, it is a mistake to dismiss the Mothers' Union just because it isn't all that it could be. None of us are. The saddest thing is to forget what we could be. Someone has to hold that vision in front of the Mothers' Union, to lead them on. Someone has to hold that vision in front of each one of us, to lift us up. I suppose that is the priestly function.

I ought to do it better than I do because I have seen the Mothers' Union as it could be, in full swing. In Sudan, where whole villages have lost their menfolk to the war, it is the Mothers' Union who teach the children, lead the worship and keep the church alive. In refugee camps and places of deprivation, where famine threatens, it is the Mothers' Union who march and demonstrate and hammer on the Camp Commander's door, demanding fair shares for their children. Mary Sumner, who claimed that 'mother power' would change the nation, would be proud of them. It is a strange contrast with this land where the Mothers' Union has become passive, lulled into compliance, while family traditions collapse around them and they know not what to do. So they serve tea. But there is more to these grandmothers than that.

If the Beaminster 'revival' bridges the generation gap, it will be a great achievement. When gathered together, they have a wealth of experience. At least three of them are clergy widows; among them Betty Fortescue-Thomas who, when the M.U. was searching for a leader, took it over at the age of 86, and pepped it up no end! She learnt her survival techniques in a hard school as a priest's wife in Baghdad before the war, and she retains them. I had been told that she had had a fall while

I was in Jerusalem, and had been rushed to hospital by the paramedics who had revived her. But there she was at the Communion this morning, full of beans and bounce at the age of 89. Truly, the M.U. is to be reckoned with. Age does not weary them and the years do not condemn. They are tireless and timeless and have so much to offer. But who will receive it?

The Team Meeting which followed was a gem! When I retire, there is nothing I will miss more. The lovely thing is that there is no agenda so there is absolute freedom to raise any issue, and no one has the slightest idea what will crop up. And no minutes are kept, so nothing is recorded and anyone can say anything, which opens the door for endless variety, and that is good for us all. Today David Shearlock, the former Dean of Truro, was with us and I thought he might raise some issues to set us thinking. Not so. It was Richard Satchell, a Reader, who set us alight with his plain spoken view of Deanery Synod. It had no plan, purpose or direction. It stumbled around like a blind man without a guide. He had served for three years which was more than enough and he didn't wish to continue. I listened quietly and said nothing. I had reached similar conclusions about Deanery Synods years ago, when I was Rural Dean. I remembered my predecessor as Rural Dean (Bob Moorhead) being taken ill and put into intensive care in Yeovil Hospital. I had been sent to tell him that we were postponing the next Synod until he had recovered. He was all wired up, with machines recording every heart-beat, but he managed to tell me that "If the Synod never meets again, it will not greatly affect the Kingdom of God." That was at least twenty years ago; now Richard was telling us the same story, and I believed him. The layer of Government called 'Deanery Synod' served no useful purpose. We have an effective and quite enjoyable Team Council and we do not need another layer between us and the Diocesan Synod. We all agreed with him and I was left with feelings of utmost thankfulness that Richard had been in the front line of Deanery issues for the past three years, and not me. If he does give up his place on the Standing Committee, I am quite sure we will not find anyone else with his unusual mix of skills. He has experience of the business world; in his working life he lived through the privatisation of the water industry which needed all his skills of man-management. As a Reader in the Church he has been preaching for the past twelve years. His rather earnest manner veils a considerable experience of the way the world is while his deep commitment to the Church wrestles with the way it could and should be.

It is a mystery to me why no one has put his name forward to become a locally ordained Priest. Every parish has agreed to keep a look-out for suitable candidates for the priesthood; the Bishop has urged parishes to select them and here is one who is totally committed, evidently wise, and has already been preaching for twelve years and acting as a Priest in all but name. Why don't they put his name forward? Perhaps the Church Councils are leaving it to me. But I have spelt out in the clearest words of one syllable that, if the local Ministry is to be truly local, the local people must make the choice. Not me. We want them to belong to the people and be of the people. Or perhaps there is another reason. Perhaps people are cautious because Richard is a 'newcomer'. There is always the feeling that long-established country people shouldn't be taken over by newcomers whose ideas might change things. And Richard would change things. He would bring the brains of business to bear. Some say the Church needs to be more like business. I fear the business model will take us further away from Jesus, from the Gospel and from ordinary parishioners. But it is the current fashion and such thinking may shape the future.

It's difficult to be a 'newcomer'. If they don't take part in things, they are thought to be unsociable; if they do take part in things, they run the risk of being accused of interfering and wanting to take over. It's like walking a tightrope. So Richard continues as a Reader, as the people wish. Yet, for some years, we have used our Readers as partners and equals. Our congregations have got used to them bringing the Sacrament and administering it; no one has objected, in fact it is appreciated. Why does the Bishop not lay hands on them in Ordination without delay and give us the priests we need? What is to prevent it? Why should they have to embark on a three-year course of training? They are preaching already, and have been for years. What would they be training for, which they are not doing already? Sometimes the Church seems to find ways of preventing anything happening. We should be the people who remove barriers to progress, not the people who put them up and then patrol them with sentries armed with Synod regulations.

In my time our Readers could have made a succession of local priests who would have been the ones "who know and are known" in the parishes. At Hooke there would have been the late and much loved Vera Davies. She had been a missionary nurse in Namibia for much of her working life and had been the District Nurse throughout our Team area until multiple sclerosis overtook her. Even then, from her wheelchair, she had established and nurtured Hooke's children's work. She was steeped in the language of the prayer book, the traditions of the Church, the prayers and poetry of psalmody and hymnody were in her blood and on her lips. And Broadwindsor would have had Dorothy Shiner who, as a school teacher, had taught whole generations who are now the parents and even the grandparents of today's Broadwindsor children. She, too, is steeped in the tradition of the Church with an unrivalled knowledge of local families, but age and failing eyesight now make impossible what could have been. Burstock would have had the late Dr. Colin Roberts as their priest; as the executive Secretary of the Oxford University Press and as an Oxford Don, he had tutored several students who had become Bishops. He had marked and assessed their papers and recommended them (or not) for higher things. Why should he have been subjected to a three-year academic course? As a New Testament scholar, he had been one of the compilers of the New English Bible! It would have been an insult to send him on a course. He could have written the whole course! In fact, before his crippling illness, he came to our Team meetings to give us all a Biblical exegesis of the texts for the coming Sunday, and every priest benefited from his learning. And in earlier times, there had been Lawrie Dover whose life was given to the Church and its traditions and whose second name should have been Loyalty. And in the present time there is Lilian Wallace who gently guides all the clergy to where they should be on a Sunday and who tactfully arranges with each parish the services they can and cannot have. She has been walking in this minefield for years without ever causing an explosion. In fact, her super-sensitive radar system spots and de-fuses trouble while it is still a mile off. All these people have done the work the Church allowed them to do and have brought blessings but, if they had been made priests, it would have affirmed them and taken untold stress and pressures off me.

It was good to have the Very Reverend former Dean at the meeting but it was Richard Satchell, who remains Not at All Reverend, who got us all talking and thinking!

In the afternoon, I wrote the Pew News leaflet along the lines the Team meeting had agreed and delivered it for typing. It will be run off the photocopier in the morning. I got in touch with everyone involved in Sunday's Remembrance Day. I am still not sure the Maiden Newton branch is really geared for Toller church. I would like a rehearsal. They say too many people are involved. All the more reason to have a rehearsal, in my opinion. Anyway, I went to Toller again, took the service sheets, agreed the hymns and the reading and that is as much as I can do.

The evening meeting of the Beaminster Charities raised some issues in my mind. I would have an easier life if I didn't see problems and issues so quickly.

The Charities are in excellent hands in that John Groves, the Clerk, has every detail at his finger tips and understands the terms of the Trust Deeds which control us. And Ralph Bugler, the Chairman, has as good a knowledge of Beaminster as any man alive. In fact we meet in the Council Office under the board which names him among the

Council's long-serving leaders. The problems which arise are not of their making.

The fact is that the charity is rich by local standards. It has more funds that it can distribute, to such an extent that we authorised £3,500 worth of Christmas hampers without batting an eyelid. Some of the applications for funding come from people who are articulate, who can write a good letter and who know how to make their case. They may not be the people who really have greatest need and who are most deserving of help. The people with greatest need may not even know of the charity's existence and, if they do, they may well be too shy to come forward, or be unwilling to expose their situation, or too proud to 'accept charity'. So the charity, with its wise investments, becomes richer but the people who have profound needs do not. We were all aware of it, we all felt a little uncomfortable about it, but none of us know what to do about it.

An even bigger issue arose from St. Mary's School's request for help with the cost of purchasing computer equipment. As Governors of the school, Janet Page and I declared an interest and did not speak or vote. The debate was significant – should the charity give the money and improve the education opportunities for the town's children or should the charity refuse the money on the grounds that the supply of equipment was the responsibility of the Education Authority, and the charity should not do their work? In the end, a small majority favoured the school but the point was well made that the more the charity does, the less the proper authorities will do. It was of extra special interest to me because I know that the school is desperately trying to find the necessary funding to retain its 7-class system which benefits children and staff so much. But the budget restrictions may make it necessary to revert to the 6-class system, which would be a shame and have a detrimental effect on everybody. The charity has the money to meet the shortfall. But if such a request were to come from the school, it would be the clearest ever case of the proper authority failing in its responsibility and being baled out by a charity, which isn't right. Yet the money is there and it's meant to benefit children. This is a classic dilemma. In the night, I woke up time and again with a different opinion each time, but no solution. Anyway, the request hasn't come, so why do I worry about the hypothetical? My successors will have to think this one through.

Thursday, 5th November

I didn't expect any fireworks today. Mary arrived at the Office in the usual way, the Pew News was ready for her to print and I had opened and answered the post by the time she arrived, which is the ideal way to start the day. It didn't last. BBC rang, followed within minutes by Westcountry TV. They both wanted to interview me about Andrew's film "Living in a Minefield" to be screened by Channel 2 on Saturday. They had seen a 'preview' and wanted to run radio and television trailers. They wanted to do the interviews in church, in front of a Sudan display. I told them the display was all set up for Remembrance Day. They wanted to come within the hour! Television people think they are gods. They expect everything on their own terms and they imagine everyone will run around at their bidding. I told them it couldn't be until the afternoon and they were quite miffed. As Joan Holland would have to change the whole display board – which she had only just put up – and as I had to change my afternoon plans, they should have been grateful, not miffed.

The morning was given to the meeting of the Strode Room trustees and a presentation to Wilfrid and Dorothy Buckingham. It marked their retirement after twenty-five years, in which they set about restoring the broken-down almshouses and raising the £18,000 to establish it in trust for the use of the town. It had taken four years of ceaseless effort, it had been completed in 1977, the Queen's Jubilee year, and Wilfrid had chaired the Trustees for the following twenty-one years, until he reached the age of ninety! It was a success story because the room had become a treasure for the town, well used and well cared for. It seems hard to believe now that it was a matter of such controversy at the time.

The story is that the greater number of people had been willing to see the old almshouses fall into ruin. No one was willing to fund their

53

restoration. The Church Council had the opportunity but was divided; they lacked the funds and the vision and did nothing. Wilfrid, a Church Council member, was annoyed. He had been unable to convince the Vicar of the time, or the Church Wardens, of the value of the property to the church, although it was on the church doorstep. So Wilfrid backed his judgment by setting up a private enterprise for the town with the result that the church lost a unique opportunity which would never recur.

It was a strange irony that my first public engagement, the day after I was installed as Vicar, was the opening of the room by the Lord Lieutenant, December 1st 1977. Immediately I regretted it had not become a church property. What a marvellous centre it would have made for the Team's ministry. It would have been the Team Office, the meeting place, the resource centre and the library which we have always needed. Joan and I would not have had to make our house available for the purpose. It would have saved us domestic strife and harassment, it would have retained our privacy, it would have prevented me from becoming the perpetual focus which is inevitable if I host the office. I doubt my successor will be so foolish as to allow the office to be in his house. Then the search will be renewed for something similar to the Strode Room. Oh! What a lost opportunity! To complete the irony, the Church Council now manages the Strode Room on behalf of the Trustees. It means the Church does all the donkey work, without the benefits. Such is life!

At least the morning meeting was straightforward. The budget was balanced, bookings were as good as ever, David Hedworth, the architect, had presented drawings for storage cupboards in the entrance lobby, which we accepted and commissioned. It is a relief to be able to make decisions and do things without the long and complicated process of Faculty Application. So the morning was far from wasted.

The radio and the television people came in quick succession. I was annoyed on Joan Holland's behalf. She takes endless trouble over the display boards in church and they are always up-to-date and topical.

She had just dismantled the Sudan display and had designed one for Remembrance Day and had put it up for all to see. Now she was asked to take it all down, which she did without a word of complaint. These displays must take her hours and hours and where she gets the material from I cannot imagine. It must cost her a pretty penny, as well as a lot of time. I wonder if she is ever properly thanked or whether it is all taken for granted. I didn't hear the television crew thank her. It was just a matter of "Put it here, the light's better there ... not that picture, it's too dark ... we want a map in the middle ..." and Joan was busy obliging as if she was one of their staff. I told her she should charge a £100 fee for her efforts – but it is always assumed that everyone wants to be on television and that they will do it all for the glamour and publicity of appearing. I didn't want to appear at all because it was Andrew's film, not mine. He had been through the war zone to make it; I hadn't even been on the journey. I would appear as a 'talking head' which seldom makes good television. When the cameras started running, I was not confident. On a Sunday, when I preach, I have prepared thoroughly and I know the listeners, inside out. This was different. I could not prepare at all because I didn't know what questions would be asked and the only thing I knew about the listeners was that they would be more in number than I had preached to in a whole year, or probably in ten years added together. And most of them probably would not know where Sudan is, and certainly wouldn't know what the war is about. I, on the other hand, knew too much; so much that it would be difficult to know where to begin, and what to emphasise, given only two minutes! So I played safe. I tried to mention Weymouth College who had trained Andrew when his English was near zero. I mentioned Sherborne Abbey who had given the camera equipment which made the film and I mentioned Salisbury Diocese which sponsored him in the first place. Better to keep it local, I thought. Afterwards, Joan put all the Remembrance display back again and I hope that I thanked her properly. She is one of many church people who work and work without a penny reward and too often without so much as a 'thank you'. It's a miracle of faith that they stick at it.

At last! An evening at home. I needed it!

It gave me the chance to go through the December service programme. It demands a concentrated session. It won't come right by luck. When every parish has made its requests known to Lilian and every colleague has made their preferences known to me, there comes the time to sit down with every door closed and curtain drawn, radio and television unplugged and phone off the hook to see if the jigsaw will fit together. The marvel is that, usually, it does. Tonight was jigsaw night. December is fairly easy because no one is away except John Whettem who is at a Chaplaincy in Cyprus. And everyone is fit except Bernard Oliver, whose eyesight is not yet restored. So the second draft got it right. It had taken about two hours. All the parishes should be satisfied; they have their wish. But there is always the risk of a late change and one change has a domino effect on the others which means going back to the drawing board, closing the doors and drawing the curtains again. Very often the change comes from the parish end. It is not unusual for one person in a parish to tell me that the parish wants one thing and someone else to tell Lilian that the parish wants another thing. The truth is that there is division in almost every parish, about the best ways to worship. Some want the old tradition, others the new. Some want sacramental services, others want family services; some want this time, some want that. They used to expect the vicar to decide and then the losers could blame him. Now they have to decide among themselves and it can cause quite a furore, especially if a minority decides on behalf of the majority. This leads to conflicting messages reaching us. But if I decide whom to believe, the losers will again be able to blame me instead of debating and resolving their own differences in their own elected committees. That is what they should do. It is all too easy to blame the vicar and use him as the scapegoat. It absolves local committees of responsibility and of blame, but it is basically unsound. It is a throw-back to the old autocratic syle which most of the congregation grew up with and which most of them prefer. It allows them to hide from debating the issues, and from facing their differences by saying "The vicar says ..." No progress that way.

So the December programme is prepared. But I doubt it is the last word. There will be some phone calls ...

At last I was able to sit down without interruption and read the pile of reports which had been waiting since the Jerusalem journey. The Cathedral's plans to honour the 900th anniversary of St. Osmund, the review of the Deanery Finance Working Party, the new Chancellor's booklet on faculty procedures and the Education Authority's recommendations on bureaucracy, all waited. I wouldn't have chosen any of them for relaxation. And I didn't find any of them inspiring. But they had to be read. Duty required it. Meantime, my lovely library of cricket books looks down on me, and my collection of biographies which I eye longingly, remains un-read. The faculty application procedures have no appeal, yet they took my time. This should not be, but is.

And when bedtime came I remembered it was fireworks night. I suppose I should have been out and about, being seen at a bonfire somewhere. And so I went to bed feeling guilty about the things undone instead of satisfied at the things done. It's a difficult balance to keep and I fail it, most days.

Friday, 6th November

It is St. Leonard's Day and I needed no reminding that it was exactly a year ago that we buried Leonard Studley of Broadwindsor on 5th November last. Today was the right day to visit Olive, his widow.

I had thought a morning visit would be better for her as I imagined that, at the age of 80, she would take an afternoon rest. But it didn't work that way. Things seldom do work the way I plan! This morning it was the office which trapped me, even though I had made a good start and answered the post before Mary arrived. The good start did not continue.

Lilian came to discuss the December services which was a help and which was programmed, but while she was there an issue blew up about the parish Christmas card. The distribution of the card is well organised under a group led by Margaret Walters. But the content of the card and its cover come to me for agreement and I couldn't agree with Mary's choice. It was a popular design which was obviously under the copyright of several charities. We would be in breach of the law. I suggested we should use local talent for the local card. Feathers began to fly and I retreated to the safety of my study, reflecting that I produce twelve magazines a year, each with a cover and twenty illustrations, and I have never been in breach of copyright because I always use local artists. Seemed common sense to me.

Lilian's patience was tested further by the unexpected arrival of two people who wanted to explain complicated items for Team News, followed by Brenda Travers with some advertisements which also needed explaining; before they left, Margaret Satchell rang, asking for advice on the Strode Room Managers' agenda which she had to draw up, and Clifford Howe arrived to discuss points of contract which I said needed church wardens' opinion as well as mine. Meanwhile, a Beaminster mother rang to cancel the Christening arranged for the 22nd and wanted to fix a December date, which we couldn't agree because Christmas interfered with the normal programme.

I don't want to become the sort of priest who works by appointments, like a doctor's surgery, but how else is it possible? Lilian was the only person with an appointment and she was delayed nearly two hours by people without appointments. This can't be the best way of doing things. By then, I had no hope of getting to Olive Studley, as planned.

One of the great mistakes is having the Team office in the house. It draws everyone, like bears to a honey pot. I become the centre of everything, including things which need not be anything to do with me. And it leaves my colleagues out of everything, unless they come in to Beaminster and force themselves into the scene. It means the office is in many ways counter-productive. It focuses attention into the centre and onto me, against our declared policy of promoting village independence and lay leadership. Mary has worked so hard, too hard, giving her time and making it her life and it has achieved a lot, but unfortunately it has also created the trap of centralisation when the intention was the opposite.

The postponed visit to Olive Studley happened in the afternoon and I wasn't surprised that her sister, Vi, was there from Crewkerne, and that she soon appeared with tea and home-made cakes. The elder son, Mike, and his wife also arrived from Crewkerne a few minutes later, as did Leonard's sister, 'Queenie'. No need to worry about Olive being lonely! The daughters had also been over at the weekend and Bill had phoned from Australia. It's that sort of family! Olive, it turned out, hadn't been well and was awaiting the result of blood tests. I only eked this out of her after she had spent half an hour enquiring after Joan and telling everyone about our Godsons Kilele and Timothy. I will start worrying about Olive when she stops thinking about others. This caring concern had been a trait of Leonard's which he never surrendered through all his long illness. In fact on his death bed he spent his time thanking everybody, including me.

Leonard remains my ideal of local priesthood. Of course the idea came twenty years too late, for him, and he remained a layman. He was the natural 'elder' of the community. He had been church warden for a generation, had held most other offices of the church, had turned the twentieth century story of Broadwindsor into a popular book and was steeped in Biblical thought and language. And, above all, he was local. Nobody more so. One of the reasons we have drawn blanks in our efforts to create a local ordained ministry is that the people who have emerged as likely candidates are not really of the locality. Certainly not in the way Leonard was. They have all sorts of credentials and qualifications gained from afar. But they lack the one thing needful – long knowledge of the local network of families.

People coming into a village to retire do not always realise that they are becoming part of a fine and delicate web of relationships which has been a long time in the weaving. Most people already have their place in the way of things. The arrival of a talented, experienced and capable newcomer can be quite a strain on the web. If wisdom is one of the newcomer's talents, he or she will stay in the background until invited to do something. If awareness of village ways is not one of her gifts, she will volunteer herself at the first opportunity, only to discover that the invisible web is tightening, and she isn't quite in it. Oh! the arts and subtleties of village life! Even people trained in group dynamics have been unaware of the impact of their own arrival on village dynamics. I learnt this a few years ago when the late John Lilley led a course of training lay pastoral assistants – not to be priests, but pastoral assistants. When I delivered one of the lectures, I found that almost all the 'candidates' were recent arrivals. I was not at all popular when I pointed out that each community already had a network of neighbourly concern and that, if newcomers were proclaimed the pastors, it would be taken as sheer paternalism by the long-established people, who had managed quite nicely for years, thank you. It isn't a surprise that the L.P.A. network has not solved much, in spite of all the capable and well-intentioned people involved. The whiff of paternalism will be even stronger, when a newcomer offers to be their priest. It is assumed (s)he will start telling the villagers how they should live their lives. Of course that is not what a priest does, but it is what many people think a priest does. A newcomer who intrudes herself into the network in such a way will find the network knows how to react. How much easier it must be in urban areas where the network is less tightly drawn.

Leonard would have had none of these problems. But he lived and died a layman, widely esteemed as the Sage of Broadwindsor. It is because of Leonard that I believe in ordained ministry locally. If it is possible for villages to produce such as Leonard, of course there must be a place for local ordination. But, conversely, the likes of Leonard are few and far between.

Saturday, 7th November

This was to be Kilele's day – off to Southampton for the big match. But I knew it would be my day as well. The Saints would win, lose or draw but we would be winners whatever happened.

For Kilele it was a visit to 'the big stadium'. The fact that it was the smallest stadium in the Premiership was irrelevant. For me, it was also a visit to my sister and as many of her family as happened to be calling that day.

For Kilele, there would be the sight of the famous Matthew Le Tissier playing for us and there would be the infamous Paul Gascoigne, against us. As Kilele had watched the video of Le Tissier's first fifty Premiership goals until he knew every goal by heart and could even number them backwards, the sight of him 'in the flesh' would have all the more meaning. For me, there would be the nostalgia of another Dell visit. I wondered if by any chance it might be my thousandth. This was something beyond calculation because my first match had been while the war was still on! Southampton had 'guest stars' in the team that day, mostly from army bases in Aldershot and Salisbury. We beat Luton by 12 goals to 3! My first match gave me the club's record never-to-be-repeated score! In the Saints' line-up, at centre forward was one Alf Ramsey who scored four of the goals and later became Sir Alfred, manager of England's World Cup winners. The memories were so vivid that I am sure I could take anyone straight to the seats we sat in on March 3rd, fifty-four years ago. I was eight years old and a love affair, which was for better for worse till death us do part, had begun. Now Kilele was eight . . . It would be my day, as well as his.

There was one problem nagging my mind which would put a shadow over the day, and another in his mind which cropped up approximately every twenty minutes. The cloud over me was that I can't come to terms with the way things have changed. I have loved football for the football, nothing more. Now it is clear that people running clubs, including mine, are in it for the money – and it is very big money. The directors, who used to be the club's biggest givers, have become takers and millionaires by clever (and dubious) dealing on the Exchange. That was when I stopped going. And the players move from club to club according to whatever contract their agents can negotiate. They are footballing mercenaries. They don't love the club they are playing for in the way I love it. How can they? They pop over from Italy or Israel, Norway or Denmark to make their name in the Premiership, or they come south from Manchester or Liverpool when their day is done, to secure a generous end-of-career contract on the strength of the name they once made in the Premiership. Loyalty, which was once the name of the game, is now not so much as named among them. Gone are the days when Terry Paine played eighteen years and 800 games for Saints – still the record for the whole country and one which will certainly not be beaten. Then there was Mick Channon who, apart from the aberration of a short sojourn with Manchester City, thrilled us for nearly twenty years and still holds the club record of 223 goals. And now nostalgia overcomes me at the sight of Le Tissier who, alone in the whole Premiership, continues the tradition of one-club loyalty. His unique skills have saved us from relegation year upon year; he deserves the Freedom of the City, and more. But he will not receive as much as the mercenaries, who come and take their pickings until something better crops up. These were the clouds hovering over me. The fact that the ticket for Kilele cost £20 and that I used to go in the boys' block, week after week, for 6d old money, reflected the changed times.

The cloud over Kilele was simply that Saints were bottom of the league, a long way behind anybody, and had won only one match. His arithmetic was being severely tested by the various calculations of who would have to lose, and by how many goals we would have to win, to get off bottom place. When he had satisfactorily arranged the results to get us off bottom place, he began the more complicated calculations of how to get out of the bottom three. The complexity of those results projected a month ahead were beyond me but he announced that we could be half way up the league table by Christmas. Would that it were so simple! But it was refreshing to know that hope does still spring eternal.

I must have seen most things that there are to see in fifty-four years of matches at the Dell and I have run the whole range of emotions from triumph to despair, many times over. The triumphs have mainly been escaping relegation in the last match of the season when Le Tissier would, like a sorcerer, produce something out of nothing at the last gasp and save the situation. This annual torture, this repeated drama would surely happen in one season too many and the signs are that this is the season. But there had been earlier triumphs, when the Saints fielded five England captains in one match (Mills, Keegan, Watson, Channon and Ball) and the Irish captain, Chris Nichols, as well. That team had led us to be runners-up in the First Division and to two semi-finals. They had played with an abandoned freedom which kept us on a perpetual high. Those had been heady days, but not typical. Our natural place seems to be at the other end of the drama, and today the next stage was played out.

Just as I had boasted to Kilele that I had seen everything there was to see in football, the referee provided something I had never seen before when Middlesborough were reduced to nine men by two sendings off. It was a desperate match – twice we came from behind to equalise, then took the lead with four minutes to go, only to give it away with a miss-kick on the goal line in injury time. Agony and ecstasy, all in one match.

Kilele's reactions were as interesting as the match. One minute on his feet, fist in the air, face jubilant. Next minute, down on his seat, head in his hands. Then "Oh! referee, where's your glasses?" followed by "Uncle, I would have scored that ..." His understanding was considerable, his involvement total. I felt I was passing a baton ...

We were back home just in time to see his father's documentary on Channel 2. Of course I knew what to expect as BBC had sent an advance copy, but there was still something special about seeing it transmitted 'live' (as they say). I felt a lot of pride (too much?) in his achievements and thought he fulfilled the dual role of camera man and commentator brilliantly. BBC got two journalists for the price of one! I await other people's comments with interest.

Tomorrow will be difficult. Not because I will have four services; that's normal. But the services will be so different. Beaminster in the morning and South Perrott will have the ordinary service of the Sunday with the theme of Abraham. Toller in the morning and Beaminster in the afternoon will have the Remembrance Order but Toller's will be geared to children, Beaminster's will not. The preacher's problem is obvious. All the sermons will have to be different, but one problem will be hidden from most people. I will not know the congregation in the way that I know them the rest of the year and the congregation will not know me. For many, if not most, it will be the only sermon they hear in the year. It provides the preacher with a different sort of a challenge. In an ordinary week, the rapport between priest and people exists from the beginning, because each knows the other. On Remembrance Sunday the rapport, which is essential if there is to be any communication, has to be won afresh. I am not surprised that a good many clergy object to Remembrance Day and wish it would go away. They hide under the excuses that it glorifies war or stirs national jingoism. It needn't do any of those things if it is well handled. But handling it well is very demanding, and that is the real reason for clergy reluctance. There is the fear of being unable to rise to the occasion and to the expectation. I feel it myself at the moment. Extra prayers required. Right now.

Sunday, 8th November (Remembrance Day)

The day wasn't as difficult as I expected. The people come in great numbers, each with their own reasons for remembering times past or people past, and I find it very moving – very moving indeed. I imagine all the memories, all the griefs, all the thanksgivings put on to a set of scales. No scales would be able to weigh them. It would be too much. I was worried about rapport, or lack of it, among people who come inside the church only once a year but, as soon as I thought of them as people whose thoughts could not be weighed, I felt respect for them and for the (unknown) reasons for their attendance. Maybe that was the beginning of 'rapport'. One thing does puzzle me. A good number of people parading or looking important were younger than me, and I was five when the war began. So what did they have to do with it? Especially in West Dorset which didn't suffer the blitz the way we did in Southampton where we had been bombed-out and had lost home and everything. Then we suffered it again in Liverpool and again in Plymouth. My father's move to three centres of destruction gave me a schoolboy's taste of things but I doubted whether some of the principal performers today had even that. Anyway, I buried that thought and concentrated on the medalled survivors and the Beaminster names soon to be called. Yes, Beaminster had not suffered the Blitz but it had suffered in other ways, as the long list of names proved. Then another thought emerged. The Royal British Legion like a preacher who 'knows something about it' which is natural. They always look a bit askance at me, because I was so young at the time. But I retire next year. So, whatever age will preachers who 'know something about it' be? Anyway, I buried that thought as well because it will not be my problem, in the years ahead.

The Toller event was very strange. I had a strong feeling it would be. From my point of view, nothing went right and I was not satisfied. The church was bursting full before I arrived but they had only 50 service sheets for a hundred or more people; the children had none. The children were all outside the church with their banners, wondering what to do and where to sit and whom to pass them to, and when. I wondered as well. So did the parade leader who was a nice man from the Maiden Newton branch who hadn't a clue because he had left it to me. This is why I had wanted a rehearsal. By the time I got all the children lined up, it was well past 11 o'clock, the time of the Silence. Eventually the banners were handed over, the Legion Standard was dipped, the anthem played, the bugle blown and the Silence kept (at ten past eleven) but, to my dismay, no names were read. Out of the corner of my mouth I whispered "Names?" to the man from Maiden Newton but there were none. I thought it very strange. I had Toller's names ready, but couldn't read those if the others weren't read. So all those people came from Rampisham, Cattistock, Maiden Newton, Wraxall, Halstock and further afield and didn't hear the names. I thought that was central to the event. I don't know whether it was a mistake or the Maiden Newton custom. Anyway, I recovered from the shock and also from the sight of all the children squatting on the floor midst the wreaths, which they kept knocking off the chancel step, and I decided the service should be greatly curtailed – partly because it had started late but mainly because all the children had no service sheet and no seats. On their way out, the people were fulsome in their appreciation. "Lovely service, Vicar," was repeated again and again, which was gratifying, though it was not my own feeling. These events require rehearsal or marshalling, or both. And the smaller the church, the more important that is. This had not been done.

I knew the afternoon would be different, and it was. The Beaminster Royal British Legion is well organised and has its own tradition. I have received the Standard of the Women's Section from Nita Spencer for all the twenty-one years that I have been here (and she did it for twenty-four years before that) and I have received the Standard of the Men's Section from David Bullock for a good many years. Sir James Spicer, formerly a professional soldier and a paratrooper, has read the lesson for even more years – excepting once when he was in hospital, and Graham Hawkins has played the Last Post and Reveille forty times in all. With such continuity and only occasional changes in personnel, the efficiency of the event is guaranteed. The order of service also repeats itself in a changeless way; even the hymns are written into the routine. This means that the only variable is the sermon, which puts a big responsibility on the preacher. I think I have done it at least ten times, but we have also heard Bishop John Waller, Bishop Geoffrey Tiarks, two or three of the Catholic priests and several of my colleagues. The one I remember best was Deaconess Carol Graham, who warmed my heart with her Indian perspective. Of course there was also the one I would like to forget, when Richard Thornburgh tried to be clever and deliberately put the Japanese view of the war on the Fiftieth VJ anniversary. It was out of place and almost led to a walk-out by the Burma Star veterans who were meant to be our honoured guests. This seemed to me anything but clever, in fact it did nothing for the integrity of the pulpit because it was a snub which is not what the privileged position of the pulpit is for. At the reception which followed, in the nearby garden of Mrs. Meadows-Taylor, the President of the Legion,

Sir James Spicer, then M.P., chose to respond by correcting the pulpit view in terms which were equally lacking in courtesy and tact. As I had already been to the Burma Star table and had spoken with them all, it might have been better to have left it at that. I understood why Sir James thought something had to be said, but his combative Parliamentary style and hectoring of the Church in general left little to choose between him and the preacher. A grey cloud hung over what should have been a sunshine celebration.

That unhappy incident revealed several things, one of which is the preacher's dilemma. Almost all the other Remembrance sermons have flown, forgotten as a dream. In fact, I have never heard anybody comment on any of them. But Richard's is remembered! The usual thing is for the preacher to drift into the expected platitudes which provide pleasant enough comfort at the time but are not sufficiently significant to be memorable. How to say something memorable, without being confrontational? That is the question.

As a result, I chose today's words, and rehearsed them, carefully. I claim two merits for them. They were original, and I believe them. Whether anybody ever comments, or remembers a word of it next week, is another matter. But the integrity of the pulpit will be intact.

The unmistakably good thing to come out of the day was that Father Jonathan, the Catholic priest, came and took his part. The War Memorial, which happens to be in our church, belongs to all. The names which are read are of Catholics, Anglicans and Non-Conformists who fell, side by side, for the common good. It is a shame if the two priests do not stand side by side in their memory. In times past (I am told) the Catholic priest used to allow his people to the church door but no further, and not to say prayers. Thank God those shameful attitudes have died the death they deserve to die. One day we will regard such separation from the Moslems, Hindus and Jews who fought alongside us as equally outdated. Their names Liveth Evermore, as well. And the God who is ever to be worshipped and adored, is One, in all and over all. If the idea of barring Hindus, Moslems and others is anathema to me, how much more so, to Him? He is the Father of all. Perhaps it takes a war to teach Christians this basic truth.

Monday, 9th November

David Wakely was on the phone before 8 a.m. There had been two deaths: Walter Coombs of Beaminster and Lilian Hawkins of Broadwindsor. Both families wanted Friday funerals. I said I would rather do one, not two, but promised to do the second if David Tizzard couldn't. It would be Rose's day off on Friday and it was David's day off today, so we confirmed the Beaminster funeral but delayed the Broadwindsor decision until we could contact him.

My other worry was that my monthly article for Sarum Link (Second Opinion) was due in at 9.00 a.m., and I hadn't written it. The speed at which these 'deadlines' come around is quite un-nerving. My 'report' for the next Sudan Committee meeting is due to be with the Secretary tomorrow, Pew News has to be written by Wednesday, the centre spread of the next Team News will have to be at the printer on Thursday if we want it to be in colour, and by Friday – when there will be one, if not two, funerals – the rest of the magazine text should be ready. And I will be preaching three times on Sunday. Those sermons won't drop out of the sky. I often think it cannot all get done, but it does … month after month after month.

However, 'Second Opinion' would not be on time. At 9 a.m., when the Editor would have been expecting it in the post, I telephoned, apologised, and asked for an extension. She gave me till 4 p.m.! Of course if I can't stand the heat I should get out of the kitchen and it would be quite easy to give up the Second Opinion feature. I have done it every month for four years, which is a long while, and a good many people would be pleased to see me quit. But so many critics have campaigned against the feature and written abusive letters to me and to the paper about it that I am extra determined to continue. Everywhere I go, clergy say "It's the first thing I read each month" or "Don't let the knockers put you down." Recently, a layman said "They seem common sense to me, I can't see what the fuss is about." That makes it all worthwhile. I don't set out to be controversial, though some people think I do. I set out to put forward common sense. The trouble is that Christians with fixed positions feel threatened. Narrow and blinkered views are not common sense and, if Second Opinion helps them look further, so much the better. The priest of the Evangelical parish who wrote and said he could no longer allow Sarum Link into his church in case people read my article is very blinkered indeed. He might be surprised to be associated with the Pope but the Catholic and Evangelical extremes meet in trying to prevent debate on issues which people want debated. If the Church does not deal openly with the issues which people struggle with, we will find that they will go their own way, leaving tiny sects which call themselves Christian, on the extreme wings. So 'Second Opinion' has its part to play in promoting debate. If this is regarded as controversial, I take it as a compliment, but the purpose is more than that. The problem this month was the likelihood of no article to be controversial about. So I settled to it, purposefully.

I wanted to write about Charles and Camilla, on his 50th birthday, wishing them well and urging them to go public and trust the good sense of the people. Everyone knows they are lovers and yet they can't hold hands or appear together in public. What nonsense! Neither of them is tied in marriage and they must be among the most mature people in the country, after all they've been through. Why should they be treated like naughty children? However, everyone else was writing about them and the public debate was well under way. So there was no need for 'Second Opinion' to raise it, and I refrained. If my purpose had been merely to be controversial, I would certainly not have refrained. Instead I wrote about the threat to democratic institutions posed by the modern media and by Murdoch in particular. This debate doesn't seem to have struck the Church as important. In fact the Pope seems to think Murdoch is a good thing, judging by the way he recently gave him an honorary Knighthood. Or perhaps that guaranteed some Roman scandals not being lit? Anyway, the article was on its way by lunchtime and David Wakely had caught up with David Tizzard who was able to do the Broadwindsor funeral on Friday. Things were looking better.

I do not like the hurry and the hassle that seems to have overtaken our lives. And I don't know anybody who does like it. And I am sure it is not meant to be like this. But what can we do about it? We live in this culture, just as we live in our skins. There is no getting out of either.

My mind goes back to college days with nostalgia. It was drummed into us in those days that, once we were in a parish, we were to make a routine and keep it. And the routine was already known. Every morning after prayers would be given to study; this was the reading time, the sermon time, the book time. Very good. Every afternoon was to be given to parish visiting. Out in the patch being seen, preferably walking. Very good indeed. Every evening was to be given to the clubs and activities which the parish ran. Excellent! It was all so clear. So neat and tidy. And so indisputably wise. And the amazing thing is that in those lovely days (two priests to one parish with one church, and not a car or a bike between us) it did work. But how suddenly that world disappeared, as if it had never been. And no priest that I know has produced a formula for the new situation. Perhaps there never will be a formula. Things are changing too rapidly. Perhaps the Team we have produced with its challenge of changing roles for both clergy and laity is as near to a 'formula' as we are going to get. But one thing about it distresses me, above all other things. We are too busy, and people know we are too busy, though they don't know what we are doing that makes us too busy. "I know you are very busy, Vicar, but ..." is the opening gambit heard daily. For a while, I replied "I am not busy" or "Please don't say that. I do have time." I said it because I wanted to believe it and because people want a priest who has time for them. A rushing priest is a useless specimen, and that is what we are in danger of becoming, or have become. My time with the 'gurus' of India and with the Buddhists of Sri Lanka has given me another perspective on time and on holiness, completely abandoned in our culture. We can never go back to what it was in my college days and any effort to copy the gurus and holy men of the East today would be artificial and we would soon be called lazy. The authentic form of holiness for the new style of priest that has become necessary, has yet to emerge.

Tuesday, 10th November

The morning post was double the usual size, and welcome. The extras were from people who had seen Andrew's documentary on Channel 2, and were congratulating me! It was a case of reflected glory. The days when I made those terrible journeys are gone – for ever, I trust. I could not go where he goes, do what he does, eat and drink as he has to do, and survive. Neither could I carry the heavy camera equipment in such heat, nor face the privations of such wildly alien conditions. It needs an African to make the journeys, and he is the man. It needs a local to cope with the language and the culture, and it suits him. It needs high training to master the camera and communications technology, and he has it. If I attempted such a journey, I fear I would be left behind quite early; health and strength would not survive the test. Yet the kindly letters arrived, congratulating me! Of course most of the writers knew Andrew was somewhere in Sudan on another dreadful journey and others knew that I had brought him to England in the first place, and had set the ball rolling. The letters were good. They recognised that I had opened the door for Andrew, which is true. But they recognised also that he had walked through the door, and the film proved it. Bishop John Baker marvelled at the gift of intuition which enabled me to choose him from among hundreds. Nadir Dinshaw, writing from Jersey, was so moved that he sent a cheque for Andrew's work. Mary Bell of Puddletown was also full of admiration. She remembered the day he had spoken of his ambitions, before he entered college. It was an encouraging change, she thought, to see ambitions fulfilled; no longer castles in the air, but solid achievements on the ground. Many other letters in similar vein set the day off to a good start.

It was the Communion service at Glebe Court this morning, which I look forward to because all the people who come have been faithful and true in the old fashioned way, all life long. Now they have reached a stage which makes going to church difficult, and it's right the church should go to them. So I went, with Lilian to play the piano and Bernard Gildersleve, a Glebe neighbour, to strengthen the singing. Together we took something of the goodwill and care of the church, and it was welcomed. David Thomas remembered singing in Welsh chapel choirs as a boy and the indelible mark the hymns had made on him; Dick Davidge had sung in Anglican church choirs and knew all the old traditions backwards; with Bernard, they made a male voice choir which even roused me to make a musical effort, though I fear I spoilt it. Marjorie Poole, life-long Beaminsterian, had prepared the flowers on the 'altar'. Mrs. Childs of Corscombe, whose family have suffered so much and strengthened each other, was there – now in great discomfort and bearing the indignities of old age with a profound fortitude. These people make up the company of the Saints and it was good to be with them. But one thing niggled me – Glebe Court was but one of many similar sheltered housing centres which had sprung up in my time. They are signs of a social revolution with which we are still coming to terms.

I remember Andrew's African dismay when he saw 'sheltered' accommodation, for the first time. "Why do you do this to the Elders?" he asked. "They are the wise ones. They have lived. They know everything." He thought they should be at the centre, advising the next generation. But now they are on the edge at St. Mary's Gardens, Abbeyfield, Hanover Court, Denziloe, Fullers and Old Vicarages at Melplash and Broadwindsor. All in my time! As a Church, we have been overtaken by the events. The clergy attempt a house communion each month but the numbers and the problems have overwhelmed us. We do not know all the occupants as Lawrie Dover used to do at St.

Mary's Gardens. When there was only one centre, it was convenient for a diligent Reader with a pastoral heart to take it under his wing, and Lawrie had done this, and sustained it until his own final illness, and even after his death Joan, his widow, continued the visiting for another ten years. His ministry remains a model of what once could be done.

The Sudan Committee's Honorary Secretary, Robin Musson, was awaiting my report to send out with the next agendas. I had drafted most of it before the postman had diverted my attention. It was easy to finish because there was not a lot to report. All I had done since the last meeting in my capacity as "Public Affairs Officer" was write to the nine Members of Parliament with Salisbury constituencies and urge them to re-form the Parliamentary Sudan Group which had lapsed with the previous parliament. Six of them had replied and the signs were that the group would re-form with Tom Cox (Lab.) as Chairman, Michael Colvin (Con.) as Secretary and our own Member, Oliver Letwin, among the contingent who would make up the number now required by parliamentary regulations. If this happened, it would be something worth reporting to the next committee, so I called on Robin and delivered the report, on time. I would not be able to meet all the deadlines in this breathtaking way if it were not for my near neighbour, Myrtle Gildersleve.

Once again, Myrtle did today, with little or no notice, what she has done time and again, day after day, for the past eleven years. She took my hand-written scrawl, crossings out, corrections, arrows and asterisks included, and returned it in short time, clean as a whistle and so certain to be correct that I have long since stopped checking. In fact it is she who corrects errors in my manuscript, not I who correct errors in her presentation. It is the unsung ancillaries, Myrtle chief among them, who have made my ministry possible. She has typed the manuscript of all my books – half a million words. She has typed all the reports I have had to produce for countless committees and has always managed to seem interested in them, which is an achievement; at least she has presented them so that they *look* interesting. She has typed Pew News week in, week out, she has typed the accounts for one parish after another and for the Team Council. It is a wonder she and her machine are not worn out. Perhaps the machine did wear out because the time came when she mastered the new technology and became computerised so that everything comes even smarter and in any type face I want, or she chooses, in the twinkling of an eye. The efficiency of the new technology is welcome but almost frightening. It has enabled me to keep pace with increased demands but there must be an end, a breaking point, to the ever-increasing demands and the way technology meets them. Or does the technology actually fuel the demands? Are we on a spinning spiral which will one day self destruct? Anyway, at the present time I have a calm controlled centre called Myrtle who with her quiet smile reminds me of the Buddhist monks who sit at peace while storms rage around them.

Wednesday, 11th November

Another big post this morning. More letters from viewers of Andrew's documentary. Several commented that the film had been truly African. The only white person to appear was a Christian Aid representative whose contribution was slight. It was the story of an African initiative, of African skills and of the bravery of the Africans who were risking their lives in the attempt to rid their land of mines. It was a welcome antidote to the images of callous cruelty and hopelessness which usually flash out of Africa. That was the general impression.

Two important visits had to fit in before the Team meeting. Yesterday it had not been possible to visit Mrs. Coombs, whose husband had died, because she was delayed in Lyme Regis registering the death. I had tried twice without luck, so an appointment was made for 9.30 a.m. She was well supported by her niece from Suffolk and she was full of praise for her neighbours and Mr. Jim Hibbs who looked after her garden and did the little repairs which would have worried them both. She was confident she would be able to stay in the home they had both loved and enjoyed. "It wouldn't be possible in Ilford," she said, remembering where they had come from, seventeen years ago. "But here it is like a big family and I won't leave it for anything." I thought that was a wonderful compliment to Beaminster and it was certainly from the heart. Her husband had been a very private man and she wanted a very quiet funeral in which she could give thanks for their sixty-one peaceful years together. Neither of them had been able to understand the horrors which had overtaken the country, with high divorce rate, one-parent families, abuse of children, promiscuous sex and so much unhappiness. They had lived their quiet withdrawn lives by the old principles and had been devoted and content to the end. I thought it was both humbling and reassuring to know that simple and good lives continue, out of the public eye.

The second visit, to Ean and Lydia Ramsay, was meant to coincide with the eleventh hour of the eleventh month because it was at that very moment sixteen years ago, that I had declared them to be "man and wife together" at a private ceremony in Beaminster Church. Now they were sheltering in Broadwindsor House and he, through infirmity and great age, was unable to get to church, and he missed it. He wouldn't go to the communion service we provided in the Common Room each month because it wasn't the same as "hearing the old words in the old church." I sympathise with that. I feel the same myself, at every house communion. But it is the best that can be done, when old age brings its limitations. Ean doesn't take to the limitations kindly. He lives surrounded by the portraits of his long line of Scottish forebears. He loves nothing more than telling the tales of their doings and soon we are enjoying a reverie in another age – of gallantry and honour, of adventure and romance. And Lydia is looking on with gratitude that for a few minutes he has male company with which to re-live the days long past. No doubt most of the time she sees him trapped in reduced circumstances and hears him fulminating against the evils of the modern age and of the church and its bishops in particular. I receive my share of this but somehow he has come to exempt me from the criticisms, which is surprising because he must know that I share with the bishops many of the views which he abhors. Perhaps the fact that I respect his ancient tradition and recognise his rare brand of holiness allows him to exonerate me from all the stains of modernism. I also like the fact that he knows that in Lydia he has a wife whose "price is beyond rubies." It was good to be with them, 16 years on, even though it meant missing the Silence in the Square.

The Team meeting began a little late, which didn't matter much. The main business as far as I was concerned was for everyone to agree the December service programme so that I could get it to the printers, poste haste. The main business as far as David was concerned turned out to be an analysis of the previous night's P.C.C. at Broadwindsor which had not been a happy one. I once heard a wise man (it might have been Bishop Tiarks, or it might have been Father Pat Waddy – no matter) say "after receiving a bad letter, put your pen away; after going to a bad meeting keep your mouth shut." I suppose the advice is not greatly different from that learnt at mother's knee, "least said, soonest mended." Two problems had cropped up, neither of them very surprising. One was the pattern of Broadwindsor services for 1999. That issue causes a problem in every parish. If it is discussed openly by the whole council, there is always a confusing variety of views but if it is decided by a small sub-committee, the majority feel left out. And nobody should be left out because people do care very much about how they worship. It would be far more worrying if they didn't. The second cat among the Broadwindsor pigeons was that the Archdeacon had said their annual accounts and report did not meet the requirements of the new Charity Law which now governs the procedure at our annual meetings. Broadwindsor was not exceptional, the Archdeacon's comments applied in six other parishes in this Team; so it is commonplace. My sympathies are with the parishes and the hard-working officers, all volunteers. They have produced accounts, to the satisfaction of auditors for years without number. Now new requirements are imposed. It suggests that the previous accounts were unsatisfactory, which they weren't. It's no wonder it causes a flurry in the dovecote! And now the annual report has to follow a certain prescribed pattern, and be sent to Salisbury. Of course it smacks of uniformity and centralisation because that is exactly what it is. And that is not the way the village Churches of England are, or ever have been. It is no surprise to me that Broadwindsor's meeting was a little agitated. I daresay a few robust personalities, for which village life is noted, spiced it all up a bit. Without them, country life would lose its colour and its character.

The good thing is that any parish which is confused by the new regulations only has to consult Richard Satchell. He is our man for these matters. He knows it all backwards. If they consult me, which they tend to do, they will get further in the mire because, however necessary or laudable it all is, I have no time for it.

I knew the afternoon would be difficult, and it was. I had to sit in one of the comprehensive school's many hot seats. It was a meeting of the staffing committee, now re-named 'personnel'.

I admire what is being achieved in education and especially at our school where results are constantly above average and where the personal care of pupils is of a very high order indeed. It angers me that, with all these achievements to celebrate, schools and schoolteachers are constantly maligned and blamed for every national ill from the divorce rate to losing Test matches. It is a marvel that there is any morale left in schools at all. It seems that 'pressure' has become the spirit of the age. Teachers are under greater pressure than ever. More requirements in paper work and bureaucracy (but so it is in farming, or with the voluntary church officers). More requirements in assessments and reports (likewise any business) and reduced resources to enable it to be done (tell me the old, old story). It is the 'personnel' committee which, under the calm and comforting chairmanship of John Darnley and alongside the headteacher, Sue Collard, has to decide on staffing requirements and share out the diminishing funds. Oh! give me a hornet's nest, a lion's den and a snake's pit rather than a headteacher's task these days!

We listened to the staffing issues, the shortages, the tensions, the 'pressures'. I had only two contributions to make and I felt they were as corn to a tiger. I made the point that teachers did not have a monopoly on 'pressure'. It was common. They must realise it was, unhappily, the spirit of the times, a fact of life. Everyone was suffering it. It was the plague of the day and it wouldn't do teachers any good to think they were the lone victims. The second contribution, which I hoped was more positive, was to recommend as much 'team teaching' as possible. It is teamwork which has saved me from the pressures which seem to be knocking out clergy and destroying clergy marriages, left, right and centre. In a 'team teaching' situation, absence is more easily covered, problems are more easily shared, difficult children are a little diluted, and the pupil's diet is more varied. All these things also apply to parish life where I have seen them all and benefited from them all, and believe the parishioners have done so as well.

Pew News was written in the evening and delivered to 'Magical' Myrtle who returned it before 'lights out'. The centre spread of the magazine, in full colour, is now prepared for the printer, alongside the December services now agreed by all the clergy and readers, all the parishes and worship groups. Phew! So far, so good. The deadlines are being met, one by one.

Thursday, 12th November

The post was bigger than ever but this time it was mostly magazine items. Good timing. People do take the deadline seriously. It they didn't, we really would be in a mess. But oh! What a life, to be ruled by deadlines. No wonder a guru from the East told me that the first thing a Westerner should do, if he wanted to be holy was throw away his watch, "the symbol of your slavery." That may be true but I am still grateful for people's promptness because – for better or worse – this is the way we are, deadlines do count and must be kept. Oh dear!

Mary arrived at the office, punctual as ever, and was pleased to see Pew News ready to run off. I also ran off, to Creeds, with the centre spread and the service rota. Must say I am pleased to get both off my plate, and on to theirs.

I called at St. Mary's School on the way back. Now that I am not Chairman of Governors, it is not strictly necessary, but I never did call as a duty. It is simply a good place to be. They have their 'pressures' and their disturbed children, and the West Dorset 'Special Unit' in addition. Yet somehow the place hums along to a cheerful tune. That doesn't happen by accident or by chance. There is a plan and purpose and everyone knows what it is because they have shared in creating it. On its own, that is not enough to keep the tune cheerful. There is also the need to nurture each member of staff so that they also grow in confidence and ability, like the children they teach. It is a mutual exchange, learning from each other. And if it is handled anywhere better than it is handled here, I haven't seen or heard of it. Chris Longridge has the touch which shows care and inspires confidence and it spreads right through the school. Some people have a way of stirring people up and creating tension – making a mountain out of a molehill. Any fool can do that, and plenty do. Much rarer, and more attractive, is the gift of making a molehill out of a mountain and treating tension as creative. This is where the school excels, and it comes from the top. I hope parents appreciate their luck. It seems human nature requires some moans and groans. They are never in short supply, anywhere, but there are few places where they are less deserved than at our school. Fortunately, this is recognised and a certain atmosphere of celebration prevails. Oh that it would in all our churches! It is sad when the church-going people don't reflect this sense of celebration. We are meant to be the "thank-you people" celebrating the good gifts. It isn't always evident. Give me the school before the synod, any day!

The big event today was Joan's effort on behalf of the church fabric funds, the evening Concert by the Madrigal Society and the Chamber Orchestra of Sherborne School for Girls. We endured all the usual anxieties suffered by anyone who promotes events – Has the publicity been adequate? Will there be sufficient refreshments? Should we have sold tickets in advance? Did all the notices get around? *Will anyone come?* There is always the nightmare of the performers assembled and ready, and the church empty.

In the event, we need not have worried, the nave was comfortably full and the performance was sublime. The girls looked so demure (I am told they are not!) and so sweet that a sure-fire success was guaranteed before a note was struck. And then came talent to match the charm. It was as delicious as any dish prepared for a queen and afterwards the wine and refreshments were enough, and to spare. Eventually, the school bus bore them all away but not until the girls and staff had chatted and laughed with everyone, which added to the general delight. Then "Ichabod", the glory had departed; the clearing up began.

Joan had called on the Mothers' Union to do the refreshments and, as they have never been known to let anyone down, it was a safe request. Their stamina is exceptional. There was Kate Hile behind the teapot – was it her five hundredth appearance? Now at times she bends almost double; it must be the cumulative weight of all the tea urns she has carried over the years. Thank goodness her David now arrives to do the staggering for her. None of us is getting any younger. And there was Betty Fortescue-Thomas, in her ninetieth year, smiling through. And there was Audrey Jones who never makes a moment's fuss, while in the background her workrate is unequalled. These people keep the wheels oiled. Without them, as the old scripture says, 'A city would have no inhabitants.'

However, one thing has puzzled me about concerts in Beaminster Church, and always will. There is a local reluctance to accept them. In fact there have been a good many objections. Surely the finest building in the town should be fully available to everyone in the town. To limit its use to worship would be to limit it to church attenders and that would be wrong. I want to maximise the use of the town's historic treasure, for everybody. It's plain common sense, but isn't seen that way. An old theology lingers on in Beaminster which wants the Church (like God) to be remote and separate. But it's a bad theology because God isn't like that. He entered the world and became available "from henceforth my dwelling is with men." So I would like to see the ancient tradition of the Church at the centre of things (like God), not on the edge of things. I would like to see the Church become once again the Patron of the Arts. I will do all that I can to patronise local talent in art, music and craft. It's good that many musicians and artistes of national repute have enjoyed their visits and commented that the acoustics lend themselves to concert performances. We must continue to seek the excellence which the building deserves and continue to promote the arts. It is an old out-dated theology which fails to see the glory of God in all his works and all his ways. If that was the way people thought when the church was first built, the builders never would have given us such a treasure. We must enjoy it and make it available for as many people as possible. And each event, in its own way, must have the mark of excellence. Tonight's certainly did.

Friday, 13th November

It was Walter Coombs' funeral at Yeovil this morning and, as he was such a private man, all I will record about it is that his Monmouth Gardens neighbours did him proud, and his brave widow must have felt very well supported indeed.

I was invited back to the reception and wanted to go and should have gone, but I had made two other commitments and couldn't keep them all. It was obviously the right moment to do a round at Yeovil Hospital, and I had promised to go on to Sherborne and watch Kilele play football for his school.

The Yeovil Hospital situation is annoying. It isn't possible to call at Reception and ask for the book of patients, as it used to be. Neither is it permitted to ask if there is anyone from Beaminster or any of our villages . . . as I used to do. Regulations forbid it. Patient confidentiality and hospital security have prior claim on clergy convenience. Therefore it is all the more important that parishioners pass the information; there is no other way we will find out. Gone are the days when I would call at Reception and ask which ward Mrs. So-and-So was in, and be told "Oh, and while you're here, don't forget Mr. This and Mrs. That from your patch." I used to 'discover' five or six parishioners, and they would all be so pleased. It is a pity these changes have happened and, when I made the point at Reception today in a very polite and peaceable way, I was roundly told that there was a hospital chaplain anyway. I let the matter drop, but I wasn't satisfied. I know the hospital chaplain and I believe he is an excellent man, but that isn't the point. Even if he was the Archbishop of Canterbury, it still wouldn't be the point. If I have a parishioner in hospital, I want to be able to visit and not leave it to a priest who is (to them) a complete stranger. In sickness or loneliness or time of anxiety it is wonderful what a familiar face can mean. As I left, I wondered how many of our people were wondering why the vicar hadn't called. I wished I had gone to Mrs. Coombs' reception.

Instead, I continued to Sherborne for Kilele's school match. This is the advantage of not having a regular 'day off'. If something special crops up, there is a chance it can be fitted in 'as and when'. And this was special, for Kilele to be selected for the school. His dad would be so proud and would have been there if he wasn't involved in greater issues elsewhere, so it was exactly the right moment for me to stand in his place. It is quite extraordinary the pride which grandparents (in my case a Godparent) feel in the next generation. And it was evident at the game, where it seemed there were more grandparents on the touchline than parents. How often, when visiting, I have heard from doting grandparents every detail of little Tommy's progress, how he can say the A-B-C and put his own shoes on – but can't tie the laces yet. As I have never met little Tommy, and possibly not even his parents, it is difficult to sustain the interest. However, efforts to change the subject seldom succeed. Grand-parenting is a great joy and, at a time of life when other activities are diminishing, it can be excessively so. So I have solemnly promised myself that I will not bore parishioners by reporting the detailed progress of Kilele and Timothy. Yet I find myself doing it! It is the fascination with the things they say. The unexpected expression, the surprising wisdom. I wish I had kept a list, a record, of them. Where do they come from? What deep wells are there inside us, from which these comments surface? And why is it that they bubble to the surface so effortlessly in a child where an adult would be inhibited? Anyway, I went to see my Godson play, and it wasn't difficult to spot him. He stood a head taller than anyone else on the field and the length of his legs and the energy with which he covered the ground reminded me of Carlton Palmer. It was difficult to tell what position he was playing, sometimes a saving tackle at the back, then taking a corner at the front and, to my pleasure, popping up in the middle to score three times. His Abbey side won 8-1 and, when they came off the field, their captain, a tiny fellow who came up to Kilele's waist, called for "Three cheers for the County Primary," just as we had done in our school days. I felt quite emotional. Then Kilele went up to their goalkeeper, who had let in eight and who looked as if he was going to cry, and said "You did well." I felt even more emotional.

Tonight was sermon time. The time was there but, unfortunately, the sermon was not. Sermons don't come to order, or at the press of a switch. It's a mystery how they do come, unpredictably for sure. Some priests set aside a time in their diary and sit in their study with Bible commentary and helpful books, until it is done. Indeed, that is how we were taught at college. Sound result I expect, but dull I fear. Other priests don't do much preparation at all; they have an idea and get up in the pulpit and "let 'em have it," as one priest put it. Those congregations deserve sympathy because a random collection of personal opinions is not what the people come for. Other priests like to practise their sermon beforehand and one diligent wife insisted on hearing it on Friday night, so that she had time to correct it on Saturday. He has now escaped, to glory.

All I know is that a sermon is meant to give food for thought and therefore the preacher, if he is to feed others, must eat well. An insatiable appetite for books of all sorts, a keen awareness of current affairs, as much travel as possible – preferably in odd and interesting places – and listening to every sort of parish opinion, has been my diet. Very good food it has been. I would recommend it to anybody and I would change it for nobody. Nonetheless, the variety of ideas has to come into sharp focus, the food has to be well cooked and served at the right time. That is the weekly teaser. I have been helped so much by the themes for each Sunday which the Church gave us twenty years ago in the A.S.B. This gave a clear directive for the people's attention and a useful focus for the preacher's words. I regret that, in two weeks' time, they will pass out of use and a new lectionary will come into use. We are told it is progress and I hope it proves to be but I fear that, without the controlling discipline of themes, there will be nothing to stop the more cranky clergy running amok. The themes have helped me, and I shall miss them, though I must admit some have been a little obscure and it's difficult to imagine this week's theme of Moses causing the crowds to flock in. Anyway, theme or not, the sermon didn't come tonight and it's a bit late in the week to be still searching. I don't want to be one of those preachers who has to say something. I want to be one who has something to say.

Saturday, 14th November

When I woke up this morning, the sermon was there. It had come in the night. There is no accounting for the way the human mind works, even in sleep, it seems. It was all very obvious and quite clear and I wondered why it hadn't come earlier in the week. The link between Moses (the given theme) and the Remembrance Day which every church had just kept was so obvious. We think our Remembrance Day has been going a long while – 80 years – but the Jews have been remembering Moses leading their escape from slavery for 3000 years. So when Jesus kept their Remembrance Day (Passover) and said "Do this in Remembrance of ME" it would have been the equivalent of me, on Remembrance Day, putting myself above all the names the people had come to honour. It would be outrageous and the people would be so offended that they would correct me as Jim Spicer had corrected Richard Thornburgh, or even put me out of the Church, and quite rightly too. It is little wonder that Jesus was arrested that night and put to death next day. This sermon could be good because it begins where people are – everyone has just kept Remembrance Day – and it takes them somewhere else – to the great themes of Biblical faith. Our journey, day by day, is from the known to the unknown, and so should every sermon be. I was still surprised that it had come, so unpredictably, by night.

After I had put the gist of the sermon down on paper, to be polished later with anecdote added, I went up to Broadwindsor's church centre. It's always a good place to have a coffee and hear the local chat.

It must be fifteen or more years ago that Dorothy Shiner first rented an empty shop front in Broadwindsor's Square – a prime site if ever there was one. The idea had filled me with excitement from the beginning. I imagined it as Broadwindsor's distinctive contribution to the whole Team area – a coffee shop, a meeting place, a theological library and a centre at which all the village church requirements of wine, wafers, candles, registers and stationery could be ordered and stored. It could even have stored the duplicator and the printer and become the office base. Most of this Dorothy has done, with a few faithful helpers, ever since! Failing eyesight has now overtaken her and she has the wisdom to recognise her limitations and retire with a good grace. Even so, she still occupies the same seat on a Saturday morning, and that is my one chance to see her. She has never seemed capable of speaking ill of anyone and, when people have been awkward, she has always had a word to explain the reasons behind it. She used to do this at every Wednesday Team meeting, and we miss it. The coffee was all right but the chatter was better. I refuse to call it 'gossip'. Gossip always implies a certain tendency toward malice or scandal, however mild. When Dorothy is around, there is no such thing. I have searched the dictionary to find a word for gossip without malice, and I can't, which is a shame.

I knew tonight's event would be good but I hadn't expected it to be so good. It was the Hooke Church Council's Party held, for the first time, in Toller's new village hall. It was advertised as a four-course dinner with entertainment and the tickets were £10 and sold out, so it was an ambitious undertaking for any organisation, never mind one as small as Hooke village.

Joan shared my astonishment at the achievement. She remembered Hooke Church as it was when we worked at the school, became engaged and got married there. She has reason to remember it – on the eve of the wedding, the churchyard was so overgrown that the path to the church had to be cleared with a scythe so that the bride could enter! Now it has won the prize for the best managed churchyard in the Diocese, among new entrants! And I remember the Easter offering in my first year as vicar, was forty pence. Last Easter it reached £100! The church 'share' at that time was £5 and hadn't been paid; now it is £1,600 and has been paid. Why, oh why, do people moan about the decline and fall of the Church of England? I don't see it. Let the doom and gloom pundits come and see a village Church Council in action! We feasted, no other word for it, for two hours before the entertainers even got on the stage. I doubt any restaurant within miles would have bettered the fare, and where else would there have been a choice of fifteen dessert dishes? It was a mammoth achievement on any reckoning. The washing-up alone must have taken some organising – eighty guests, four courses each. And then, lo and behold, the same people who had prepared and served the feast and cleared the tables were on the stage to do their party pieces, cabaret style. As far as I could see, every Church Council member did a turn, with a few other village stars adding to the home-grown fun. I felt rather guilty that I hadn't taken any part – although one of my 'Letters to God' was read as a feature. Quite a compliment when a sermon is used as entertainment!

The whole affair was remarkable and a very far cry from the rather staid 'Sale of Work' of yesteryear. Perhaps the most remarkable thing is that one church warden, Pauline Wallbridge, had masterminded the feast and the other church warden, Ena Anderson, had masterminded the cabaret, even to writing the script and the limericks which wittily summed up our Bishop and all the Team clergy. It was a stunning show and I felt elated because I could see how things had changed. Thirty years ago, Hooke Church had been on a hit-list for closure, and it certainly had been in a poor way. It has climbed the mountain and reached a fresh peak tonight. Pauline and Ena may not think of themselves as mountaineers but they and their colleagues have matched the Hillary/Tensing team.

Sunday, 15th November

No two Sundays are alike, at least not for a priest with fourteen churches to get around. I fear Sundays may be all alike for those who go to the same church at the same time each week, but that is not the way we are. I reckon it's the variety which has kept me on my toes, feeling fresh and looking forward to each Sunday. There were two different things today, and both were good.

At Netherbury, it was the choir. It seems to grow in numbers, strength and confidence, week by week. And now it is robed and looks stylish too. Netherbury's music has been something of a weakness for some while. Suddenly, it is a strength. Robina Pollock knows she is not the world's best organist but she has persisted in taking lessons for years and she was wise enough to ask for a couple of strong voices to stand near her, to keep organ and congregation together. It was a mustard seed, if ever there was one. Something good is happening at Netherbury and I can't quite put my finger on what it is. I used to find the atmosphere turgid, from the moment I went into the church. It wasn't the welcome; the church wardens or sidesmen were unfailingly courteous, but the building always felt cold and dark. It was more like going into a morgue to identify a body than to a celebration of the mighty works of God. There was once a tradition of churches having 'dim religious light' and Netherbury had never outgrown it. It was all part of the penitential package. We didn't go to church to be happy, we went to church because we were miserable sinners. And if we froze to death, it was no more than we deserved. Church was, after all, to be endured. Well, that's the way it was and every church is at some stage on the path of recovery from that unhappy theology. The Reformers' pre-occupation with sin always was unhealthy. They passed their gloomy neurosis on, under the guise of piety. It is only now that the phoney mask is being stripped away. Netherbury took a big step in the right direction when the new lighting was installed after eight years of to-ing and fro-ing with English Heritage and other interested parties. It is a beautiful old church and now the people can see the beauty of it, and the priest can read the print in the altar book without bringing his own torch. The children's work which has also begun may develop now. Previously the environment was just too depressing for children to prosper. Playgroups and primary schools are warm (by law) and colourful by design and the church needs to match these expectations. Anyway, Netherbury was a good experience today. Choir and light ... *two* more steps along the way we go.

Melplash also provided a different sort of occasion. We were to dedicate a wrought iron Paschal candle stand in memory of the late Nell Stevens. Her family had turned up from near and far for the occasion. Nell had left Melplash Church fifteen years before she died but she had always retained her affection and her generosity, though she worshipped in Bridport. I didn't preach about Nell because the funeral address had been some while ago but I did refer to her kindly affection for me, in spite of the fact that I was the one who had turned the nave of her church into a badminton court. When it was first proposed at a P.C.C. she had all but fainted away. However, the changes had taken place and had worked well ever since. At the time, the church was heading for bankruptcy. The annual oil bill for heating the church (£400) was greater than the total income. The drastic alterations left only one third of the space to be heated, substituted electricity for oil and the income from renting the nave to badminton players more than covered the year's heating bill. The finances were cured at a stroke. And so was the worship. Suddenly we were all close together, so that the singing improved as well. The great glazed screen on folding doors was the design of Guy Hereward of Toller, who did it for nothing. It remains a masterpiece and architects still come to view it. The puzzle I can't solve, though I was at the centre of it, is how we ever got a Faculty for it. I do remember that when we were halfway through the work a letter came from the Chancellor refusing permission. Either things were more lax then than now, or perhaps the Chancellor saw the wisdom of it in the end. Anyway, it was done and it was done entirely by local labour, and I never heard anyone regret it. The church had been built when great expansion was expected. The expansion had never happened, leaving the people of Melplash with a building far too large for its needs. The changes brought the whole building into good use while retaining all the original features. If only every Church Council, as Melplash in Nell Stevens' day, would take an imaginative look at its building and see how it can be brought into fuller public use in the week, and be more suited to the worship on a Sunday. Anyway, remembering Nell brought all these memories back into my mind. But when I looked around the congregation, it was a shock to see only three survivors from those days. To the rest, Nell was just a name, not a face, and the changes were of no interest – they had never known anything else.

There was a phone call from the Hooke Church treasurer this evening. Their epic effort last night has given them £700 clear profit. They worked for it and they deserve every penny of it.

One way and another, it's been a very good weekend again. And the whole magazine text is ready for the printer tomorrow morning. Tailpiece included. It hadn't seemed likely a week ago, but wonders never cease!

Two weeks later ...

Monday, 7th December

I have made a resolution today, and I am determined to keep it. It will not be like New Year resolutions – here today and forgotten tomorrow. This is a Christmas resolution and I will put it to the test. I am resolved not to join the Christmas rush.

The Christmas rush is a disease and it is contagious. I don't want to catch it. Every sort of pressure builds up to spread it, yet it is anti-Christmas under the guise of being pro-Christmas. The commercial pressure to spend, spend is enormous and grows every year. In fact the national economy demands ever-increased spending, the High Street stores depend on the Christmas boom and, if it is a slow Christmas, their share values drop, the recession will take over, jobs will be lost, interest rates will change. They need a Christmas rush; it is the way our consumer-driven economy has developed and that shows how fragile the whole structure is. The boom and buy consumerism cannot go on booming. Eventually it will bust. The rich nations will become too bloated, too demanding, too dependent on goods and comforts. If we continue to consume the earth's natural resources at the present rate, we will go down in history as the most selfish, destructive, profligate and ruthlessly greedy generation of all time. And the maddening thing is that it all comes into focus at Christmas which should be the season of simplicity. It has become the reverse, the most complicated time of the whole year, and certainly the most rushed. I am determined and resolved not to be rushed and not to join the spending spree. But if we all did that, it would bring the economy down. Oh! How complicated it has all become! And of course if I stand a little apart from it all, people will think I am unsociable or even a little Scrooge-like. So my resolution not to join the Christmas rush must have a positive side. I will visit as many bereaved people as possible. I will visit as many lonely people as possible and I will get around the hospitals. That will be nearer the Christmas spirit, but it's sure to make me rush, and that is the problem.

It really needs more than a few individuals to stand outside the rush. We will be swept aside unnoticed. It needs a mighty prophetic voice in the political world which will dare to call for a sacrificially simpler standard of living instead of the ever-increasing growth rate, which must one day, like the ulcers it causes, burst. Last year, I heard of a person who, while most of us feasted on Christmas Day, sat in a public place with a bowl of peanuts and a jug of polluted water. It was a sort of John the Baptist acted parable pointing to the way the world is. No doubt he was written off as a crank. We really need a political movement built on his vision. Who in the present consumer craze would have the nerve to join the movement? It's hard enough to try and stand outside the whirligig that Christmas has become. I shall try. That is my solemn resolve and, as a start, I have cut my Christmas card list from a hundred and fifty to twelve. However, I shall be disappointed if people cut us off their lists. I love receiving Christmas greetings. That's the dilemma. It's all become too complicated. But I have made my resolution and I shall put it to the test and we shall see what happens.

The morning post brought a problem and it was the sort of problem which I am no good at solving. There are some things I am good at and some things I am bad at and one of the things I am worst at is faculty applications. This is why I wish that any alteration anyone wants to make in any church could be done in their name and not mine. Then they would have to deal with the correspondence and the costs and all the problems which arise. Not so. Every faculty application has to be in the name of the incumbent, all correspondence comes to the incumbent, all questions have to be answered by the incumbent and all costs fall on the incumbent unless he gets the Church Council to indemnify him. At the moment, there are no fewer than six faculty applications in the pipeline – the millennium window at Stoke Abbott, the millennium window at Toller, the St. Francis statue at Netherbury, the organ renovation and internal decoration at Netherbury, the organ renovation at Beaminster and the installation of an aumbry at Beaminster. It was the Diocesan Advisory Committee opinion on the aumbry which arrived in today's post and made me wish that applicants had to do things in their own name, not mine. The letter recommended that the architect be consulted as more information was required about the excavation into the wall – I thought we had done that on site with the Archdeacon and the architect two years ago. Also the Committee did not support the proposed 'gothic-style' lettering, but they did not say what style of lettering they would support. We could go on sending one style after another for years until Tony and Margaret Greenham, the donors, lose patience or interest. The letter also said that the proposed door had no lock and the Reserved Sacrament had to be secured – but surely it is obvious that the safe door has the lock and the wooden 'door' is only a facade. Also, I had asked in my letter that the D.A.C. would make their own recommendation for an aumbry lamp and we would agree, to avoid any further delay. The letter said that they would have to consult the new Chancellor, Judge Wiggs, whose ideas might differ from those of the former Chancellor, Judge Ellison. So the Advisory Committee has to take advice! And finally the Committee stated, flatly, that the name of the donor family should not appear on the outside of the door where the public would see it, but on the inside of the door where they would not. I can't imagine the donor family being pleased with that, though I do know there has been a recent policy of preventing names appearing on church walls.

Some years ago, the people at Hooke were disappointed when a memorial naming Mrs. Dorothy Wallbridge was refused. She had been a much-loved church warden for 43 years. The church at Broadwindsor had been refused permission for a plaque which named Dr. Solomon Caesar Malan, a former vicar and leading oriental scholar. I understand the wish to prevent the accumulation of names on the walls of our churches; of course there has to be a limit, but it is a change of custom not clear to everyone. For generations, it had been permitted, as the walls of all old churches show. The old memorials now create a good deal of interest and root the church in the midst of the local history. Yet the new policy is understandable; no one wants the church cluttered with the names of families who can afford to buy themselves a space. It would be a throwback to the days when prominent families bought themselves the most prominent pews. But in the long run the effect may be that the church's roots in the locality will be less evident.

On the face of it, the policy is a disincentive to would-be donors. But it need not be. Alec Walbridge has given a hand-carved screen and a lighting system which displays the ancient corbels, but his name does not appear. Harry and Patricia Palk gave a beautiful hand-made oak bookcase to celebrate their wedding but their names to not appear. The Symes family at Netherbury have given two sculpted statues, with a third on the way, and no memorial name to be seen publicly, though all is recorded in the church inventory. Perhaps this anonymous giving is the only sort of giving the new system will allow. In the end, it may be for the best. At the moment, it causes some upsets, as it did among friends of Dorothy Wallbridge and among the Orientalists who wished to honour Dr. Malan.

Thank goodness the Fabric Committee is meeting tomorrow. They will have to consider the letter and decide how to act. But whatever is decided, it will have to be in my name and it will look as if it is all my doing, when it is completely beyond my control and not my doing at all.

Lo and behold, who would believe it, but another package, hand delivered, arrived mid morning and woe is me! It was the paperwork, the photographs, the artist's design and the drawings for the Netherbury statue of St. Francis. Another faculty application, two in one morning! And this one had a note attached, saying that page 3 was missing. Well, where is it? I can't send if off incomplete, it will come straight back. The Diocesan Committee will not meet until the new year. The best thing I can do, in accord with my resolution, is put it all on one side in a safe place until after Christmas. That is not my style. It goes against the grain. I don't like problems to pile up in safe places but it is the only way to keep the resolution. Meantime, perhaps page 3 will turn up.

This was not the start to my new resolve that I wanted. Wakelys rang to tell me of two Beaminster deaths, to add to the four funerals we had already, making six in the week. This is awful for the families, so close to Christmas, and it's awful for us because nothing takes more time or absorbs more energy than the preparations for a funeral. The sensitivities are always intense, the complications within families are often considerable. Country funerals are not like urban funerals. "I did four in a day, quite often," an urban priest once told me. But he admitted he didn't know the people and used to ask, as the funeral party arrived at the crematorium, "Man or woman?" so that he knew which prayers to offer. Pathetic. Such priests are no more than functionaries. They are cyphers. I don't see how that sort of funeral ministry will survive into the next century. People might as well have a secular event and do it themselves. Here, we know the people, sit with the family beforehand and usually know the background story. This is emotionally demanding and it takes time, but it is worthwhile. In thirty-three years, I have buried only about five people who were not known to me. That is the difference between town and country ministry.

Both today's deaths were sad; I suppose all deaths are, especially at Christmas. But I was sorry that Jean Watts, who I thought was settling so well at Hanover Court, had collapsed and died. Her family will meet me on Wednesday. And Kathleen Bridge had died in Dorchester Hospital after having her second leg amputated. Her husband will also meet me on Wednesday. Meanwhile the four other funerals are in the care of David Tizzard, two of them today in Beaminster, the other two in Broadwindsor. Thank heavens for such a colleague.

Tuesday, 8th December

I have resolved to be calm and to side-step the Christmas rush. It was difficult to do that today, but I will start it seriously tomorrow. Today's programme didn't allow me to side-step anything. It was a series of happenings, all arranged for me, and they fitted together like pieces in a jigsaw.

The Glebe Court Communion was at 10.30; I couldn't stay for the coffee and chat because the Kingcombe Coffee Morning for Sudan was expecting me. It was typical of Mrs. Thomas that she wrapped up two warm mince pies for me to eat on the way to Kingcombe, which I did. The Carol Biss and Elsine Trendell enterprise at Kingcombe raised £200 and was a good occasion because of the superb backcloth of the Kingcombe Centre and all the paintings which were exhibited and for sale. It was tipping with rain and the mist was swirling round but inside the Centre it was all warmth and welcome, with more mince pies. I went on to Toller and called on a Toller lady who had written to complain that Team clergy never attended their money-raising efforts for the church. Unfortunately she was out, in Bournemouth for the day, but I had just attended one of their money-raising efforts and my colleagues had both told me that they had been to recent events as well. Nonetheless, had she been at home I would have apologised because the perception is that we are not seen enough. It is the non-church attenders who feel this most. The church attenders see one of us each week, which keeps information flowing, but others can very easily feel estranged and when they raise money for the church it is disappointing. It is a weakness in our system and if anyone could show us a better way, we would welcome it.

There wasn't time for lunch because, by the time I got home, colleagues were arriving for the Team meeting which, for the first time in my memory, had been moved from Wednesday morning to Tuesday afternoon. This was meant to give us extra time to discuss the new baptism and initiation rites which would come into use in the year 2000. In fact, we didn't discuss them at all. Christmas arrangements seemed more immediate and more pressing and I had to be at the M.U. Christmas Party by 3.30 for Peggy Turner's 90th birthday celebration. As she has been a real stalwart and is still doing needlework for church funds, it would have been a shame to miss that. Then by 4.30 I had to be with Brenda Travers to collect all the advertisements for the 1999 Team News, which have to be at the printers a week early, because of the Christmas rush. I don't know how Brenda does it. She must have called on dozens of businesses. I can't estimate the hours it must have taken her. She passed them all on for me to sort out, with explanations that this one wanted the telephone number changed, that one wanted the wording changed, another wanted to reduce to one twelfth of a page, another wanted to enlarge to one sixth of a page, this one wanted to move to the back page, that one wanted to go to the top of the page, another wanted to be inside the cover, this one wanted the logo smaller, that one wanted the logo larger, another wanted to be in for the summer months only, this one wanted to change the wording every month, that one wanted to be in alternate months only. She told me she had collected £6,000 advertising money in 1998 and I reckoned we had earned every penny of it. One thing is for sure, it is her endeavours with the advertisers which have kept the price stable at 25p. We used to produce a 24-page magazine; now it is 40 pages with the centre spread sometimes in full colour. Yet we have made only one price increase in fifteen years, and we still break even.

There was nothing for it in the evening but to lay every single advertisement on the floor, alongside the relevant magazine pages, and staple them all together, with the alterations highlighted and hope that Kathy at Creeds would make sense of it all. Sunny put his tail down, lay down by the door and didn't move for three hours. If he had stirred even once, he would have blown that lot across the room and into the fire and Team News advertisements for 1999 would never have seen the light of day. Sunny has a great sense of crisis. He knows how to read the signs. His patience is remarkable. He hadn't had any exercise, just as I hadn't had any food, except Mrs. Thomas' mince pies and the M.U. tea. But the day's jigsaw had fitted together, and Creeds will get the adverts tomorrow, on time.

The resolve about the Christmas rush will start tomorrow.

Wednesday, 9th December

The resolution against Christmas rush began in earnest today and it didn't get off to too good a start.

The first thing that happened was that a huge morning mail brought a good batch of Christmas cards. Very nice really, apart from the fact that they were all from people I had cut off my list when I reduced it from a hundred and fifty to twelve. It will be a shame to cut ties with the people who sent from Australia – they will probably think I am sulking about the Test matches. Or that I am dead. Also, we see little enough of cousins and the remoter relatives without cutting the remaining link at Christmas. I will have to re-think this part of the resolution and I can see the number of cards will have to be upped. Maybe to fifty, or something like that.

The second thing that happened was worse. The Sarum Link editor rang to say that 'Second Opinion' was due. Because of the Christmas rush, it had to be a week early; the paper is due at the printer tomorrow. I suppose I should have known, or guessed. After all, it is the same with Team News. I have written to every contributor asking for everything one week early. They have obliged, and I will be able to deliver to the printer in the morning. Jane Warner is in the same situation with the Link. There is no avoiding the Christmas rush unless I get ill and go to hospital or persuade a doctor to order me to bed. But I wouldn't like that. I would be most unhappy. So I turned my mind to Second Opinion and wrote quickly, from the heart, about the Christmas rush being the very opposite of the Christmas spirit. It's not a joke. It's deadly serious. The whole Christmas business has taken on a life of its own, with no connection at all with the message from the manger. I call that serious. Why do we all go along with it? Because we can't get out of it.

Anyway, Magical Myrtle typed the screed and it was winged on its fax way minutes before I had to preach on John the Baptist at the 10.00 a.m. service. He had the right idea – camel hair clothes with sandals, and a diet of locusts and wild honey. That would end the consumer culture, and that's what I preached to a group of the faithful, who looked a littled startled.

The day improved after that. Roger Peers had suggested a 'working lunch'. He wanted to up-date me on the Beaminster Fabric Committee meeting; I thought it an excellent idea. Joan usually leaves lunches prepared but the Christmas rush has invaded her school because it's their last week and I haven't seen her since reports, kiln firings and end-of-term happenings took over. Roger's suggestion of 'a little cold meat' turned out to be a three-course feast. No better way to work. His own commitments – all voluntary – are so many and varied that the only way to meet with him is when he is sitting down for a meal. Formerly the Curator of Dorset County Museum, he now goes on archaeological 'digs'; he researches Dorset's poets and novelists; he lectures all over the U.K. and abroad on matters of literature and antiquity; he is an active member of conservation societies and he travels in the Far East digging up history. If there is a more interesting man in Beaminster, I haven't met him. And, in the midst of all these commitments, he manages to be our church warden and accept oversight of the building. His love of architecture and his pride in Dorset's antiquities make him the ideal person. I am not an expert on buildings, but I know one when I see one and when I took the initiative and invited him to be church warden, it was one of the best things I did for Beaminster in my twenty-one years. I will always remember hearing his address at the funeral of Gertrude Bugler, who had been Thomas Hardy's 'Tess'. We shared the pulpit that day. He spoke of Gertrude's place in the Dorset history of drama and literature; I spoke positively about Hardy's theology which is usually treated negatively. Roger was still curator of the Dorset County Museum at the time and was not yet fully resident in Beaminster. It was then that I first thought what a wonderful church warden he would be. And in due course it came to pass. Praise be! I wonder if Beaminster knows how expertly it is served. Anyway, it was a good lunch and all the building problems had been put into good hands except the issue of the faculty for the aumbry which had to be referred back to the donors.

I arrived back from Roger's at the very moment Jean Watts' daughters were knocking on the door to make the funeral arrangements. Christine had flown back from Hong Kong and had seen her mother before she died; Maggie had caught the first flight from Spain but had arrived just after she died. With David, their brother, who had also been there, they asked that family members should take their part in the service. The son wanted to pay a tribute and his wife had chosen a poem she wanted to read; one grandson, Duncan, would read a poem which had been found as a bookmarker in Jean's prayer book; another grandson, Darren, wanted to play the organ and sing a song "Let it Be" at the end of the service. I thought it was marvellous that all this planning was in hand and I also thought it was as Jean would wish it. She was so motherly to us all, not only to her family. But I made sure of one thing. I asked to see the poems which would be read and to hear what the son intended to say. I will not risk a Diana fiasco, however well intentioned. And I will add to the son's personal memoir our local view of Jean as the faithful servant of the family of God. Grieving families are sometimes so wrapped in their loss that they are not in the best position to see the wider view, which, I take it, is the priest's job. But it's lovely when the family all have their own ideas to contribute. The end product will be a long way from the Order in the old Book of Common Prayer, which doesn't allow any sense of celebration, or give any place for the personality.

As Jean's daughters left, I went round to call on Dennis Bridge whose wife had died in hospital. She had survived forty-four years with diabetes, injecting herself with insulin twice daily, while retaining a high humour and strong spirit. In the end, she had lost both her legs and it is hard to see how she could ever have coped at home again. We looked at old photographs with his brother-in-law, Peter Warren, and we made the funeral arrangements peacefully. There will be a lot of loneliness after 49 years of marriage, without close family at hand. That is a sadness which takes a special sort of courage to face and in Beaminster it is all too common.

I returned home to the message on the Ansaphone that Bernard Rosewarne, formerly of Culverhayes, had died. Barbara, his widow, has asked for Lilian (also of Culverhayes) to do the funeral. They had both been devout Methodists, lifelong, but his long illness and residence at Saint James' Nursing Home have separated him from the new Methodist ministry in Crewkerne, so it is a special privilege for us to be asked to officiate. It will mean we have eight funerals in six days. Even death cannot escape the Christmas rush.

Thursday, 10th December

I woke up with a fresh determination to control the Christmas rush and not to surrender my resolution. Peace and goodwill would be absent if I continue to rush and have no time for my own reading and for other people's happenings. Also today was the day to see Kilele in 'Joseph and the Amazing Technicolour Dreamcoat', his end-of-term show. At breakfast time, it all looked perfectly possible and felt very peaceful. I like early starts to the day when it is completely dark and no one has stirred and neither the post nor the paper has arrived. It's easy to plan the day and make everything look neat and tidy. It is when people wake up that the trouble starts.

The magazine was ready and delivered to Creeds the Printers as soon as they opened. Every local editor had done her stuff (they are *all* women) and had responded to the Christmas rush, without fuss. So I delivered it on time; even the January services had been agreed and were all in order. It was short of a New Year message on the first page but Doug Beazer had promised to do a summary of millennium plans and I was confident about that. The January issue would be thin, 36 pages – though that would be considered fat in most parishes. Anyway, it was a peaceful start to the day and a positive victory over the Christmas rush to have the whole magazine off my hands and onto Creeds. Let them do the rushing.

Back at base, the mood changed. An Ansaphone message from Rose Bullock said that she had been taken to hospital last night after the external growth on her leg had burst. She had called Richard and Margaret Satchell to the rescue, they had rushed over and taken her to hospital. She was now under doctor's orders – no driving and no standing, pending a consultation. She would not be able to do any services on Sunday and there must be a question mark over her Christmas availability. Fortunately, she was not doing any of the eight funerals and so there was no need to make any re-arrangements in that sensitive area; but for Sunday services I would have to return to the drawing board.

The amazing thing is that, like good elastic, the Team stretched and her Sunday duties were covered very quickly. Jack Broadhurst has always said "Call on me if there is any sickness; I don't mind short notice" and, sure enough, he agreed to go to South Perrott for their communion service. No one would believe he is ninety! In old age, people usually close down a little and withdraw into a smaller circle. Not so with Jack. Out of respect for his age, I have offered to keep him in a smaller area, close to home, but he refused. "You can't control where illness will come," he had said, indicating that he would go anywhere. And so when I asked him, he didn't hesitate. He isn't worried, but I am. I have nightmares about him having an accident in these narrow lanes on the winter's ice or when visibility is poor. I feel a bad conscience, that there is something immoral about asking a man of his age to drive around the countryside on our behalf in mid-winter. I hope against hope that he will be all right and the parishes will appreciate his effort.

Rose's second service was to have been a Christingle at Drimpton. Fortunately, Lilian and her sister, Margaret, were going as guests and so the leaders of the children's work, Jane Marsden, Jenny Beck and Julie Pearce simply asked Lilian to take over. As an ex-headteacher, she won't have the slightest difficulty in adapting. Drimpton will be well served. They will reap the reward of having done all the planning and preparation themselves. Drimpton has had its problems in the past but it is definitely on the mend and the fact that it could change so effortlessly from Rose to Lilian is a good sign. In the old days when the priest planned and controlled everything, that wouldn't have been possible.

Rose's third service was Evensong at Stoke Abbott and I was free to fill that. It pleased me that the Team could expand and embrace a problem and solve it. The parishes would scarcely notice the change. Nine out of ten people wouldn't be aware that anything untoward had happened. And Rose hadn't had to do anything about it. I cannot understand why so many people, clergy and laity, are so sceptical about Teams. Here was a classic example of the value of teamwork. Neither the priest who was ill nor the parishes who would have been without a service raised a finger, and all was covered. That would not happen in an ordinary parish where a priest, even at his last gasp, has to find his own 'locum'. An incident like this shows me the extent to which the Team has protected parishes, but the parishioners probably remain blissfully unaware of it.

In the midst of the phone calls which fixed all these new arrangements, there was space for a call to come in. It was another death. I scarcely believe it! Old Mrs. Barter, formerly of North Street, had died in the Bridport Convent Home, eighteen months short of her century. The funeral is requested for next Friday; that will be nine in quick succession.

I hadn't planned any of these things in that private and peaceful hour before breakfast. Perhaps in the priesthood we should plan nothing and respond to everything. That would be interesting. It would be a very different style of ministry. When I took my sabbatical leave ten years ago and travelled through India, I was taken up with the idea of responding to situations rather than trying to control them. In fact I wrote the whole of "First World, Last World" from that perspective, and I believed it. But, when I returned, it didn't work. We are geared to planning, budgeting, targets, aims and schemes. Anyone who simply responds to events is considered to be either idle or inefficient, or both. It takes a very strong man indeed to resist the purpose of the planners.

Planning is the whole mode of the Western world, of business and of capitalism. That is the way we are and that is the way we are expected to behave. That does not prove it is the Gospel way and I very much doubt that it is. Anyway, there was one part of this morning's pre-breakfast plan which I could salvage – I could still call on Canon John Whettem, now housebound with his left leg in plaster. John was in terrific form, laughing at his situation, though it wasn't funny. He and Mary should have been in Cyprus for an eight-week Chaplaincy. They would have wintered in the sunshine and they would have had Christmas in a top hotel. And they would have been brilliant at the work because they are born pastors which is the main need for holidaymakers who end up in hospital or some other trouble. Instead he will be stuck indoors for the English winter with his leg up. I told him Rose was in the same situation, but with the other leg. Coming out of John's house, I bumped into Fred Holland who told me he at last had an appointment with the eye consultant and it was on the Monday coming. This was good news for him but, if they go ahead with his operation, he will also be unavailable at Christmas. Whoever will go down next?

I returned home to the news of another death. This is quite unbelievable and brings the number to ten. This time it was the former Broadwindsor church warden, Victor Thompson. He had died in the hospice at Taunton and the funeral will be at his new home in Chard. We won't be involved until his ashes are interred with his first wife at a memorial service in the new year. Peggy, his second wife, will be well supported in her own parish, so there is no need to respond for the moment, which is a relief as I haven't finished preparing for Kathleen Bridge's funeral tomorrow, never mind Jean Watts' on Monday or Mrs. Barter's. Somehow it doesn't seem like Christmas.

Joan got annoyed this evening. I had promised to go to Sherborne and see Kilele in "Joseph and the Amazing Technicolour Dreamcoat" but, with Rose out of action, I went to Hooke's P.C.C. instead. Joan said I was too conscientious and Hooke could manage perfectly well without any clergy. I didn't agree. All these Church Councils deserve a priest and they should have one. They have more responsibility than at any time in history and the clergy should show their support. Not so long ago, the vicar was obliged to be Chairman of every Church Council. To get out of the Chair is reasonable enough but to get out of the meeting altogether is going too far. I knew Hooke could manage without a priest present and I knew Hooke wouldn't complain if they didn't have one, but that wasn't the point. The Council had just put on the amazing four-course dinner and cabaret entertainment and the least we can do is show appreciation. I was not being over-conscientious; it was common courtesy after such a feast; besides they had their Christmas services to plan and how could they do that without a priest? I had been looking forward to seeing Kilele on stage, and I was sorry to miss it. I rang him up to say I was not coming and it didn't seem to matter to him in the slightest. It mattered far more to me. Anyway, he sang me his song over the phone, mourning the supposed death of Joseph.

> "There's one more angel in heaven
> There's one more star in the sky
> Joseph we'll never forget you,
> It's tough but we're going to get by.
> There's one less place at our table
> There's one more tear in my eye,
> Joseph, the things that you stood for
> Like love and peace, never die."

It hardly filled me with Christmas cheer, but at least he was tuneful.

So Joan took him to the concert and I went to the Church Council where we gathered in front of Ena's woodburning stove. It ended with home-made mince pies and John's own brew of mulled wine. Church Councils can be very enjoyable – and so they should be!

Friday, 11th December

The hour before breakfast was utterly peaceful; the only sound was Sunny licking himself clean all over. This time I didn't try to plan the day because that doesn't seem to work – events take over, as they did yesterday. Today I tried to imagine what might happen and how it would be wise to react. There were three fixed points which had some certainty about them.

The first was the Yeovil funeral of Katie Bridge at 10.30; the second was in Dorchester at 3.30 to discuss with Peter Parker advertising for Sudan Church Review; the third was that Joan would return from Sherborne in the evening, exhausted at the end of term. The fixed points of a day are in many ways the easy part – even if they are difficult. It's possible to prepare for them, because they are expected. I know the people who will be involved. I can picture their faces and I know something of their temperament. The fixed points are seldom the problem. It is all the things which crop up in between – in the post, in the office, on the phone, or in the town. There is no planning for these. Yet they are probably the key to a genuinely responsive ministry as opposed to a controlling or directive ministry. I favour the responsive ministry because I believe it is Our Lord's way; but the church is geared to a directive ministry because it has always been that way. The people expect both. And that creates the pressure point. Is it humanly possible to be both responsive and directive?

I cheated today. After Katie Bridge's funeral, which was very well attended and must have given great encouragement to Dennis, I went on to Sherborne and, for three hours, I was hidden away. I met Timothy from school at noon and heard that he will soon be staying at school all day and that he had had two full days as practice already. Anna had left his lunch, wrapped in polythene, and, because I had none, he said "We can share, Uncle" and he carefully divided all his food into two. Later we went to meet Kilele from school and he was happy with his performance in the "Dreamcoat" show, though he was far more concerned about Saints' next match at Everton on Saturday. He is beginning to think that we need a new manager. I said we needed a new team. He replied that the manager had bought the team, and that the manager trained them, and therefore it was his fault. The logic was unanswerable, and I fell silent because it is evident that relegation stares us in the face. "Don't worry, Uncle," said Kilele. "If we win on Saturday

105

and Blackburn and Nottingham Forest lose, we will only be one point behind and we can easily get that by Christmas." The enthusiasm and the optimism made me smile, though the realism is that there is nothing to smile about.

Sherborne to Dorchester is a direct route and the meeting with Peter Parker of the Sudan Church Association was hopeful. It has puzzled me for some while that our little local "Team News" earns £6,000 annually from advertising and yet the "Sudan Church Review" which is nationwide (and beyond) earns nothing at all from advertising. If it could earn even £1,000 a year, I would be able to edit it in full colour. If church publications want to be widely read, they must keep abreast of popular trends and be presented in full colour. I believe that there are many businesses, church and secular, which would be pleased to contribute £100 to the suffering Sudanese, in return for an advertising spot. Peter agreed and, with Liz Green to assist him, he promised to begin enquiries. I am happy to continue editing the Review, but I am not the right person to be involved in its finances.

I was home by 6.00 p.m., expecting Joan at the end of her school term. Should I take her out to supper as a celebration, or would she bring food and expect to cook it? I had kept the evening free and would do whatever seemed best. Sometimes she comes home exhausted, deflated and defeated and doesn't want to go anywhere. Other times she comes back elated and excited and ready to do anything. That is the way the end of term affects every teacher I have ever known. They work flat out, targeting a certain point, like an athlete timing his sprint to cross the line. Then the collapse. I waited and waited for her return, to see whether the mood would be high or low. Only one thing is certain. When she is home, life will be different. When there is only one person in the house, it is easy to be selfish. When there are two people in the house, everthing has to be considered from a second point of view. It won't be so easy to eat when it suits me, I will have to eat when it suits her! Everything becomes negotiable and subject to democratic discussion. In "Journey to Kars" Philip Glazebrook muses on the merits of travelling alone and concludes there is a lot to be said for it. When the pressure is intense – as on a long journey in a hot climate with a different language in an alien culture – it is quite enough to cope with oneself, never mind having to consider the feelings of another. And the approach to Christmas could be considered a long journey. On the other hand, Joan will undoubtedly deal with the Christmas fare which is quite a complicated matter, she will wrap all the presents and make sure they go to the right people at the right time, she will order the Christmas tree and dress it and she will make all the lights work, as she does every year. In other words, her return will be a blessing, but a mixed one. And that is what marriage is, a series of compromises and consultations. I don't believe the people who pretend to have found some perfect idyll of continuous delight. It is much more creative than that. It will be annoying when she opens my study door and enquires why I haven't lit the fire, but it would be desperate if she didn't. And she will be annoyed when she is busy and I ask her what time supper will be. But she admits life would be terribly dull if I didn't. So she was due back and I prepared myself for the changes that would follow – for better, for worse. It was nine o'clock when she rang, still in Sherborne. A late kiln firing had been necessary and she had to be at the carol service in the morning so it was common sense to stay the extra night and return for lunch next day. I agreed, and wrote in my diary that she would be back for tea, possibly. There was bread and cheese in the kitchen.

Today's effort not to give way to the Christmas rush has been the most successful so far. But only because I cheated by going into hiding between the fixed points. Perhaps I need not feel guilty about those few hours because an old priest, who refused to have a telephone in his house, once told me that from Monday to Friday he never went out beyond his own garden. "It only invites trouble," he said. He made a concession on Saturdays when he used to spend an hour in the village square. "That's enough to pick up all the news," he said. That era is well and truly gone, though some people still describe the clergy as "six days invisible, one day incomprehensible." I wonder if that old priest was as lazy as he sounds. Perhaps he was thoroughly recollected and able to respond deeply when called upon. That we will never know. At least he knew how to escape the Christmas rush, and any other rush.

Saturday, 12th December

Joan arrived home at 3.00 p.m., bringing lunch with her. I decided not to say that I had already had a lunch of soup and cheese. It wouldn't have been tactful. So I sat down to a second meal, making a great fuss of the speed and efficiency with which it was delivered, though I felt as if I was being fattened up for Christmas. Before the late lunch was served, everything had to be brought in from the car. She said the car was loaded. It certainly was. I carried in two 56lb. bags of dog food, two cartons of bottles, *two* Christmas trees, a box of vegetables, three or four boxes of fruit, two huge cardboard boxes of groceries, two boxes of crackers, big bags of crisps, packets of nuts, a box marked 'Fragile' and a holdall which I presume was her clothes. It filled the hall. I had the sinking feeling that Christmas was upon us and that, if I thought I had already faced the Christmas rush, then "I ain't seen nothing yet." It had arrived, with my wife. "Where is all this going?" I asked in a faintly peeved way. "Most of it into your stomach," was the basic reply. That was an appalling thought. It couldn't possibly be true. All those boxes of things, filling a hallway, couldn't possibly be eaten, could they? What are we? Gluttons?

Two things were clear. One was that Joan was doing her best for the national economy. This is what we are meant to do, spend and consume. And this is evidently what we are going to do, because it's Christmas and that is what people do at Christmas. The second thing which is now clear is that the tension, the rush and the palaver when there are two people in a house is not twice as much as when there is one, but about twenty times as much. The battle I thought I was waging against "Christmas rush" had been a mere "phoney war". Now Joan is home, let battle commence. But there can only be one winner, and it's not me. I might as well surrender and avoid the fight. "Blessed are the peacemakers" could be my excuse, but I did quietly enquire why there were *two* Christmas trees. "One for us and one for Sherborne," she said.

I could see what this meant – we would have to go over to Sherborne, which she had just left, to put the tree up. I decided it wasn't the right moment to make that comment. In any case, all would be revealed in due course. In fact, it was revealed sooner than I expected. I was carrying the big bags of dog food into the garage when she said "We'll have to go over to Sherborne soon." I kept my peace. "Because all the presents are there." I had noticed the plural *"we"* but I still said nothing, possibly hoping it would pass by if I didn't draw attention to it. "I thought we could go tonight," she said. I knew I had tickets for the Beaminster Singers' Concert in church tonight and that it would be a good local event with lots of people we should meet and a nice way to set the Christmas scene. But I also knew I had disappointed her in the week when she had tickets for Joseph and his Dreamcoat. Tactics! Compromises! Oh! Isn't marriage exhausting? So I dumped the dog food and asked why Sunny needed 112lbs. of it for Christmas. "Oh!" she said, "you never know if the roads will snow up; better to be safe …" Well, Sunny, you'll be well looked after! I was considering the question of the concert tickets when she said "Put the Sherborne tree back in the car, ready for getting the presents." I've seen something like this on television. I think she is called Mrs. Bucket (Bouquet) and he is called Richard. I have a fellow feeling for Richard; he is quite adept at keeping the peace. There are times when agreement or compliance has the mark of wisdom. I knew very well that I needed a cover designed for the January magazine and that Joan was the best person to do it at such short notice. If I insist on going to the concert tonight and she has to go to Sherborne tomorrow, there is no way she will have time to do the magazine cover. But if I go to Sherborne tonight and I casually mention the cover on the way back, she may find she has time to do it tomorrow. Oh! What tangled webs we weave! No wonder Our Lord advised us to be harmless as doves – and *wise as serpents*! It's a dangerous thing for a man to take on a woman in the arts of the devious, but I quietly put the tickets for the Beaminster Singers' Concert in the waste bin and said I had always wanted to go to Sherborne and collect the presents. "How nice to go to Sherborne," I lied. "It will be good to dress the tree tonight." And so we went, against all my inclinations, expectations and the plans made in the peaceful hour before breakfast. "Blessed are the meek" said Our Lord in the Sermon on the Mount and I gave every appearance of being very meek as I put the Christmas tree back in the car. But it was all part of a greater plot to get a magazine cover. Oh, marriage! It is such fun, so creative of the arts of subtlety. But would we bother with all this finesse, I wondered, if we didn't love each other?

At Sherborne, Kilele answered the door. "We lost," he said. Of course I had heard the scores and knew all the details; it had been a one-nil defeat at Everton. "We're now more bottom than we were before," he announced. I knew that too. "Never mind," I said. "We've brought the Christmas tree. You can help us put it up." "The Manager is the problem," was Kilele's response. I asked if he knew where the decorations for the tree were kept, but he said he was going to bed, and that's what he did. Do these footballers who pocket their thousands of pounds each week have the slightest notion of the effect of their performances on the supporters? I doubt very much that they have the love for the team or the club that we have, even though they are in the team and we are not. I want my team to win, I long for them to win, but these days some players are nothing more than rogues and mercenaries. So there we were in Sherborne, but Saints had lost and Kilele was going to bed, so it wasn't the right moment to decorate the tree.

However, we did collect all the presents and on the way back to Beaminster Joan said she thought she would be able to do the cover for the magazine, in the morning.

Late at night, I was still struggling with the Sunday sermons. The Gospel was all about John the Baptist preparing the way for Our Lord. And he was clothed in camel's hair and ate locusts and wild honey. He wouldn't do the national economy much good. Maybe he is the corrective we need to the spend, spend syndrome which has overtaken us all.

Sunday, 13th December

Sunday is not only the best day of the week, but the easiest. Nothing is less true than "This is your busy day, Vicar!" Sunday is the only day of the week with clear fixed points and scarcely ever an interruption between them. It is also the only day in which I am certain to be doing the things I was ordained to do – teaching the faith and leading the worship. It is also the only day in which I am certain to be free for six hours and, on some Sundays, from noon till bedtime. No wonder Sundays are the easiest day of the week!

Today was no exception. There were four services but I had something to say and I enjoyed saying it. It is easy because the people do their part so well. Every church was well prepared – the lesson readers were clear and it was obvious they had prepared thoroughly; the intercessors had thought about the prayers which they offered with sensitivity; the hymns had been chosen thoughtfully and the organists played them in a way which encouraged the congregation; the Sacristans had prepared the altars with the bread, the wine, the shining silver and the Advent candles ready for lighting. In every church the way had been prepared, the priest's job was made easy. This is normal in cathedrals and in the great parish churches which employ a verger but I doubt it is normal in the smaller village churches of the land, but it has become the norm here and it makes the biggest possible difference to my Sunday. From the moment I enter the church, I have a sense of expectation. The people are gathered and all the background work has been done. Now the priest must respond, and deliver the goods!

This is a far cry from the way things were, not so long ago. A few incidents of yesteryear are etched indelibly in my mind. There was a time – before the Team came into being, when I was on my own – that I arrived for the Toller service from Melplash a few minutes late and feeling very rushed. The congregation were in their pews. The organist was at his seat. But, before we could start, I had to light the candles, prepare the altar and put the hymn numbers up while everybody watched me. Later, when I questioned them, they all said they thought "holy things" should be handled by the vicar, not by them. On another landmark occasion, a Melplash church officer phoned me (I was ten miles away at Toller) to say that the candles on the altar were alight, and what should she do? I told her to blow them out (the service had ended three hours earlier). She said that she hadn't liked to do that, because the vicar had always done it. Perhaps this is why I appreciate Sundays so much. I know where we have come from, and it is very encouraging.

Every Sunday has its special character. I have never known two the same. And one of the distinctive features today was the Advent gifts which had been made by the children of the Team at their 'Fun and Learning Day' and given to every parish church. At some point in the service, the gift needed to be unwrapped. In the modern ASB service, I thought it fitted well at "The Peace", when we greet each other; that was the moment to receive the gift. In the old prayer book service, I thought it would be better at the very end, after the blessing; it is never wise to intrude into the flow of the old service. In each church, the gift was well received, whether it was done in the middle or at the end. The people were visibly moved by the thought of all these young children busily making a Christmas gift for every parish. At Broadwindsor, I chose Jim Hardman to do the unwrapping. I chose him simply because he was the nearest person to the parcel, but I couldn't have made a better choice. He entered into the spirit of it with a few timely wisecracks as he put the figures of Joseph and Mary into the crib that was being built week by week. I thought the whole idea of the gift of a home-made crib for every parish was brilliant, but it remains a marvel and a mystery how David and Jill got the children to make fourteen of them in the time. It was good that so many people went to have a look at the figures. They were made out of card, held together by glue and sellotape. I would estimate the cost at around five pence a figure, possibly less. Yet I had the strong feeling that the people would choose them in preference to a £100 crib set. I sensed a strong statement about the true Christmas spirit coming from these home-made cribs and I hoped every parish was opening them publicly, and appreciating them properly.

One thing marred my morning. It was at Broadwindsor. Everyone was leaving the church so cheerfully after the little present episode, when someone came up to me and said "Have you heard the Test score?" I hadn't, but I froze on the spot because I knew by intuition or by his tone of voice that it would be dreadful. "We lost the last six wickets for twenty runs," he said, "and the Australians are 150 for 1." The whole of this Ashes series is turning into a nightmare. I wish I was not interested in sport. I wish I could give it up. The constant disappointments repeated day after day in Saints' football or English cricket are too painful. People who are not involved don't know how lucky they are. How peaceful and untroubled their lives must be! But for me there is this constant dashing of hopes, this constant cloud of pending doom. Why I am not a chronic depressive, I do not know. This morning I was downstairs by 7.00 a.m., an hour before the 8.00 a.m. service, to hear the radio commentary from Australia. But with great self restraint, a discipline any Buddhist monk would have respected, I sat there and never turned it on. I knew, instinctively, the news would be bad and that I would go to the service fuming at their latest follies and inadequacies. This latest news proved my instincts exactly right. But at least I found out after the three morning services. It spoiled my lunch, but not the services. But what can be done to lift the English game? The Moslems, the Hindus and the Buddhists all beat us now. I never thought Buddhists would become great cricketers, but they are the best of all. I don't mind losing

to Buddhists. It's when those heathens from Down Under thrash us that I get rattled.

Monday, 14th December

There were too many little things happening today, and one big thing, which was Jean Watts' funeral.

The first of the little things was a 9 a.m. meeting with the Beaminster church wardens, the Chairman of the Finance Committee and Clifford Howe, the Director of Music, to review his contract. This should be done every year, according to the Royal School of Church Music, and it hadn't been done for four years. It turned out that in the original contract, Clifford was expected to play at a certain set of services, which were now quite different. We made the adjustments and it was all cheerful and painless. In one way, the contract is a nonsense because Clifford does well beyond anything for which he is paid, and he does it with good will because his heart is in it. He has built a choir with youngsters, as well as the faithful regulars, until the numbers are too great to fit in the choir stalls; he has fostered good relations with the schools; he has supported every event which has encouraged the search for excellence, especially concerts and diocesan choir festivals. None of these things are mentioned in the contract. He does them because he loves it. Contracts confuse me. I have never had any sort of a contract, with the result that I have very little understanding of them and a great dread of the day when clergy will want a contract and start working to their rules. May I not live to see the day.

The next little thing was that Creeds needed the magazine cover and the late items, including the centre-spread pages about Father Pat Waddy's 70th anniversary of priesthood. Joan had done a suitable cover, by digging out an old photograph of a winter's scene which might be very effective but the Pat Waddy centre-spread was not ready because the tributes from the Bishop of Salisbury and the Archbishop of Canterbury had not arrived. And they were the main features. There was nothing for it but to telephone their offices and enquire. In both cases, the letter was on the way, caught in the Christmas postal rush, but the Fax machine solved the problem and ten minutes later I was on the way to Creeds, with both tributes. Modern technology, much as I loathe it, had come to the rescue. Creeds promised the whole text would be ready to collect for proof reading by 5.00 p.m. Their speed astonishes me; it must be the new technology again, though I would like to think that the way I present it helps.

The next little thing was a cross-country dash to Hooke where Rose Doughty and her worship group had met to plan the crib service on Christmas Eve. Joy Edwards, Rosemary Brandon and Theresa Colton, with Rose, make a good team for children's work. They never fail to come up with something different for the festive occasions, and something in which the young folk participate. There is always a trauma or two about whether the youngsters will know their part or rehearse properly but my experience is that somehow it comes right in the end. Their briefing was more than a little 'iffy'. If so-and-so comes, we will do this; if not, we will do that; if someone else is here for Christmas, this will happen but, if they are away, it won't. It seemed to me that the priest would have to go to the service with a general picture of the theme but with an open mind about how to adapt to circumstances on the day. I don't mind that. The most important thing is that several people are putting their minds to it, are thinking about how Christmas should be presented and are busy making costumes for it. The church will probably be full, because so many people will have been involved in the preparation. All the priest will have to do is let it happen, and not mess it up, by intruding too much.

The same could be said of the big event of the day, Jean Watts' funeral at Drimpton. I had never known a family plan every detail so thoughtfully and also provide the family members to carry it out. All the priest had to do was let it happen, but I very nearly messed it up.

I had promised Gwladys Roberts, the organist, that I would be first there and go through the music arrangements with her. At the age of 91, she deserves special attention, especially as a grandson was due to take over the organ and play a modern piece. Gwladys is amazingly game but this hadn't happened to her before, so I promised to be there early. But I didn't keep the promise. After my morning trips, Joan wanted the car; so I took Andrew's car for the funeral but, after a couple of hundred yards, the petrol warning flashed – nearly empty. I diverted to the nearest garage and filled up – only to find that as I had changed into my cassock, I hadn't brought my wallet – no cash, no cards. I couldn't pay. They let me off with the signing of an I.O.U. but it was embarrassing and time-consuming and, when I arrived at Drimpton, the church was bursting full with people spilling into the porch and the vestry. Gwladys was playing and it was too late to even think of briefing her. I had promised to be first to arrive and I was the last. I had to robe with people breathing down my neck, but it was all in a very good cause. I was pleased Jean Watts was to have a terrific send off.

The family excelled themselves. The son welcomed everybody and paid his own tribute and his wife read a Gibran poem; one grandson read two poems and another grandson claimed the organ from Gwladys and led the singing of "Let It Be". All the priest had to do was pray, and make sure he didn't intrude too much.

This was not an ordinary funeral and, although everyone loved Jean Watts, not everyone would have been comfortable with her funeral. I can't help wondering whether this will be the pattern in the next millennium. The totally impersonal nature of urban cremations demands the pendulum to swing – possibly to the highly personal style of today's service. The church needs to embrace and affirm the style, or funerals will simply go secular and by-pass church and clergy altogether.

After the cremation in Yeovil, I called on Rose in Mosterton en route to Creeds in Broadoak. Rose is not well and the prospects of her availability in January look thin. Richard Satchell had taken her to the consultant and the result confirms that an operation will be necessary and that, in the meantime, she must neither drive nor put much weight on the foot. A drear prospect for her and for us. She seemed calm and peaceful enough. It worried me that she wanted to spend Christmas there, on her own. David and Jill had invited her, as Joan and I had done, and as lots of others are sure to do, but at the moment she wants to be on her own. I would have thought that her family might come and swoop her up, but she intends to stay where she is. We all cope with things differently and she is adamant she knows what suits her best. Our Team meeting on Wednesday will have to do a lot of re-thinking of the Christmas schedule and the programme at the printers for January is now not worth the paper it is written on.

Creeds had the whole magazine text ready for proof reading and when I delivered it to Vivien for proof reading her eyes sparkled and she was ready to start. At home, I laid the whole lot on the floor. Sunny stretched out in his corner and sighed. He knew he must not move for three hours, and he didn't, by which time the entire text was in an order which will make sense to the reader. Nothing has been left out and very few additions had to be made. It was one of those good months when things fitted well. When Vivien's corrections come, it can go back to Creeds and be printed, ahead of time. But because of Rose's absence the service programme will be riddled with errors.

I reckoned the day's mileage – to Creeds at Broadoak, on to Hooke, across to Drimpton, over to Yeovil Crematorium, back to Mosterton and then to Creeds again, was about ninety miles. The good thing about the journeys is that they make nice quiet intervals between the events and give a little breathing space – unless I am short of petrol and without a wallet, then it is breathless and bad for the equilibrium, and for everything else, as at the funeral today. That must not happen again.

Tuesday, 15th December

David Tizzard was on the phone before 8.00 a.m., and it was good news. Calls before 8.00 a.m. are usually David Wakely with bad news and, as we have had eleven of those calls in a fortnight, this was a welcome change. David was buzzing – he usually is – with the news from the 'Crisis' centre. Yesterday was the first day of our annual appeal for the homeless. Gifts received in kind have filled 60 sacks, while gifts in cash passed £600. As there are still four days to go, the possibility is that we will have to get a second lorry to transport the sacks to London, and that will mean a second driver as well. It will not be too easy in the midst of the Christmas rush; lorries and drivers are not necessarily available at short notice in Christmas week. I am sure of one thing – if anybody can find a lorry and persuade a driver, it is David, so the best thing I can do is keep out of the way. When David gets an idea, or a project under way – look out! He has the style and the weight of one of those Churchill tanks that became so famous in the war but, unlike the tanks, he moves with the speed of a modern missile. Things will happen! I am told that guided missiles are a marvel but that, when they go off-course, it's the devil's own job to retrieve them, and the result is invariably explosions with disastrous consequences. Thank God that David is well guided by Jill and that our Team meetings and his many friends have a share in keeping things on course. Church life will never be pedestrian while David is around; there will always be beams of energy flashing this way and that, catching people unawares and sweeping them into the latest scheme. This is what we need and let us rejoice in it. Even so, when I put the phone down, I was resolved to keep out of the way for a while lest I became swept away in the tornado and find myself driving to London on Christmas Eve with a lorry load of 500 sacks of blankets, jackets, woollies and all the other valuables people bring to the 'Crisis' centre.

This centre, each Christmas week, has become part of the local tradition. We have been doing it for ten years and its success grows every year. It is now expected. People wait for it and save their gifts for it. It is in the calendar. I have noticed many times in country life that certain things which recur regularly gather their own momentum. They get in the blood stream and they just happen. Everyone knows their role and are ready when the call comes. But therein lies a fatal flaw. It is too easy to think it will happen automatically. Wrong. It still needs fine-tuning every year and a radical review occasionally, otherwise it will become repetitive and dull and eventually lose its flavour. Even a success cannot be repeated again and again. In fact the more successful something is, the harder it is to repeat it. This is the blessing of being in a Team – Peter Swain ran the Crisis Appeal his way for a few years, followed by Peter Steele who added his distinctive flavour; now we have David in partnership with Ralph and John Bugler in one of Beaminster's prime sites, twenty yards from the Square. No wonder it is surpassing all previous efforts.

Doctor Tony Barter called at coffee time to arrange his mother's funeral on Friday. She was in her ninety-ninth year and had kept a sturdy spirit until the last few months, which had to be spent in the nursing home at the Bridport Convent, for which he was fulsome in praise. He is keen to pay the tribute at the crematorium and that is a great help to me, and I've no doubt he will do it very well, but I warned him it isn't easy for any son to do this, however mature the man. We agreed that the way in which an ever-increasing number of people are living well beyond their allotted span of three score years and ten and can live alone, happily, well into their nineties, is one of the marvels of the age.

It is one of the mysteries of the age that other people do not. The passage into old age does not seem to follow any recognisable pattern or have any logical rationale. Some of the most brilliant minds become clouded and some of the lightest spirits become heavy. I suppose everyone approaching old age has a fear of losing their faculties and becoming foolish. The terrible thing is that there doesn't appear to be any way of living that will guarantee your way of dying. It is an undeniable fact that some of the sharpest people, whose life and work have been an inspiration, simply lose their minds. The illness may be given a fine-sounding name but it isn't much different from what was once called senility – and there is nothing fine about that. It is tragic. Alastair Bannerman calls it 'an agony'. And he should know. He has now made four hundred journeys to visit Elisabeth, his wife of fifty-eight years, since the disease took her out of circulation. Elisabeth was an entertainer all her life; she danced and sang every hour God gave. She taught half of Beaminster to dance, fifty or more years ago. She sang in choirs, presented children's plays in church and read the scriptures for all to hear. If there was a warmer heart or a sparklier spirit, lead me to her. And now? The mind is veiled. She speaks a language of her own in a world of her own. Alastair, himself 84 years old, spends hours upon hours trying to tease a memory out of her. He will play music, look at family photographs, sing songs, bring toys and card games, but she chatters on, in her own language and in her own world. The sons come, week upon week, supporting their father and bringing fresh stimulation, but the recognition is fleeting, and passing. Oh, wretched disease! Oh, most foul and beastly mockery that such a one, any one, should come to this!

Tonight, Joan and I were Alastair's guests. After his exhausting days of endless vigil, he likes to spend an hour or so in the evenings with the glass and the friends that cheer, and we enjoy it too. I've heard about his days in the Gielgud company more than once, of how he fenced with Olivier, trained with Alec Guinness, played opposite Flora Robson and I know that, long before the second glass, Shakespeare sonnets will be flowing – all from memory – and we will be carried to another world, yesterday's world which, like his Elisabeth's world, is gone for ever. But Alastair is not a yesterday's man. Tonight we heard that he continues his tennis playing once a week and that he had played twenty games of men's singles that very morning, the women considering it too cold to make a doubles! And he wanted Joan to cast her professional eye over his latest paintings – landscapes of the hills and valleys of Beaminster with which he has heartened himself after his hospital visits. And before we left he handed me not one but two poems for Team News. "It's the painting and the poems that keep me sane," he said.

There are so many people grieving for loved ones who have not died. Much easier to cope with the grief of death, which is at least final, and understandable. Alastair's efforts to live with the grief that is neither final nor understandable impressed us tonight, as they always do.

David Tizzard rang late this evening, still buzzing. The Crisis shop has filled a hundred and fifty sacks and the gifts have passed £1,200, last year's record, with three days still to go! He gets as excited as a schoolboy, which is faintly funny and very infectious. This Crisis effort means more to him than to most people because he has spent a lot of his thirty years of priesthood at 'the other end'. In one inner city spot after another, his parishioners have been among the 'receivers', the victims pushed to the margins. Suddenly he finds himself at the 'giving' end and the pleasure and the urgency are evident.

Wednesday, 16th December

The morning post arrived with a strong Christmas flavour which should have put me in a good mood, but didn't. The post included my pet hate, Christmas letters which are photocopied 'round robins', two of them. No doubt there will be more to follow. I understand people trying to avoid the Christmas rush. I respect that, I am trying to do that myself. Sending a circular is one way of doing it; the writer covers fifty or a hundred people with one missive. Very convenient for the writer but to my mind they are not letters at all. They completely fail to communicate. They cannot possibly enquire of or relate with the recipient, who is just one among a hundred. And so they are always about the writer and his/her family and activities. They read like annual reports. And they always emphasise all the family successes: "Charlie was the senior King in the Christmas play ..." I don't know who Charlie is, and there is no evidence that there was a 'senior' king anyway. This particular circular didn't have even my name entered by hand – the computer said "Dear Everyone ..." It was not even signed by hand. Immediately, it went in the bin, and so will any other circular that comes. This device is not *solving* the problem of the Christmas rush, it is *surrendering* to it.

The magazine text, proof-read and corrected, edited and illustrated, with new advertisements in place, was ready for printing and I delivered it to Creeds as they opened their doors. It will be printed before they close for Christmas, I will store them for the holiday period while the world goes out of shape, and release them when things return to normal. What a relief! The printer won't re-open until 4th January – imagine beginning the process at that late stage. It has been worth the rush and everyone has seen the point and done their part.

I returned to hear continued negative news about Rose. She has to sit and wait, sit and wait, sit and wait. There is nothing else she can do, and little anyone can do to help her, while she waits. The results from the laboratory will decree what happens next. For her sake, I hope it is decisive and leads to action, even if the action is surgery. And for our sakes too. It's always better to feel something is happening. David and I were one priest short at Christmas last year, and it never occurred to us that we would be back in the same situation at Christmas this year.

The Team meeting had to consider the situation. I said we faced two problems and that we shouldn't mix them up. One problem was fulfilling the promises already made for the Christmas programme. The other problem was the longer-term plan for January, and possibly beyond that.

My hope was that the clergy Team would somehow stretch and fulfil all Christmas promises with a priestly presence. I considered it would be a dreadful let-down if a parish didn't have a priest at Christmas. It would be bad for them and give them reason to talk about the decline and decay of the Church of England. And it would be bad for the Team, giving the impression of neither caring nor coping, at Christmas of all times. At Christmas dozens and dozens of people come whom we don't see at any other time. If we didn't fulfil the Christmas promises, with priests, we would be sending defeatist signals, especially to those once-a-year worshippers. Fortunately, David Shearlock, in the first year of his retirement, was ready and willing to do extra on Christmas Day and to take Rose's place at midnight; Jack Broadhurst, in the ninety-first year of his life and the twenty-fifth year of his retirement, was equally willing to do a Christmas Day service and I was able to fit in two extra events – the Mosterton Christingle among them. Lo and behold, all was covered, and by priests. We will not be sending negative signals at Christmas.

The second, longer-term, problem is different. I cannot in conscience expect priests who have retired from the hurly burly to return to it, to rescue us. They have served diligently for thirty or more years and have earned their peace. We should not put them in a position where they again feel a duty laid upon them, week in week out, and in the winter weather. It will be wrong if we allow retired priests to solve our problem by doubling their efforts. Fortunately, David T. agreed with me, one hundred per cent or more. After Christmas I will write to every church warden and advise them that, during Rose's absence through illness, we will revert to the arrangements agreed for the Interregnum. The services Rose would have taken should be led locally, by the church wardens or persons deputed by the church wardens. Every parish has been supplied with the recommended Order for Morning Prayer and the people responded well, last time. The plan will have to be put into operation again. It's a pity, but it is better than allowing retired priests to veil the whole problem, by putting their own health at risk. We depend on them too much already. Better to expose the problem. I am convinced that, if we do our part at Christmas for the festive season, the church officers and congregations will want to do their part in the new year.

There is no telling the ways of women! Or, if there is, I am not privy to it. When Joan returned from school on Saturday, I prepared myself for all the fun and the frustrations of being together again. But I have scarcely seen her since. It's quite embarrassing when someone rings and asks where she is. I am expected to know, but I don't. Since coming home, she has been to see her mother at Parkstone, delivered presents to the Wimborne part of the family, been to London for an exhibition, delivered chairs to Sherborne for the Wells Cathedral Concert, gone on a consumer spending spree (I don't want to know where) and now says she will deliver the Southampton family presents when she goes to Salisbury (I don't know what for). I just nod and let it happen. I am sure I could be Richard in "Keeping Up Appearances", without acting. Someone telephoned tonight and asked where she was. This has happened three times today and so I said "In Scotland." I hadn't planned to say it. It just came out spontaneously. The person the other end said "Oh, all right," and rang off. Didn't seem the least surprised. She came in a little later, having gone out "for ten minutes". She had delivered our offerings to the Crisis shop where she "had a lovely time" for two hours! It would have been quite nice to see her again if I hadn't been going out as she came in. And I noticed she was unloading from the car a third Christmas tree. "What on earth is that for?" I asked, which seemed a fair question because neither of the first two trees is up yet. "Don't worry," she said. "It's going to Amos" (her nephew). Amos, it turns out, is moving into a new house today and will be calling tomorrow with a van to relieve us of surplus furniture. "He is sure to need a Christmas tree," she said.

Thursday, 17th December

The morning mail brought another wretched Christmas circular. I passed it to Joan without reading it. She said she would tell me any important news but she never did, so I guess there was none. It probably said John was in his final year at university, Mary would be starting next summer and Granny had had a spell in hospital, but was doing better now. They all do. It is more than likely that we had never met John, Mary or Granny, but that is the nature of circulars. I don't call them letters and I will never answer them. In the same post, came a proper letter from Peter Swain; eight hand-written pages with a ninth added by Pauline. I have put it in my folder. It deserves a proper reply and it will get it in the new year. If Peter, who is rector of the huge parish of Leominster, has time to write by hand at Christmas, then anybody can make the time if they have the mind to do so.

David T. arrived, late morning, bustling and beaming. He had been for his long-awaited medical check-up. We heard every detail of what had been done to him, which was a lot, and he seems to have responded well to everything, including electric shocks. They seem to have a diagnosis at last. The muscle spasms and the exhaustion he has been suffering are said to be 'Chronic Fatigue Syndrome'. In my opinion, his body is trying to give him good advice. It is controlling and correcting him, which is more than anyone else can do. If I was locked with David for long, I would have chronic fatigue syndrome! His constitution is protesting, and preventing a disaster. What clever and balanced mechanisms our bodies are; we should listen to them more carefully.

A letter from Father Jonathan, the Catholic priest, fell on the doormat this morning, while I was out. I wish I had been in, and had been able to welcome him and offer him a coffee or something a little stronger. His letter invited us to "Ecumenical Carols" at the Catholic Church on the first Sunday in January, at 7.30 p.m. We must try to respond positively. I am committed to two Toller christenings that evening and David will be leading Blackdown's big Christmas effort at that very moment. However, no opportunity to work or worship with our fellow Christians should be lost. I will have to return from Toller quickly and join the service a little late. I don't want to miss it. The division of our churches remains one of the scandals of Christendom. Anything we can do which proclaims our goodwill publicly, should be done.

The best thing we ever did was share Beaminster Church with the Catholics while theirs was being re-ordered and enlarged. For six months, we shared the building. If that was not a public statement of goodwill and brotherly concord, what is? It reached a very happy peak when the Catholics said "thank you" at a service in Beaminster Church on 10th May, 1993. The date should be written in gold letters in the annals of our churches.

That night, the Catholic priest and I shared the sermon. We recalled the day that the Pope (Paul VI) had given the Archbishop of Canterbury (Michael Ramsey) an Episcopal ring. It had been an historic public gesture; an announcement of engagement with intent to be married. We then celebrated the sacrament and it was a revelation to many people that the two services are now so similar as to be interchangeable. He and I even said the Eucharistic Prayer simultaneously, though at altars side by side. There then followed two of those magic moments that sanctify a priest's ministry and will remain with me all life long.

The first happened as the two congregations lined up in the aisle, each to receive the sacrament from their own priest. One Catholic parishioner, having received the consecrated bread from his own priest, broke the orderly line to receive the consecrated wine from me. It was technically improper behaviour! But everyone knew it was also a sign of how things should be, of how things could be and of how we all wished they were! It was a brilliant public statement, an acted parable. Without any words, we were reminded of the way Our Lord called us to be.

The second happened after the communion. For me, it was a thing most wonderful to see so many of the Catholic congregation, having received their communion, join the Anglican line and seek a priestly blessing from me. This would have been impossible a few years earlier. But it happened. It was an affirmation of new friendship, from old rivals. Old wounds were being healed and a new chapter was being written. I don't know why we didn't all stop and applaud the Catholic gesture. Anyway in a suitably modest English way we exchanged gifts and so we buried the ugly hatchets of our unhappy history.

Unfortunately, nobody knew how to take all this goodwill forward and we have returned to our separate ways. We still haven't learned to do together all that we could do together. But on that memorable night we shared something unique and we enjoyed a foretaste of what one day will surely be. Of course there were people who did not approve. They stayed away. There are always people who cannot see the vision, who prefer to stay with the known. That is the mentality which stops the Catholic and Anglican archbishops from joining hands and walking down the Garvaghy Road together.

Nowadays, we all see the almost unbelievable sight of a uniting Europe, healing the wounds of horrific wars. What a shame and scandal if the Churches are the last to forgive. Why do some people perpetuate the bitterness of four hundred years ago? That is a sin against God and a shame on us all. That night we were all saying "It's time to move on ..."

Now, there is an invitation from Father Jonathan and we must repond as fully as circumstances allow. I hope my good intentions will not be swept aside in the Christmas rush.

Tonight brought one of the social events of the year. It was Wakelys' Christmas Party, held at the Windwhistle Inn, near Chard. Wakelys are so much more than funeral directors. They are a family business, run in the old style, which is rare these days. The family emphasis was strong tonight. The brothers, David and Clive, were good hosts, the next generation, Simon and Leah, were playing their part graciously and I had the privilege of a place next to the patriarch who began it all, Jack Wakely. At least fifty staff and family feasted sumptuously, and it's certain a good time was had by all. In many ways Joan and I were intruders, though we knew almost everyone present and couldn't have felt more comfortably at home. But I was the only priest present. It seems that David has developed the idea that there should always be a priest to represent the clergy of the area. As the clergy work so closely with Wakelys and have so much respect for their work, it seemed a very nice way to end the year. I would like to think that Wakelys always find the clergy as co-operative as we find them. I fear this may not be the case where clergy over-protect their day off or have developed a work-to-rule attitude. Bereavement should always have first call, certainly above any personal convenience.

One thing struck Joan and me quite forcefully, but very cheerfully, tonight. It was this. Sunday services are not the most important thing in a priest's ministry. The social round is vital too. Joan recalled her early days, at Toller, when she did not take easily to the social happenings. She had been greatly put off by the wife of my predecessor – Frances Johnson – who gave her advice which she found daunting. "Now never forget, my dear, that you are the First Lady of the Parish." It was intimidating advice, suited to an earlier age. Joan was a professional potter and had no intention of being the traditional vicar's wife (i.e. unpaid curate), let alone "First Lady of the Parish", whatever that means. Possibly as a reaction, she opted out of most village events in those early days. How different now! She is a professional person in her own right and the expectations which people have of a vicar's wife have changed out of all recognition, with the result that social events have become a joy and no longer a duty.

Sunday may still stand as the day the vicar must be on parade, and people may still speak of "his busy day" but that is less than the truth. In country life sociability matters, more than in urban life. In country life, the entire population still regard the church (and therefore the vicar) as *theirs*. In town life, the population may not have the slightest idea who the vicar is. In the country, the vicar belongs to everybody and the people will think (s)he is a good vicar if (s)he is seen everywhere, and a bad vicar if (s)he isn't seen everywhere – regardless of whatever is served up on Sunday! In the town, the vicar belongs to the congregation, and that is often a fairly small number, rather as the Catholic priest and the Methodist minister are responsible for quite small and easily identified groups of members. Not so the country vicar. It is a different ministry, in which the social events are the key to people's hearts. Priests who come from urban settings are often not ready for this. It is demanding, especially on time. Three or four hours at a wedding reception may not be the chosen way to spend a Saturday afternoon/evening but months or years later every guest will know which priest to call in the hour of need. It is through the ceaseless round of social happenings that pastoral knowledge is built up and pastoral care becomes real to people who wouldn't know a good Sunday service from a bad one. Now that door-to-door visiting is ineffective and out of fashion, it is essential to have other ways of meeting people, and that the clergy grasp every opportunity. The alternative is drear and dire. If the clergy fail to meet and know the people, the village clergy will become as marginalised as the town clergy. The great privilege we have is that we belong to everybody. This birthright belongs to the Church of England, and to no other, and it will be lost if clergy think that what happens on Sunday is more important than what happens in the week. It isn't.

Jack Wakely reminded me of all this tonight. He remembered our evenings at Yeovil Football matches and a meeting at Taunton Cricket Ground and the happy hours in the bars afterwards. I am lucky to have a job in which duties and joys become one flesh.

Friday, 18th December

The morning mail brought a quantity of Christmas cheer, but it was a mixed blessing because so many of the well-wishers were people I had axed from my list when I took my vow against the Christmas rush. This action now seems both unkind and negative. It is a shame not to remember old friends and people from the past, at Christmas. There was nothing for it but to get out last year's list and go through it again, with a more generous spirit. The result is a reinstatement for sixty-five people who had been ditched unwisely. I will not send cards to people whom I see day-to-day; that has always seemed an absurdity. If you greet them in the street, why do you have to put a greeting through the letter box as well? So the list of the reprieved is for those I will not see at Christmas. I wish I had done these cards earlier. Changing my mind at a late stage adds to the sense of hassle which I am trying to avoid.

The morning post brought more than Christmas cheer. It also brought the latest batch of news from The Sudan, via our Committee Secretary. It was a fat wadge of papers and it was tempting to put it on one side in the "After Christmas" pile. But, when it had been there for a few minutes, curiosity and conscience got the better of me, and I decided to read it. Curiosity is provoked by The Sudan because the situation is never static and the news is never dull; there is always at least one drama unfolding, often more than one. The continuing horror of the Sudan is that, no matter how terrible the situation becomes and no matter how often we think they have reached rock-bottom, the next news somehow manages to be worse. In addition to the natural curiosity that surrounds any horror, there was also a niggling conscience at work. Here we are surrounded by tinsel and trappings and there they are, without the necessities of life. Here we are in a consumer culture, devouring more and more. There they are in a survival culture, living and dying with less and less. Somehow I couldn't shelve the papers until "After Christmas". There is more of the "no room at the inn" reality of the Christmas message coming out of The Sudan than there is coming out of the High Street. So, for curiosity and for conscience, I read the papers, until it was time to go to Yeovil Crematorium for Mrs. Barter's funeral.

Dr. Tony, the son, spoke about his mother in terms which made me wish we had been in church where he could have spoken as long as he wished, instead of at the crematorium where the conveyor-belt system limits us to a strict time-clock. He recalled her London years with the visitation of the Zeppelins in the First War and the Doodle Bugs in the Second and then the more comfortable Dorset life and her thirty years of voluntary stewarding at Parnham, going back to the distressed gentlefolk before the present regime of the Makepeace craftsmen in wood. Beaminster is only a small place, the villages even smaller, but the sum of experience gathered in them never ceases to amaze me.

On the way back from Yeovil, I called on Rose again. She had perked up. The antibiotics were doing their job and clearing her system. The dressing was cleaner each day and she felt more like herself, but the result of the biopsy is still awaited. Meantime, it is a pretty bleak outlook for Christmas but the steadfast determination to be on her own remained. I don't know how I would react in her situation. I guess I would get a good fire going, surround myself with Christmas cards to remind me of the past and books to feed me for the future. But we are all different and feeling ill destroys all norms.

I knew the afternoon would be a delight, and it was.

It was St. Mary's School end-of-term service, and it was in church. It was at this service last Christmas that the church heating system had finally failed. It had been stuttering and blowing out foul fumes for a while. Some people had questioned whether the fumes could be toxic and it was obvious to me that, with the church full of children, we should not take the risk. In fact the system never fired at all and we had been left bitterly cold; a most unseasonal and unfortunate way to welcome the children and parents of Beaminster to the opening of the Christmas festivities. Today the old system, now renovated, was firing well, and the weather was exceptionally mild and the children and parents would have shed their coats and woollies gladly, but the crush of the crowd was such that there was not even the elbow room to remove a coat.

The school had decided to act the Russian legend of Baboushka and to present it 'in the round' which is ideal in Beaminster Church where there are no pews to obstruct the action. The church was bursting full, with even the standing room around the walls taken. The service was well planned and well presented and even more well received. It was possible to sense, and almost possible to see, the parental and grandparental pride swelling over us all. It is quite astonishing that a small child carrying a candle can have such an overwhelming effect on so many people. Rational analysis can't explain such things. Is it something to do with the hopes we all transfer on to the new generation? That they will actually achieve what we have only aspired to?

The service and the school term had an unexpected end. Just as I thought the Head was dismissing everyone and wishing them 'Happy Christmas' he called me forward and said the Governors wanted to mark my twenty-one years as Chairman (now ended) with a presentation. Out of many wrappings came a large painting. As I hadn't even gathered my glasses, I couldn't see which way up to hold it. And as I hadn't gathered my wits either, I was strangely lost for words. I got the picture the right way up and saw it was a celebratory drawing of Beaminster Church tower and all the properties around. This was an original work and a generous gift but all I mumbled was something about surprise. In fact I can't remember what I did say, but I know I quite forgot to say 'Happy Christmas'. This was a lost opportunity. I should have thanked my fellow-Governors of the past 21 years, who have actually done all the work and I should have said that everyone of them has done it entirely 'for love'. None takes a penny out of the school, and all put a tremendous amount into it. In a culture and climate of "gimme, gimme, gimme" to have the governors of the school as givers, not takers, makes the work a pleasure and the school a treasure. Unfortunately, I didn't say any such thing.

In the evening, I closed the doors, drew the curtains and had one of my shutdown sessions. Joan was out, I don't know where, probably delivering presents or reviewing the school term with colleagues but, wherever it was, it gave me a clear run. Christmas greetings were properly written (no duplicated circular nonsense) and all the sixty-five who had been axed were now restored. Even writing their names on the envelopes brought back memories, writing a distinctive message inside was easy and natural. I won't dismiss them lightly again. It was an error. Better to live with the Christmas rush than to forget the friends of yesteryear.

Saturday, 19th December

Lots of things were due to happen today and I didn't see how they could all fit in. The first essential was to meet Father Pat Waddy at his Christmas base in Toller Whelme and discuss details of his 70th anniversary of priesthood which I am hosting tomorrow morning. The next essential was to get the Christmas tree in Sherborne up and dressed in time for Andrew's return from Sudan, which is also tomorrow morning. Then I must get his car cleaned and ready to pass back to him, and I must get all the Sudan papers and his correspondence in order on his desk and somehow I must analyse his thirteen-page fax report, and translate it from his African English to the sort of English which C.M.S. will expect in an official report. Thank goodness Father Pat is preaching tomorrow, and not me. That is one less thing to think about. Of course I am preaching in the following week, eight times in four days. But that is next week. Today I am concerned with tomorrow. How wise Our Lord was when He said "Sufficient unto the day, is the evil thereof." So I will get through today and be ready for tomorrow, and leave it at that.

The real problem was how to meet Andrew at Heathrow. He would be bringing his mother into the country for the first time, and the question was, would I get back to Beaminster in time to host Father Pat's anniversary? Andrew's flight was due at 6.35 a.m. I could start at 4.00 a.m.; that was not the problem. The problems would arise if the flight was delayed, even a little, or if his mother was delayed or investigated by the immigration people. Her papers were in order, Andrew had assured me, but that did not guarantee instant entry. It was touch and go whether the timing would work. Joan had offered to meet Andrew in my place but I didn't like the idea at all. I had met him on all his homecomings from Sudan and the drive from airport to home had always been a valuable de-briefing time. And I couldn't imagine Joan driving through the night and then being equal to the rest of the Christmas programme. On the other hand there was no way I could possibly put at risk the good order and proper presentation of Father Pat's anniversary. That had to be the first priority, even over Andrew's return ...

I called on Father Pat at Toller Whelme in time to join him for his breakfast tea. I don't know when I last saw him but the rapport was instant, as if we met every day. He was bubbling, like champagne, in readiness for tomorrow's event. He practised his sermon on me, without a note and with much mirth. I persuaded him to take the President's part and to bless the bread and the wine as well as preach. He pretended to defer to me but I knew he really wanted to preside, and so he should. It will be his day. The people will come to hear and to see him, not me. They can see me at any time, but Father Pat, very rarely. The marvel is that, at the age of 94, he is still telling new jokes. I am already repeating mine! He was walking with a stick and limping quite heavily but he remained as sharp and witty as ever. "I'm going rotten," he said, "but, thank God, it's from the bottom up ..." We made all the arrangements in detail and, as we talked, I realised more and more that I had to be there early to make sure everything he needed was at hand. It seemed I would have to accept Joan's offer and let her meet Andrew at Heathrow.

Over at Sherborne, the boys were waiting to decorate the tree and clean Daddy's car. Timothy had stopped counting the days for his Dad's return and got down to hours, but he didn't like it. He thought one day sounded a lot closer than twenty hours. Kilele was trying to explain that it was really the same because a day had twenty-four hours, but he wasn't having much success. We decorated the tree with some difficulty and it was just as well that Joan had made sure every bauble was of the unbreakable variety. They all hit the floor at least once before they hung on their branch. But at the end Kilele was describing it "Lush" and Timothy said "It's all shiny, Uncle," at least ten times. We then got the car cleaned, outside at the car wash and inside with dustpan and brush and wax polish. Preparing for Christmas and for Dad's return was a double excitement, but there was a third issue pre-occupying Kilele. The Saints were at home to Wimbledon and winning one-nil at half time, and Blackburn were losing. "There you are, Uncle, I told you we would be off bottom place before Christmas." He sounded triumphant, but it was only half time. I warned him that a lot could happen in the second half, but he was buoyant. Oh, the hope and confidence of youth! I've been following the Saints too long; I know all the pitfalls. I no longer let myself get excited; the disappointments are too many. Oh, the miserable caution of old age! So we waited for the results, all the possible points permutations being worked out and then, behold! We had won 3-1 and Blackburn had drawn, so we were off bottom place before Christmas, just as Kilele had predicted.

The greater issue was whether Joan should go to Heathrow, or me. The pendulum had been swinging toward Joan all day. She now announced that she could deliver all the presents for the Southampton family en route. She would get there at about 5 a.m. I wonder if all families have this delivery problem at Christmas. There must be easier ways of handling the festive season than this. I still wanted to go to Heathrow but I could see it was becoming unrealistic. The decision was made at midnight when we rang 'Air Travel' enquiries at Heathrow. The flight was running 30 minutes' late and wouldn't touch down till 7.00 a.m. That was decisive. I could not possibly get back in time; that half hour made all the difference. So Joan took off for Heathrow. I knew I wouldn't sleep, so I set to work on Andrew's faxed report and, three hours later, the style was adjusted and it was in order for him to check and type into his computer for printing. It was 3 a.m. when I went to bed, imagining Joan on her way to Heathrow and Andrew with his mother on the way from Uganda, both travelling through the night. There was no doubt, I had the better part of this deal.

Sunday, 20th December

Joan telephoned at 8.30 a.m. She was with Andrew and his mother, and all was well. A quick calculation told me that it would be possible to reach Beaminster for 11.00 a.m. if she drove flat out with no delays anywhere. But this was dismissed immediately. She was going to take Mama Allam to a changing room and get her into all the winter clothes she had taken to Heathrow for the purpose and then they were going to have a hot drink while the lady got herself orientated. I knew that would take an hour or so. Joan wouldn't be back for the service; thank goodness I hadn't gone. So I arrived at church to welcome Father Pat and everyone else, with an hour to spare and time to rehearse every detail with him which, at the age of ninety-four and on such a special occasion, was what he deserved. Joan had been right all along.

The service was a very powerful experience, for me and for others. Who could fail to be moved by the sight of such an aged man putting his heart and soul into worship, as he had done for seventy years? Who could imagine that a man of ninety-four would preach without a note, with a voice as clear as a bell and with learning and humour undimmed? I felt proud, even though it was not my achievement, but his. Even to be the host was to shine in reflected glory. I liked the opinion of a priest who happened to be in the congregation, Canon Barney Milligan, who said afterwards that he had been enchanted by Father Pat's "charm and holiness, an unusual combination." At the 'Peace' I read messages of congratulation from Bishop John Baker, the Bishop of Sherborne, the Bishop of Salisbury and the Archbishop of Canterbury. They were all unnecessary. The quality of the man spoke for itself. I thought his sermon, delivered from a chair on the chancel step, was a profound expression of priesthood and, when I drove him to the reception, I congratulated him on it. "Oh!" he said, with great disappointment, "I lost my way. This is what I meant to say …" and then followed the 'forgotten' half of the sermon which was even more profound than the half we heard. There was one part delivered to me privately which I was pleased had not been said publicly – that when he eventually dies ("after all this waiting around") there is only one person he wants to speak at his funeral – me. May God delay that ordeal for many years to come.

Around about this time, Joan steamed in from Heathrow, ready for the reception at the home of Father Pat's daughter and son-in-law, Stacy and Giles Marking, in Toller Whelme.

In nearby Netherbury, another happy event was taking place. David was presiding over the re-opening of the church after a month's closure for repairs. The great organ was still in pieces, spread on the floor, but a small keyboard had been brought in, the choir was fully robed and it was back to 'business as usual' for the carol service.

The repairs to the rotting floor had been urgent and unexpected, hence the temporary closure, but the response of the church officers and David had been immediate and so efficient that the place was re-opened within the month, and was full for the event.

This little episode has confirmed a view I have held for a while, which is that organs are a mixed blessing. Most of them were installed around a hundred years ago and the likelihood is that they will all be due for major repairs and renovation in the next few years. Thousands upon thousands of pounds will have to be raised, sometimes by small village communities. Will they be worth repairing? We will be told by 'officialdom' that they should be repaired and that modern alternatives are discouraged – but 'officialdom' doesn't have to find the money; the villagers have to do that. And it is not just a question of money. It is also a question of what music is best for worship, and it isn't necessarily the organ. We may yet find that Hardy's Melstock minstrels were right.

When we find four or five local instrumentalists to lead the music, it invariably provides a warm sense of participation, not always possible when the organ dominates. There is another issue, too. How many young people are learning to play the organ? It is more and more common for villages to be unable to provide their own organist, so that they have to provide transport (and sometimes a fee) for a visitor to play the organ, though there may be other musicians in the village. If the costs involved in organ repairs encourage Church Councils to examine other musical possibilities, so much the better – for church funds, for worship and for the participation of young musicians.

In the evening, I was at Burstock for their carols which, for the first time in my experience, included a christening. There are probably some learned liturgists somewhere who have solid reasons for refusing christenings in the Advent season, or at carol services. The plain fact is that liturgical niceties, like Royal protocol, mean next to nothing to most people. There was a very strong historic tradition that the flag shouldn't fly half-mast over Buckingham Palace, but that meant nothing to the people when Diana died. Similarly, there are all sorts of "do's and don'ts" in Anglican tradition, but they are lost in the mists of time and mean nothing to most village people.

In fact, if the 'purists' had their way, we would not even have been allowed to sing carols tonight, never mind have a christening as well. The old tradition, which I tried to keep at one stage, was that carols should be sung in the Twelve Days of Christmas, from 24th to Epiphany, never in the Penitential season of Advent. It made good sound sense in its day. But its day is gone. Imagine all the schools being refused carols at their end-of-term services. Imagine turning away the M.U. and the W.I. and all the other organisations who want to sing carols in church. Imagine forbidding the choirs to go round the villages bringing Christmas cheer to the elderly and housebound. It would be a quick way to make an enemy of everyone and earn the reputation of a Scrooge-like misery. Yet it was once a tradition that worked. One of the skills needed today is to distinguish which old traditions still have a positive future and which ones can be quietly laid to rest. My fear is that the new Liturgies and new Prayer Book will be the work of learned liturgists rather than of pastoral priests. If this happens, clergy will have to sit very lightly to the rules, as I did tonight at Burstock with carols and christening in Advent.

It was good that Barrie Hill, the church warden, and his wife, Jane, provided Christmas cheer in their home afterwards. Not only did it continue the excellent local traditions of hospitality but I soon assessed from the comments that no-one had the slightest care that anything non-liturgical had happened!

I went to bed content that Sundays in Team Ministry are neither tedious nor repetitive.

Monday, Tuesday and Wednesday, 21st, 22nd, 23rd December

I lost the battle to avoid the Christmas rush. It was an unequal struggle from the first, though I tried hard for a week or so, but in the end I was overtaken by events to such an extent that the last three days, and nights, merged into one long grey blur. It was not as I planned it.

I know it rained, almost continuously and that I splashed through the lanes and that every church path seemed to be awash or bogged with the mud running down from graveyard mounds, and that several changes of clothes were necessary. Joan said the washing machine was working flat out, that every drying spot was in use and that I was on my last clerical shirt.

I know that there was shopping to do, which annoyed me because the long-term buying for Christmas began in the summer and the detailed buying began in earnest earlier than ever. Why was there still a last minute rush? Joan said mince pies, milk, bread, vegetables, the turkey, the pheasant and various other things had to be left till the last minute. I didn't see why, though she said it added to the atmosphere. That was the point. I was trying to subtract from the atmosphere, not add to it. It wasn't the way I had planned things.

I know that the Christmas tree had to be put up, which meant climbing into the loft to get the paraphernalia, and I know that the lights didn't work (again), and that we did all that palaver by night. I know that I put all the cards up and that it took me until 2 a.m. and Joan complained that the sellotape would damage her paintwork. It would have been more tactful if she had said how nice they looked. I also know that I fed the fire efficiently with big old logs that kept it burning all night so that it wouldn't need to be laid in the morning and that Joan said the room was far too hot and we would have to open the windows.

I also know that she went off to Parkstone to collect her mother, who arrived with two King Charles spaniels who peed whenever Sunny came anywhere near them, so that Joan spent a lot of time running around with bucket, Dettol and sponge. Oh, Christmas joy!

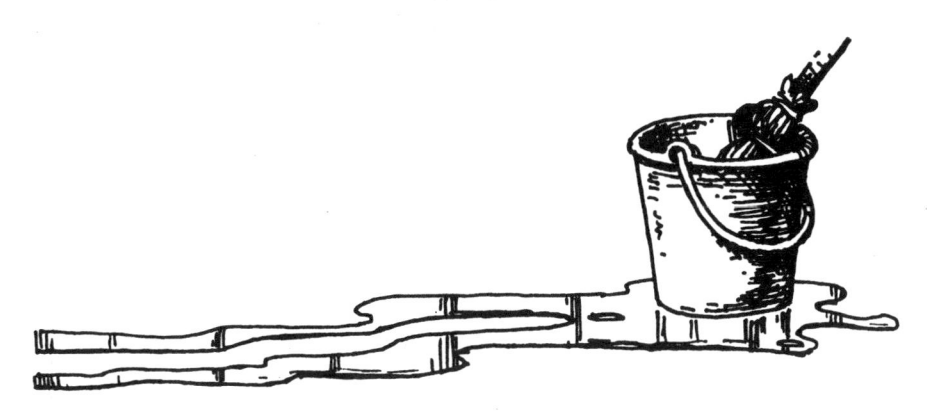

Apart from that, the days just merged and left me with a constant sense of dis-ease. I didn't get to the hospitals, as I had planned to do. I didn't visit many of the lonely or bereaved and, each time I started to do so, someone called. It would have been a shame not to say "Come in," especially at Christmas, and that took another half hour. As most of the people who called were among the lonely and the bereaved, it was not wasted time and the warm fire and the mince pies were welcoming, I hope. But it wasn't what I planned.

I would so like to be calm and recollected. I would so like to exude peace and goodwill to all men, especially at this season. I would so like to be holy, but the question I am always asking and to which I have yet to find the answer is – wherein lies holiness?

> *Lord, I tried to go shopping yesterday*
> > *But I gave up,*
> > *It was chaos everywhere.*
> > *In the stores,*
> > *little kids screaming, wanting more.*
> > *Tired Mums, trying to say 'no'*
> > *It's all money, money,*
> > > *food, food,*
> > > *drink, drink*
> > > *and ever more expensive presents*
> > *I came home.*
> > *I was disgusted. For Your sake, Lord.*
> > *Your Feast Day has become a farce.*
> > *I mean, that's not what Christmas is about,*
> > > *is it, Lord?*
>
> *My son, you misunderstand me, said the Lord.*
> > *When I came into this world*
> > *It was to be in the midst of chaos.*
> > *If I had wanted to be*
> > *All quiet and cosy*
> > *I could have stayed in my heavenly home,*
> > *But I wouldn't have been any earthly use.*
> > *If I had wanted to be*
> > *All Peaceful*
> > *Would I have come to Bethlehem,*
> > *That cockpit of the world?*
>
> *My son, if you really want to find me,*
> > *Look in the chaos,*
> > *Look in the mess,*
> > *There I am, in the midst,*
> > *That is where holiness lies, my son.*

Christmas Eve

I awoke to the frightening thought that Christmas was upon us and I was not ready. In spite of all the early planning, I was not ready. I would have to do three services – the crib service at Hooke, the Christingle at Mosterton and the midnight at Beaminster – to be followed in the morning by another three – the Beaminster, Melplash and Toller Christmas communions. And I was not ready. Imagine Christmas arriving and all the crowds gathering, and the priest not being ready! I have had nightmares like that.

Of course no priest should have to do six services in quick succession and Dean Shearlock had spotted this when we were planning the programme and he had generously offered to do two of mine so that I was reduced to four, which had been an enormous relief. Now Rose's illness means her services have to be covered, and so I am back where I began, with six again! It isn't the taking of the services which is the problem, it is the preparation beforehand and with a special occasion and children involved, that needs to be detailed, preferably with rehearsals. It is the preparation which is the problem, and I felt I hadn't done it.

Before these worries could be eased, two things happened. News of a death in Mosterton came through. This is the worst day of the year for a family to suffer bereavement and they deserve special attention and sympathy; but it is also the worst day of the year for the priest to give it. While I was pondering what to do and how to fit visits in, David T. rang. He knew the family, and said he would take over the visits and the service. Oh! What a friend we have in David!

As for the services, I need not have worried. When I arrived in Hooke for the Blessing of the Crib at 4 p.m., the church was filled to the doors, extra seating was being put in the aisles, while angels, shepherds and kings were having last-minute briefings in the porch. A large table, rude and bare, which was to take the crib, was in front of the altar, the lights were dimmed, the candles flickered and "all heaven was a tip-toe". Theresa Colton, Rose Brandon and Joy Edwards had done their stuff.

They were ready. The preparations had been made, but not by me. I sat back and let it happen. The crib figures arrived one by one, to appropriate carols, while a dozen children read an adapted narrative. It wasn't until all the children of the village had made a tableau around the crib and had sung Holy Night that I was called upon. By that time, everyone was so relieved that they had done well, that a prayer and a blessing was enough, and more would have been too much and spoilt everything. "Happy Christmas" everyone was saying, with much hugging at the door. "Wasn't that marvellous?" and one or two people added to me, "You do these children's things so well!" Of course I knew I had done next to nothing. It was a local idea, a local presentation by the local people, and that was why the church was full, and why they all thought it was so good.

At Mosterton's Christingle, two hours later, it was much the same story. The church was packed to the doors; even the gallery was in use with twenty or more faces peering over the balcony, and there was the sort of general hub-bub which I expect at the Dell, before a big match. "What is the plan?" I asked the church warden, Dinah Brazendale, as soon as I arrived. "It never goes according to plan," was her un-nerving answer and her co-warden, Graham Fry, added "We play it by ear," which was even more disturbing. In fact I could see eighty or more oranges on the altar, all prepared as Christingles, and I could see a big empty barn at the font, waiting to become a crib. So there was a plan and, when I was shown at least thirty crib figures, fashioned in clay and hand-made by the village children, I knew the preparation work had been done. They would be brought to me and placed in the barn during the first hymn, I was told. Evidently, the preparation had not only been done, but well done, because the service rolled on without a hitch, except that the lights failed twice, but the people continued singing as if nothing had happened, and the twinkling candlelights added to the effect, the only loss being the organ accompaniment. I wondered how eighty Christingles could be lit and distributed during the course of "O Little Town of Bethlehem" but it happened without fuss and I noticed a bucket of water and a bucket of sand in a corner in case of mishap. The church wardens were better prepared than they had admitted! My part was to explain the symbolism of the Christingles, receive the offerings and, apart from that, let the children have the limelight, and make sure I didn't spoil the ambience. "Lovely service, Happy Christmas, Vicar" was ringing out from the porch where the atmosphere was of a home win as the crowds jostled to get out. I thanked the church wardens and all the Pakes family (Sue was at home with 'flu) because they had taken the entire responsibility for everything. Again it was locally organised, and locally produced and that's why it was packed out. If it had all depended on me, as it would have done in the old days, there would not have been that sort of local response. In fact I checked the old registers which showed that in the last year before the Team ministry the Christmas Day congregation was six and no other Christmas service was recorded. On the way out, Dinah repeated the remark she had made on the way in. "You can never be sure things will go according to plan." She thought rigid plans wouldn't work and we all had to be ready to adapt. 'Eureka' – like a bolt from the blue she had given me my Christmas sermon, though she didn't know it. I went home as fast as possible to write it ...

The sermon notes I had prepared for Christmas went straight in the bin. I had not felt happy with them, but now I had an idea which was new to me and which I could enjoy and put forward with relish, and it would spring from everyone's Christmas experience. So I closed the door, even on mother-in-law, and gave Dinah's idea my total attention. It would all be about plans. Our Christmas plans and God's plan, begun in the crib. Did the life go according to plan? Was the cross in the plan? If so, what a devil God must be, to plan something so violent and repulsive. Perhaps God, like the Mosterton planners, knew a rigid plan would not work. Just as unpredictable children might ruin a tightly planned service, so unpredictable humans would ruin a tightly planned scheme. God would have to adapt again and again. The truth shown in the crib is that "God proposes". The truth shown on the cross is that "Man disposes". These radical thoughts flowed from pen to paper for a couple of refreshing hours until it was time for the midnight service. At last, I was ready. Thank you Dinah. This Christmas sermon is for real. No platitudes.

Christmas Day

I am told that midnight services in a good many town parishes have had to be stopped because of unruly behaviour, caused by party goers and gatecrashers. Even when I was a curate in Leeds, 30+ years ago, there was a problem at midnight – the vicar was burgled both years during the midnight service. Beaminster, by contrast, is the very model of decorum. It is hugely attended, the choir lead the singing of the popular hymns, tonight it was Canon Barney Milligan (making his Beaminster debut) who preached a Christmas word, and all was in order, and completed in five minutes over the hour. It was, on any reckoning, as good a midnight service as any country church is likely to produce. Although I was happy with it, I also had one misgiving. I couldn't help compare it with the two home-grown events earlier in the day at Hooke and Mosterton. They had such an expectant atmosphere, bubbly and sparkly, "all heaven a tip-toe." The Beaminster midnight was staid by comparison, a ritual presented from the front, which the people observed. The afternoon services had belonged to the people, been presented by the people, and I had been the observer or 'overseer'. The contrast of one following the other so rapidly was quite stunning. No doubt the church needs both and no doubt both have their place. Perhaps we have got the balance right and I should not have any misgiving, but I have. Everything tells me that the great old tradition of liturgy and language which I grew up with and which has become my love and my life, represented by the order of the communion rites, is on the wane. And everything tells me that the informal, the unstructured, the homely has a popular appeal which is growing. The two styles must learn to live together, though there aren't too many priests who are at ease and comfortable with both styles. My misgivings are not personal. I do enjoy both. The misgivings are because I doubt that the popular has the capacity to shape the minds of a generation. Perhaps it's all right for starters, but not for much more.

Back at home, I opened one present before bed. Like a big kid, I scrambled under the tree to find the one from Joan, which was easily recognised because everything else seemed to be bottle shaped and I knew hers wouldn't be. It was rectangular. She is good at framing, so I imagined a photograph of some recent happening. How far from the truth! It was a wood engraving of cricket at Lords, c.1843. I cannot imagine a finer gift, to such an extent that, although she also opened one, I haven't the slightest idea what it was or who it was from. Lords, in 1843, with the male spectators on horseback and the ladies in carriages. And they probably knew the Book of Common Prayer by heart. An age that is gone. But what a beautiful memory in the engraving.

The morning services underlined the evening misgivings. The three communion services added together – Beaminster, Melplash and Toller – didn't equal the number which had crowded into the tiny church at Hooke yesterday for the Crib Blessing. The services which are home-grown and non-liturgical have a popular appeal which leaves the traditional liturgy (old or new) in the cold.

The service at Toller was a classic case. Sixteen people turned up, rather fewer than on an ordinary Sunday, but the church wardens were purring with pleasure because there had been a full house for the Crib Blessing on the previous evening, a hundred people filling even the ringers' gallery. Later, I heard an even more vivid story from Salway Ash, telling the same message. Their Sunday congregation averages only eight for the regular liturgical worship but, on Christmas Eve, no fewer than a hundred and eighty people had filled every square inch of space available for 'Carols at the Crib' But on Christmas morning for the celebration of the sacrament, for the communion of Christmas, they were down to six, one of whom was the celebrant's wife. The signals are the same from Seaborough where the Christmas Eve carols filled every nook and cranny, and the Christmas Day Communion drew a dozen. The pattern is clear. The people are making a statement and it is a statement which raises many issues. Our Team meetings will have to consider what they are. That should be fun.

Sunday, 27th December

So many people are saying "Did you have a nice Christmas?" I don't know what to reply. Evidently theirs is over, because the question is in the past tense. If I am to 'have a Christmas', it is about to begin. But the signs are that the hoped-for break will not happen. The communions for the housebound were completed this morning and I was pleased to do them. Old Ernie Wildern, aged 97, knew every word without looking at the service book, and remembered his days in Beaminster choir and especially when he was the boy chosen to sing the solo opening to "Once in Royal David's City". That must have been before the First World War but he recalled the detail as though it were yesterday. Irene Wakely, at 90, was a youngster by comparison and she also knew the whole Liturgy by heart and even said the whole Christmas Gospel with me, though I needed the book and she did it from memory. It is this depth which will be lost if home-grown services ever replace the liturgical. Ernie and Irene speak the language of Biblical and Prayer Book faith which is passing. Is anything growing in its place? If so, our job is to identify it and nurture it. But first we have to find what it is.

Those communions and the afternoon carols would have made a very pleasant day and I could have returned home to celebrate. All was done as far as it could be done. Time to meet up with Andrew and his household, play some games, make the fire roar and open one of the bottles. But not to be. Kathleen Wiles of Fairfield had died at home, while we were singing carols in church. And, within an hour, came the news that June Holliday had died at Culverhayes. I recalled her husband's death, also at Christmas, in a car crash as they went on holiday. Christmas always takes an excessive toll; the week following Christmas, when clergy would choose to take a break, is invariably a time of grieving in such sharp contrast to the celebrations of the week before. And now there is even more tragic news that the Christmas baby, Jamie Lee, has died, on the fourth day of his life. We now have five funerals pending. But it does make the question "Did you have a good Christmas?" impossible to answer. A clergyman's Christmas is a very strange thing; no wonder other people cannot understand what it is like. So many different expectations from family and from parishioners conflict, that I find it difficult to understand it myself.

The best bit of Christmas for me arrived as a poem from a parishioner, Mada James. She expressed my theology of Christmas more clearly than I could myself. We must be doing something right, to produce such thinking:

Forgive us, Lord, that we have decked
Eternal truth in tinsel trappings.
Swaddled the Babe of Bethlehem
In layer on layer of Christmas wrappings,
Strung fairy lights in place of angel's glory
And turned the Word into a children's story.

Yet on this night,
Still, as when worlds began,
Eternal light
Holds all things in its span.
And God, forgiving, loving,
Reaches down to man.

Thank you Mada! You have said, so simply, all that I have been struggling to say.

One month later ...

Wednesday, 27th January, 1999

This has been a difficult month, as difficult as any I can remember.

We had twenty-two deaths over Christmas and the New Year, which is far and away the worst spell I have ever known. Even the crematoria have been crowded out.

We have had eight Church Council meetings, all of them reviewing the annual accounts, worrying about the new format of the annual report and wondering how their programme of services will be carried out in 1999. That is something that worries me too and which I cannot answer as long as Rose remains ill. And now it is clear that David is not at all well either.

We have more people in hospitals than I have ever known, and the hospitals are far apart. I try to reach Weymouth, Dorchester, Bridport, Yeovil and Taunton; and then there are parishioners in Bristol, Poole and Southampton which I regard as beyond reach.

I have more requests for house communions than I have ever known, and I have been so occupied burying the dead that I haven't done any of them.

I can just about live with all this until someone says "Did you go away for Christmas?" or, worse, "Have you had a good holiday?" Then I explode, either internally which is bad for my blood pressure or openly, which is bad for my reputation, and their blood pressure.

So this journal has missed a month, which is probably just as well because it would have been a month rather like the weather, unrelieved gloom with very rare sightings of sun or sky.

Today I thought I would restart the record of events. It seemed the right day because there wasn't a funeral and the Team Council was due to meet and the Council always has something worth recording. What's more, most people seem to enjoy it, which is more than can be said for

Synod and quite a lot of other church meetings.

The Team Council meetings have a nice atmosphere. It might be because the members have got to know each other over the years. It might be because they are not an executive and don't have to make decisions; they are consultative and only make recommendations. It might be because they don't have responsibility for buildings or for finance, and can focus their minds on education, worship and ministry. I like it that way, and so do others, so I try to keep it that way. I used to tell them they are the equivalent of the House of Lords – wise elders without executive powers, but worth listening to. Now that the House of Lords is on the way out, I've dropped the analogy. I suppose the difference is that these 'wise elders' have all been elected and have a constituency to report to. Anyway, for whatever reason, I like to see the 36 representatives, three from each of the twelve parishes, gathered round the tables, looking for all the world like the United Nations assembly, but behaving better.

As chairman, I have a custom of putting an 'estimated time of arrival' against each item on the agenda, so that people know it will end at 9.00 p.m. I've noticed that after that time people always begin to fidget, start gathering up their papers, turn up their coat collars and unconsciously give other signals that it's time to be going home. I've never known a good decision made after 9.00 p.m. at any meeting, but some very bad ones. But tonight the whole timetable was very nearly thrown. Two matters intruded into the meeting unexpectedly and both prolonged their spot on the agenda. I did some quick cutting on other items and we ended at nine precisely. A good bright end sends people home cheerfully and looking forward to the next one!

The two unexpected intrusions were important and couldn't have been cut short. First, after we heard a progress report on Rose, who will not be back before Easter, we heard the unscheduled news from David T. that he is also ill. The diagnosis is Chronic Post Viral Fatigue Syndrome and he explained how it came about, its progression through the body to the brain and into the nervous system (I was quite lost, but listened) and then we heard all the symptoms from short-term memory loss, dyslexic vision, headaches, broken sleep, nightmares, muscular exhaustion, sweating, lack of concentration, and some other things (as if that wasn't enough). The treatment was also complicated but my concentration was weakening by then. The upshot of it all is that he is meant to reduce his workload by two thirds and his Sunday services to two, maximum. The consultant had told him that covering fifteen villages amounted to 'slave labour'. There wasn't any comment from anyone. I suppose they were all a bit stunned and fearful that he might take a turn for the worse and have one of his collapses, there and then. Not only did this put the evening's schedule out, it would put all the carefully calculated service schedules for the month out as well. It had been a triumph to get the February programme completed in spite of Rose's absence. Now it would all be wrong again! It's as well I am not the despairing type, or given to depression. I'm sure genes have something to do with it. My mother was an incorrigible optimist, even in the midst of the war when we were bombed out and saw every possession go up in flames. All I remember her saying was "We're still together!" and "We'll sleep at Mrs. Mann's tonight; she makes lovely soup." All these things were passing through my mind while David was listing his symptoms.

The other intrusion diverted the meeting even more. After Lilian had said her piece about the service programme and had pointed out some of the complications we cope with, John Maccoy of Hooke rose to ask why, with all these complications plus the new situation of even more clergy illness, Beaminster had three services on some Sundays while the villages have one. "And," he added, "even that one service may have to be taken by a church warden." This put the Beaminster representative, Jane Rose, in a tight corner, especially as I could see all the others nodding their agreement with the questioner. It is an anomaly that Beaminster has three services and John Maccoy was right to raise it because the issue has been itching away under the surface for a while. I have told Beaminster Church Council so many times that I don't think three services are justified, or necessary. For fifteen or more years they

150

managed with two, an early morning communion and one other of their choice. In recent years, just when the clergy pressure has been greatest, they 'up' the request from two to three. And the reason, in my opinion, is only because they cannot agree among themselves. Some say the second service should be at 9.30, some say 11.00, some say family service is needed, some say the eucharist is the proper Sunday service. Others say there are too many 8.00 a.m. services and that is the cause of the problem. So, in an effort to keep everyone a little bit happy, they have a bit of everything. The villages which have only one service on a Sunday have a blessing which Beaminster is losing. They all worship together while Beaminster is fragmenting into different congregations, all because they have too many services. These were my personal opinions as Jane rose to reply. She made a good job of it, considering she was caught unawares. She said that the communion congregation had grown old and that children's work was developing. That is true. She said that the children who came, and many of the parents, were not confirmed and would find a liturgical service intimidating. She said that family services had therefore become necessary, as a stepping stone. It all sounded very logical. The Beaminster Worship Group is grappling with a profound problem, which is a nationwide problem and, because Jane was looking discomforted and had been caught unawares, I said so. But a sharp response came from Jane Marsden of Drimpton. She pointed out that every parish faced the same problem and that they had to solve it with compromise in the community, not by multiplying the services. The meeting was suddenly very lively and someone wanted to propose a sort of a censure motion on Beaminster. I asked for that not to be put because the Beaminster representatives could see the mind of the meeting and promised to take the problem back to their Council. That was enough. In twenty years we have never had any parish censured for anything – not even Drimpton when they went bankrupt and had to be financed by everyone else. A censure motion would be very divisive and one of the reasons Team Council meetings have been so enjoyable is because the fourteen churches work together so well and support each other so cheerfully. The censure motion was dropped, everyone realised it would have been heavy-handed and John Knight closed the subject by reminding everyone that we are a Team and that anyone who hasn't got exactly the service that suits them, or at the time they want, only has to go a mile or two to find it – and still be within the same family. Oil on troubled waters, indeed.

The meeting was well behind my timetable by then, but David T. was visibly fading and took two minutes instead of ten on his children's work item, so that we caught up and ended as the clock struck nine. I had reached my goal, but not by the expected route. A lot of life is like that.

As soon as the meeting was closed, people surrounded John Maccoy; among them were David T. congratulating him and saying that he agreed entirely and Richard Satchell, taking the opposite view. We haven't heard the last of this. To me, it is extraordinary that we get so fired up about times and forms of service. If I had focused on Jubilee 2000 and the desperate hunger of half the world, I doubt I would have made an eyelid bat.

Anyway, it was refreshing to get home and see Oxford holding Chelsea to a draw. And they would have won but for a referee's blunder in the last minute. And King Hussein has announced his successor. His brother is stripped of the inheritance which will pass to Abdullah, the half-English son of Toni Gardiner, his second wife. I shouldn't think this does much for domestic bliss. Queen Noor obviously wanted her son to succeed and not Toni Gardiner's. The stage is now set for a massive family feud which could have colossal repercussions in the Arab world and beyond. I hope he hasn't also made a last-minute blunder after playing so well for so long. Oxford's effort and Jordan's excitements put our Team's trivialities into perspective and I slept well. Perhaps I should have spared a thought for David and his nightmares, but I didn't. Someone has to keep well, and if I do it will be because my other interests take my mind off our troubles.

Thursday, 28th January

I expect telephone lines were buzzing this morning after last night's excitements and the news of David T.'s illness, but I wasn't available for any of it.

I had to go to Salisbury to deliver four cartons of gifts for Sudan and I reckoned that I could turn it into a hospital tour that would begin in Bridport where John Cox was laid low again, continue to Dorchester where Joy Beazer had become an emergency patient, drive on to Salisbury and do all the necessary business, including gathering a hundred Lent books, and then come back by the A30 to Yeovil Hospital and to Heather Penman, Mary Gardiner and Geoffrey Fry.

I don't know what Sunny made of it. He sat in the back while the rain poured down ceaselessly. His ears soon dropped, then his jowls, then his shoulders and after that he settled with utter resignation to the inescapable boredom. I thought it was a lovely outing. Nine hours away from the telephone and all other harassments. No need to think about David's sweats or Rose's treatments. No need to placate the Beaminster families who couldn't get their children christened because there is no 11 o'clock service. No need to see the pile of hospital visits growing; I was cutting it down to size. And in between the hospitals I listened to "African Requiem" on tape as I tootled through the storms. It was pleasant and leisurely and rewarding as each of the patients was progressing and was surprised to see me on such a dreadful day. Only John Cox missed out. Bridport Hospital said he wasn't there, which I believed because it is such a small hospital that they always know who is where. Then Dorchester Hospital said he wasn't there, which I also believed because of their sophisticated computer system. It turned out to be partly my fault. He is 'John' to us, and always has been. Officially, he is 'Harold' and computers obviously don't know nicknames.

The others, who had suffered severe and unexpected setbacks, were smiling broadly! Where do people get their courage and their humour from? What deep wells have we all got? Mary Gardiner had fallen while crossing the road in Yeovil and had broken her back, which was now encased in plaster. Heather Penman had collapsed in a heap while shopping and, judging by her bruises, had landed on her face. Geoffrey

Fry had a burst abscess treated and, while they were working on him, they found and removed a stomach cancer. Joy Beazer had suffered acute blood poisoning which had put her into a coma, hanging between this world and the next. And they all laughed. Every one of them made a joke. Hospital visiting doesn't need to be sombre. And all agreed that the nurses were sweetness and light, and the Health Service was doing a wonderful job. Perhaps we are especially well served in this district and perhaps we are not typical of the nation as a whole, but I thought the Dorchester Hospital looked as good as the Dorchester Hotel and the choices on the menu made me wonder how I could get a bed.

All was well in Salisbury too. The Church House officers are always so welcoming! I suppose it is because I go so seldom that I have a certain curiosity value. If I was a regular visitor, it might all wear a bit thin. The receptionist actually welcomed the four big cartons for Sudan, which I thought was very tolerant of her because they obviously obstructed the foyer. Jane Warner, the Sarum Link editor, was appreciative of 'Second Opinion' which shows she has broad shoulders as well as a broad mind because it causes her more aggro than any other feature but she recognises its value. Richard Trahair, the Property Officer, agreed to send the Beaminster Team treasurer all the clergy allowances for vicarage decorating, which is more than he is obliged to do. He has always been helpful on vicarage matters. On the day we were hit by lightning in 1982 and part of the roof was blown off, he arranged for Baileys, the local builders, to take charge. We were covered with tarpaulins within an hour and had a new television installed in time to watch England play Holland that very night. Chris Dragonetti, the accountant, who must be one of the most troubled people in the diocese, never gave a sign of anxiety when I asked him for the Sudan Church Association accounts. Church finances seem to me to be one great nightmare. When I was Rural Dean, I could see the problem of getting in the quota payments from my small group of parishes. The accountant has to get the money in from three hundred reluctant parishes while he keeps the whole diocese afloat and within budget. And now he has taken on the Sudan accounts as an extra, in an honorary role. The man is mad, or an unsung hero. Why is it that Church House bureaucrats are so readily maligned? It seems one of life's injustices because we need them. There is something in human nature which makes us transfer our own bad feelings onto someone or something strong enough to take it without buckling. I suppose Church House is strong enough.

It was a good day, until I got home. Nine Ansaphone messages awaited me, two of them deaths. The families want to know my availability. Next week looks awful – three Church Council meetings, a Clergy Chapter, three midweek services, a memorial service, a cremation, a School Staffing Committee, the Strode Room Managers, the Beaminster Worship Committee – already. And now two funerals, to add. I wish people would stop dying for a while.

Friday, 29th January

It is the early hour in the morning, before it is light, that saves my sanity. The silence is unbroken, nothing stirs. I like the dark mornings of the winter. They add to the silence, which isn't broken until the crows start cawing in the trees. Even Sunny, once he is fed, doesn't stir, his head prayerfully between his paws. Some days I read the psalms, slowly. Other days I look at all the pictures on the walls, collage upon collage from round the world which make it easy to call to mind the state of the world and the people who are caught up in it all. It was a Buddhist, who claimed he didn't pray, who told me that "no loving thought is wasted." Who can tell where the boundaries of prayer are? Is it a matter of words? I doubt it. To begin the day with loving thoughts is creative. It can't do much harm! I am heartened by the story of the Indian farmer who was pushing his cart home from market one evening when the wheel fell off. He was a devout man and the delay meant he missed the hour of prayer, so he sat by the roadside and said to the Lord "Lord, I haven't got my prayer books with me and I can't remember the words, so I will say the ABC three times and You fit the letters into the order you think best." It's a comfort to my style of praying that the Lord told his angels "That was the best prayer I received all day ... it came from the heart, and it trusted me." This gives me hope that the hour at first light is more prayerful in God's eyes than some might think. Eventually the silence is broken by the morning post plopping onto the doormat, and then the action begins.

The morning post excites me, every day. I always gather it with a high sense of expectancy. Why is that? It nearly always brings problems or complaints, or both. I know that very well and yet I still have an insatiable appetite for it, and always imagine the next envelope will bring a blessing. I must be an incurable optimist, because usually it isn't like that at all. But today it happened. Out of an envelope came a cheque for £1,260.60 made out to me. It was accompanied by a letter of apology which said it was reimbursement for over-payments. It was from the Tax Office. I always had a vague feeling I was paying too much but, as I never have understood those long forms, I had left it to them in the certain knowledge that they know best. It was the Beaminster Church treasurer, Bert Osborne, who came to my rescue. He gathered my papers for me, guided the form filling, told me the things I could claim for and announced it was a very simple case and my code was too low for such a small income. I thought a low code was a good thing to have, but apparently it is the reverse. Anyway, Bert took control and advised me properly. Now my code is higher, which is good, and £1,260 fell out of the envelope, which is even better. Every church needs someone who understands these things and I wonder if Beaminster people have any idea how well they have been served by Bert. When he took over, in my fourth year, the church had no reserves and was unable to meet its quota payments, which were around £3,000 a year. And now Bert is retiring. And the quota, which has risen to £26,000 a year, is fully paid and the reserves, invested for the fabric and the organ, exceed £80,000. It's a story of water into wine and I wonder that the economic miracle hasn't brought more smiles and much rejoicing. Bert's work, like that of so many treasurers in the village churches, is either taken for granted or not understood at all. If it were not for Bert, I would still be overpaying the tax man and I wouldn't have had that lovely surprise in the post this morning. I imagine the care he has given my affairs is typical of the way he has cared for Beaminster Church affairs.

There was another 'modern' funeral this morning in Beaminster Church. It was George Roderick who was being laid to rest but the 'modern' feature was that the son, Ian, gave the address while one grandson, Peter (aged 14), played a movement from a Grieg piano concerto and another grandson, David, read a poem. This is the way it must be in the future, to restore the personal touch which has been lost in over-crowded areas by clergy who don't know whom they are burying. It was profoundly moving this morning to see the loving care which had been taken in the preparation and to see the way the whole family was strengthening the participants. The grieving process was well and truly under way and the family was at one in the effort. Nothing I could have said or done would have achieved that so strongly. George had served in the Indian Army and it was there that he contracted the polio which plagued him for 55 years. In his tribute, the son read a letter written in 1944 by an Indian subaltern. It expressed, with wonderful insight, the things we were thinking about George, 55 years later. The words of the service were ancient and traditional; the presentation was personal and progressive. This must be the shape of things to come but not too many families would be able to carry it off with such style, while grieving.

The parish magazines, 1700 of them, were ready on time this

afternoon, and I brought them back to the Rectory by 5.00 p.m. Within half an hour, every parish had called, collected their cartons and the delivery had begun. Not so long ago, I used to drive from parish to parish delivering the boxes. I covered 40 miles, it took three hours and sometimes longer if distributors were out or had locked their gate, or there was no parking space. Many times they were left in the rain. And sometimes it took a week or more for the distributors to get them through the letter boxes of the customers. Not so now! Today they were winged on their way while still hot from the press and people will complain if they don't get them tomorrow. That is how it should be.

Saturday, 30th January

This was the day set aside to edit the Sudan Church Review, and it worked very well. Some jobs are more enjoyable than others and this is the most enjoyable of all. I edit the parish magazine twelve times a year, at forty pages a time, which is four hundred and eighty pages, and I've been doing it for twenty years which adds up to ... a lot. I know it is popular because the village editors panic if even the smallest item is omitted, the advertisers compete to get in it and there is never a shortage of items – in fact there is a surplus. So it must be popular, but people take it for granted. It just comes, automatically, like the milk.

How different with the Sudan Church Association and their Review! It comes out only twice a year and is only twenty pages each time. The whole year is only the equivalent of one month of 'Team News'. And yet it is received with rapture. Letters and telephone calls follow each publication, praising the product and congratulating me as if I were some sort of genius! I suppose the difference is that in the parish I am known, seen and have become an everyday part of the furniture. We don't keep talking about the kitchen table and saying how useful it is, though we do kick it occasionally, when we are rushed. That's parish life! On the other hand, most members of the SCA don't have much idea who I am and it is probable they have never met me, so the elements of surprise and mystery surround me. I understand why the Queen's advisers keep the Royal Family slightly removed from the public. The mystery remains! Familiarity does breed contempt. In parish life we see so much of each other that we take too much for granted. We should be more appreciative. I shall start in the morning, by thanking the first person I see. It will probably be the paper boy. That will give him a surprise. I shall continue, thanking the next person, and the one after that. I wonder how long before it will wear thin, or before people will think I am peculiar. I find the SCA appreciation encouraging, and we should encourage each other. We are meant to be the "Thank You" people. I wonder what the reaction will be when I start!

Editing the Sudan Review is straightforward. All the contributors keep the deadline given; they all write good English which doesn't need correcting; they all write the number of words requested, and they all know their subject. The Review has stood the test of time – well over fifty years. The recipe was good when I took it over. It only needed a little fresh spice and a slight stir, which I gave it today.

The hardest part is not writing the articles. The hardest part is bringing some hope to an apparently hopeless situation. Famines, massacres, political oppression, tribal conflicts, make good reading for sadists, and no one else. We used to pray to be preserved from "sedition, privy conspiracy and rebellion." Sudan has them all. We used to pray to be preserved from "plague, famine and all pestilence." Sudan has an abundance of them too. Facing these dark and dreary clouds is part of the job. Finding the silver lining is the other part. One without the other would make it less than a Christian publication, and less than the truth about Sudan.

When the day began, I knew the time was going to be given to the Review, but I wondered when there would be time to prepare for tomorrow's sermon. The funny thing is that, by the time I ended the Review, the sermon was also coming nicely to the boil. It's good the way one thing feeds another.

Sunday, 31st January

Fifth Sundays provide an opportunity. There are only four a year and people seem to like the idea of a different day in which they can leave their own church without a sense of guilt, and visit another.

The host churches today were Beaminster, which was reviving Mattins, and Broadwindsor which was keeping Candlemas.

Mattins has almost died out in the C of E and it is easy to see why. Today's service had three Canticles, a psalm, four hymns and an anthem – nine pieces of music! It requires a lively organist and a capable choir. It is a musical event, and very few villages can cope with that. I have been to village Mattins services which have sent me home for a brandy, sometimes a double brandy. When organists can't play the settings and elderly congregations can't get the note, it is close to a nightmare. John Ruskin's description of church music in 1856 as *'bestial howling and entirely frantic vomiting up of hopelessly damned souls through their still carnal throats'* is exactly how I have felt when I have tried to lead the singing of Mattins in churches without choirs. They shouldn't attempt it. The wife of a former Bishop of Salisbury, Dr. Alix Reindorp, gave me some sound advice after she had come to a service in one of our villages. "If you can't sing, don't," she said. But there remains a popular folk memory of Mattins and a sadness among some people with long memories that it is no more. Others have a different memory. Joan's recollections of Mattins in her childhood are "excruciating", and she is not alone.

So the Beaminster effort to revive Mattins has people for it, and people against it. I'm for it, but only because I trust Beaminster's choir which must be the finest church choir for miles around. I doubt there is any choir comparable between here and Sherborne Abbey. If any church can present Mattins it is Beaminster, and that is thanks to the choir. They were magnificent and the old Canticles seemed to fill the great building and bring nostalgic memories flooding back. Of course I was in a privileged position, sitting only a yard away from them. I might not have found it so uplifting if I had been in the midst of the congregation, most of whom looked rather pained as they struggled with the Canticles, even with the choir to lead them.

In all the time I have been in Beaminster, people have been lamenting the loss of Mattins, the loss of the Authorised Version of the Bible and the loss of the Prayer Book. Their ignorance appals me. There is no truth in them. They just use any stick to beat the church, and the vicar in particular. The Prayer Book is not lost. I have used it faithfully and diligently every Sunday of my ministry. They just choose to stay away from it. Beaminster still has more than half its services from the Book of Common Prayer but the critics who 'lament the loss' stay away. On the principle of "use it or lose it", they will have only themselves to blame when it is lost. Those who complain about the loss of the Authorised Version are no better. When I read the entire Gospels aloud in church – Matthew, Mark, Luke and John – fifteen hours of public reading of the Authorised Version, only one of the critics turned up. The rhythms and cadences are captivating, the flow of the language is magical. I loved every minute of the fifteen hour marathon. But I learnt from it that the people who complain that I have abandoned these things don't value them as much as I do. I offer them Book of Common Prayer, week in week out; Authorised Version in full, publicly for fifteen hours, but they are not there.

Today it was the turn of Mattins, and it was the same old story. Three people turned up who wouldn't ordinarily be there but the rest of the seventy people would have been there whatever the service. It reminded me of an occasion in Toller Porcorum when Admiral Sir

William and Lady Crawford made a great fuss about the loss of Mattins. At one meeting after another they demanded its return. Eventually they chose the date, it was to be the Patronal Festival of St. Peter. The day came and so did the Mattins service, but they didn't. They were sailing in the Azores or somewhere. The rest of us, without a choir, suffered the bestial howling.

It was a bit like that today. The service came, at the traditional time, 11.00 a.m., and there was no other service anywhere in the fourteen parishes. It was the golden opportunity, but in fact the numbers attending were about twenty fewer than for an ordinary Sunday. But there was no bestial howling; the Venite, the Te Deum and the Jubilate were heard at their best. Wonderful sounds from the past, suited to cathedrals in the present, but in village churches I doubt they have a future.

Monday, 1st February

No problems today. In the morning, the Strode Room managers met and all seemed to be in good order. The 1998 accounts showed that income from bookings exceeded costs and that prospects for '99 were equally good. Jane Rose had received an offer from Marjorie Harborough to clean and repair the curtains. The meeting accepted the offer. Marjorie is a remarkable woman. She never pushes herself into anything, yet she is endlessly doing the things that need to be done, all over the town. She is of that special breed that puts the community first. Even so, we realised that the life of the curtains would be limited, even after Marjorie's repair.

Next, the Bridge Club had complained that they couldn't see the cards because of inadequate lighting. Colin Smith agreed to recommend a plan of spotlights to the architect and the trustees. Next, a neighbour had complained that the black waste sack was sometimes broken into by a dog or a cat, causing smelly litter. We agreed to buy a plastic dustbin with a clipped lid. Someone else had complained that there were not enough sets of cutlery for a full wedding reception; Bernard Thorpe agreed to buy knives, forks and spoons up to fifty of each. The Recorded

Music Club still hadn't got the cupboards they had always wanted – but the contract has been given to Baileys and their joiner will start work soon. The room will need redecorating before long, but we left that until the cupboards are fitted. It was a cheerful meeting. The problems were easy to deal with, the people willing to get on with them and the funds available when necessary. I wish all meetings were like that.

The afternoon meeting was a bit different. Our Lyme Bay Clergy Chapter had to pool their ideas and experience of funerals, no doubt to help each other. The approach to funerals has changed out of all recognition in my time. They used to be absolutely bleak, penitential affairs, in the spirit of the Book of Common Prayer. We used to begin *"Man that is born of a woman hath but a short time to live, and is full of misery."* The hymns were chosen in the same vein. "Abide with Me" came as regularly as clockwork with the depressing line *"Change and decay in all around I see ..."* lamenting the present and fearing the future. A dirge-like atmosphere prevailed, very few people sang because it was so evidently a time of pain and grief that singing seemed out of place. The gloom was unrelieved. All has changed! "Abide with Me" has lost the top slot and has been replaced by "Now thank we all our God", "Morning has Broken" or "Praise my Soul". The service sheets carry a new title and are invariably called "A Thanksgiving for the Life of ..." The address recalls happy memories and often makes people smile; the prayers also reflect the blessings of the life. In short, the atmosphere has changed from a dirge for the life lost to a celebration of the life lived. It is altogether more uplifting to the public, more comforting to the mourners and more true to the Resurrection hope. But something has been lost. The old tradition told us of the awe a man should have before his Maker, at the dread day of judgement. The final prayers were for forgiveness, for sins to be 'washed away'. Now it is possible to omit this, which had been the main purpose of the service, and probably no one would even notice the omission. The fashion now is for the 'Scott Holland' reading: "Death is nothing at all ... I have only passed into the next room ..." What nonsense! Death is very real, very final and the departed is irreplaceable, and these facts have to be faced, not hidden. If we allow a funeral service to become entirely a celebration and if we pretend that death is not a final parting, we deceive ourselves and delay the grieving process. Death has become the 'taboo' which no one will talk about. We live as if it won't happen and if we have funerals which pretend it hasn't happened we are following a fashion but not facing the truth.

The other issue is the way clergy cope with the funeral address. I know one priest who believes that the point of the service is to emphasise the resurrection and therefore he has one sermon delivered at all funerals because the doctrine is the same and is not affected by the person. I think my task is to find signs of God's grace, and reveal them and I have five hundred mini-biographies of local people, to prove it. They make a library in themselves, a modern social history of the district and they represent thousands of hours of listening, thinking and writing, of which I do not think a minute has been wasted. Imagine trotting out the same address, uniformly, year after year, regardless of who was being buried. I would have done it five hundred times! And the people would know it by heart, before I started.

The best funeral story I have heard is about a very awkward woman who, in her lifetime, complained about everything, moaned to everyone and generally managed to make life miserable. When she was dying, the vicar visited regularly but still received the usual dose of criticism. We all know the type. When the funeral came, the people wondered what the vicar would say about her. He said that he had done his best to prepare her to meet her Maker, but he couldn't do anything to prepare her Maker to meet her!

It seemed absurd to have spent all day at meetings. This is all too common. I had organised curtains and dustbins in the morning and the clergy had enjoyed their favourite occupation, talking, all afternoon. Is this the job? No, it isn't – but it has become the job. The morning meeting was laid upon me – I am chairman of the thing. The afternoon meeting was an inescapable duty, laid down in writing as an Episcopal requirement. A vicar's life can easily become one long series of meetings. No doubt a bishop's life is even more so. This is not good. Meetings can become an escape, a hiding place from the people. Meetings can give an inflated sense of self-importance as if we were some sort of executive or businessman. The professional man's briefcase can soon replace the simple man's sandals, and it has done. So I was determined to do at least one visit. Pat Shirley had died and I called on her life-long friend and companion, Peggy. She had been to register the death in the morning which was her first outing for a year. Her friend had died in a nursing home which she had not been able to visit because of her own infirmity. There would only be four people at the funeral. I stayed a while and heard a lot about the old (wartime) days and the post-war years when they worked voluntarily at St. Martin-in-the-Fields where they worshipped and knew all the great church figures of yesteryear. Old age can be very lonely.

There are extraordinary happenings today, beyond our borders. The mighty men of the media are working us into a furore against the England football manager – *because of his religious views*. They even say he is unfit to hold the office and should be sacked. I thought he had the job because of his football credentials, not his religious views. Does a football manager now have to be a theologian? This is a witch hunt. The Press have hated Hoddle for some while, perhaps because he replaced their man, Venables; perhaps because he kept them at a distance and demanded privacy for his players in the World Cup; perhaps because he upstaged them by publishing his own book on the World Cup. Now they have trapped him into declaring a belief in reincarnation which includes the theory that the disabled must have sinned in an earlier life. What has that to do with his competence in football? And why is the freedom of speech, so excessively treasured by the Press, denied to Mr. Hoddle by the Press? And why is Hoddle not allowed to promote his personal view while the militant Islamic terrorist Abu Hamza is allowed to spread anarchy and terror at home and abroad under the shelter of Free Speech? The Prime Minister is in on the Hoddle-hunt now, joining the pack like wolves onto a lamb. But will any of them correct Abu Hamza? Not a word. Stony silence. Sorry Glenn, you are a soft target. If I were you, I would refuse to resign. I would stay, because before long people will realise this is an hysterical outburst which has nothing to do with football.

Tuesday, 2nd February (Feast of Presentation)

Glenn Hoddle has resigned. The chase was short. When the Nationwide Building Society joined in by threatening to withdraw their £8 million sponsorship, the Football Association defence of their man ended. Money talked. This is the sad spectre of sponsorship at its worst. The sponsor, who is meant to be the strong supporter, can very easily become the mad master. And this is madness! The way Hoddle has been sentenced without trial and has lost his £350,000 a year *football* management job on a *theological* point is certainly more bizarre than anything he said. In medieval times, heretics were hunted down and hounded out. Are we going back to those days – with Prime Minister and Press leading the pack? And what was the theological point that was such dynamite?

Hoddle thought that past sins caused present sufferings and pointed to the disabled as examples. Nothing new in that. It is there, large as life, in the first of the Ten Commandments that we are told we should make children learn by heart ... "*I am a jealous God and I will visit the sins of the fathers upon the children unto the third and the fourth generation ...*" It is there in the Book of Common Prayer which we are told we should use more often. "*Almighty God, who in thy wrath didst send a plague upon thine own people ...*" It is even in the prayer for fair weather "*Almighty God, who for the sin of man didst once drown the whole world ... we for our iniquities have worthily deserved a plague of rain ...*" This horrible teaching has got into the nation's bloodstream, like a virus, which is why people say, at any time of distress "What have I done, to deserve this?" The idea of sin causing suffering is deeply in the human psyche. If a football manager is dismissed for pointing out the effect of this on the disabled, who will dismiss the preachers who continue to proclaim it from the pulpit? It is time that the church refuted, once and for all, the ugly theology of a

God who demands punishment and retribution. But we won't. It would show that the Bible is not infallible and that the Prayer Book is not the last word on Doctrine. So we silently watch Glenn Hoddle being sacked by popular demand for saying things which some clergy continue to believe, with the Bible and the Prayer Book to back them.

It is the Feast of Presentation in the Temple today, so I took the chance to do a couple of house communions. Sunday is the best day for house communions but the faithful housebound should be remembered on high days and holy days, if possible.

It is a long Gospel today. It is the whole narrative of Simeon and the Nunc Dimittis, of old Anna and her prophecy. I suppose it is one of the loveliest of the many lovely stories which has inspired poets, painters and preachers down the years. But each time I read it today, I felt uncomfortable. The familiar words had changed and were familiar no more. Simeon now says *"Master, now you are dismissing your servant in peace ..."* For the thirty-five years of my ministry, we have repeated the daily prayer *"Lord, now lettest thou Thy servant depart in peace."* A small change but it was enough to confuse Betty Tiarks who knows it all by heart and likes to say the Gospel aloud, even though she has no book.

The new version of the Bible which we are given in the new Lectionary, the New Revised Standard Version, doesn't appeal to me. It is the chosen version and must be well thought of, but I can't see why. My suspicions were aroused at Christmas when the ugly word 'what' was intruded into the famous Prologue to John's Gospel *"He came to what was his own"* we heard. How does this improve on *"He came to his own"*? The fly leaf tells us that "all archaic words have been eliminated" and that "English words that have changed meaning have been updated." Was there something wrong with *"You will become fishers of men"* because last week I had to read *"I will make you fish for people."* As I read it, I saw someone put her head in her hands, while two others laughed. I am sure it was not the laugh of good cheer but of despair. The truth is that this version has been chosen because it uses the inclusive language which is politically correct and will prevent rows with the powerful feminist lobby. I can't see any other merit. I wonder how the Bible would read today if we had changed it to suit each fresh fashion or each vocal lobby down the centuries. The strangest twist is that the version is American. The Americans have many talents but I doubt the use of the English language is chief among them. Why should the land of Shakespeare be given an American translation? It is a puzzle to me how these things pass through General Synod. The members are well fed at Synod and rather elderly; perhaps they fall asleep at the vital moments. Or perhaps some subtle scholars blind them with science. Or perhaps there is a natural deference to the opinions of bishops. Whatever the reason, common sense has gone out of the window.

Joan was due back for one of her flying visits tonight. She wanted to come to the evening service for the Feast of Presentation. She hasn't been to Beaminster Church since Christmas midnight and is beginning to feel out of touch. She goes to the Abbey in Sherborne and enjoys the grand style of mainstream Angilcanism, but it isn't the same as being where you know everyone and feel you belong. The first time she went to the Abbey on her own, she felt nervous. In fact it was two or three Sundays before she gathered her courage and dared to go. This is interesting. What is it about Church which makes it so forbidding? Church people are no more frightening than any other people, in fact in a village they are often the same people that run the W.I. or any other group. Yet it is the Church which alarms people, so that even Joan was nervous of going alone. But once the effort is made, the fears prove quite unfounded.

Tonight, Joan's good intentions didn't work. By the time she arrived, the service was over. I wasn't surprised! She burst in at 9.00 p.m. I can't imagine what time she thought the service was. It was all for good reasons. Children at a boarding school demand attention at all hours; potters with kilns to fire depend on the power of the electric current; then there was a week's supplies to buy for me. By 9.30 p.m. the week's washing was whirling round, and so was I. The car had to be unloaded; a sack of coal burst in the boot which was a hell of a mess to clear up. By 10 p.m., egg and bacon was served. I haven't eaten at that hour for months or years. Her visits disrupt my routine. By 11 p.m. she was hoovering right through the house and by midnight all the radiators were full on, the house was a furnace, but the washing was nearly dry. Her life is more of a whirly gig than mine. At least I am based in one place.

Wednesday, 3rd February

Our Team meetings are at an all-time low. We have met every Wednesday for twenty years, but today there were only three of us and one of those, David, was half ill and didn't want to stay long. There used to be eight or nine of us, regularly. The funny thing is that the Wednesday communion, which precedes it, is at an all-time high and has never been so strong – thirty-one people today! And that is the interesting thing. People think that the more priests there are, the stronger the Church will be; the fewer the priests, the weaker it will be. Some priests may think that too. It is an illusion. For the past three years, this Team has seldom been at full strength. After Richard Thornburgh left, we were a priest short for a year until David's appointment. Soon after that, Richard Legg left and we were a priest short for six months until Rose came. Soon after that, she became ill and we were short again. Now David is ill as well. And the churches? Never been stronger! The congregations are either stable or up, everywhere. The annual accounts show quite astonishing growth; even Drimpton, the poor relation, has recovered. There is a lot to be said for being a priest short. The people immediately take more interest, accept more responsibility and the extra involvement always leads to raising more money. I won't be at all surprised if David's illness makes the churches even stronger! The basic structure is in position for lay leadership and with clergy illness it comes into action better than when we are healthy.

As for me? Someone has to be the scalded cat and do the running round. Funny it is the old'un. Godson Timothy, still only four, said "Uncle, when you are ninety-nine, will you still be running round and round?" While I was thinking of an answer, Joan said "No, Timothy, he will be dead long before that if he doesn't stop running round." Timothy wasn't satisfied. "Aunty Joan," he said, "I think when Uncle is ninety-nine, he will just go back to one and start again." Joan didn't have an answer to that but the sad thing is that a four-year-old has the image of me "running round and round." And he is probably right, but how can I prevent it in the present situation?

Joan would like me to retire, here and now without delay. She says that, according to my own theory, it would make the churches stronger. She is sick of working in Sherborne and providing for me here. She also gets emotional because she imagines me dropping dead while everyone is praying for Rose and David. It would be a pity not to enjoy the new house after all the work she has put into it. But her idea of my retiring now, in the midst of all these troubles, is absurd. It is as stupid as the woman who said "Are you going on holiday soon?" And she was one who should have known better. I wasn't rude in reply, which must be worth lots of Brownie points.

It was Melplash Church Council tonight. They also have problems with a good deal of sickness. In fact Joan Wilkinson, who was our hostess, only came out of hospital this morning and spent the entire meeting propped up in a special chair-bed. It reminds me of the days when Harold Wilson's government had a majority of only five and the halt, the lame and the blind had to be wheeled in to save the day. It is wonderful how the Church Councils vary so much from village to village. In the Melplash Council, everyone is on Christian name terms and the business is pushed through by Nell Buckler, the chairman, efficiently but with a lightness of touch. The accounts were received and endorsed, another good year. The Quinquennial repairs were discussed, Guy Busk is meeting the architect on Friday. The offer of a flag pole to be erected on the tower for the Millennium was welcomed, John Spencer will meet another architect to discuss that, on Monday. The church wardens offered to lead Mattins once a month to help out in the present situation. They seem keen, so I accepted. John Spencer and James Best will take it in turns, which is excellent. It makes a complete contrast with Beaminster whose contribution is to compound the problem by adding an extra service. The whole meeting was conducted with great good cheer around the sick bed and all was over by 8.30.

I was home in time to write Pew News and deliver it to Myrtle before 10 p.m. I started to draft the March service rota, but gave up at midnight because we can't staff things unless some parishes change their requirements. Quite a few phone calls will be necessary tomorrow, and I expect they will all be understanding and co-operative.

Thursday, 4th February

There was Victor Thompson's memorial service at Broadwindsor this morning, Patricia Shirley's funeral at Yeovil this afternoon and Toller's Church Council in the evening, which was enough for one day. Unfortunately, as often happens, a mixture of the unwanted and the unexpected cropped up as well.

The unwanted was the breakdown of the office printing machine. I have no idea how it works, I never use it and I am the last person to know how to put it right. But I was the nearest person so I was called, by which time the office floor was thick with reams of spoilt papers and Mary, hot and bothered, was turning purple. She was going to call the engineer from Southampton. I suggested she called Barbara Harris from Styles Close. Mary said she knew as much as Barbara and if she couldn't repair it, neither could Barbara. So Mary called Southampton and I called Barbara. As Southampton was a two-hour journey and Styles Close was a two-minute journey, Barbara got there first and in no time at all the machine was running smoothly and the Southampton engineer had to be stopped. I didn't wait to find out whether Mary was pleased the machine was working or angry that she hadn't repaired it. I was in danger of being late for Victor's memorial service.

Victor Thompson had died before Christmas and the funeral had taken place in Chard. Peggy, the widow, was graciously bringing his ashes back to Broadwindsor to be interred with his first wife, Ruth. This gave the people of Broadwindsor, where he had lived for twenty-five years, the chance to show their respects. I admired her for doing this. It gave her a second ordeal, for our sakes. She asked for the service to be a celebration of his life, so that is what we tried to do. It wasn't difficult because Victor was highly regarded as a warm and generous local character, as well as a faithful servant of the Church. He is the twenty-seventh church warden I have buried in this Team. I reckon that must be a world record, but it is not one to boast about. My very first funeral in these parishes was a church warden, Edwin Hansford of Toller, in 1973. This means there has been one a year ever since, on average. It doesn't sound so bad when it's spread out. The only parishes which have not buried a church warden in that time are Salway Ash and Seaborough. Stoke Abbott has bid farewell to four! These twenty-three men and four women have served for between four hundred years and half a millennium! The service given to the church voluntarily is simply staggering and every one of them has had an integrity to match the high office. Even in the disagreements I can think of only two who were disagreeable, and they made peace before they died. I doubt any parish priest has had a more courteous collection; it's just a pity I have buried twenty-seven of them.

It is interesting to see the way the gender balance has changed over the years. Of the living church wardens now in office, the balance favours the ladies, 15-13. Another significant statistic is that, of the church wardens I have buried, twenty were 'local' and seven were 'newcomers'. Of those now holding office seven are 'locals' and twenty-one are 'newcomers'. I have lived through a social revolution!

Back in the office, the machine had gone wrong again. Mary was wading in waste paper and her face had gone the shade beyond purple. She said the man from Southampton was on his way. I advised her to go home and take a rest. She wouldn't. I called Barbara H. back. She repaired it quite quickly, again. I called Southampton. They said they would call their man on a mobile and divert him to Bournemouth. Again. They must think we are a funny bunch. With that, I set out for Yeovil and the next funeral, buying a Kit Kat on the way for lunch.

I knew Patricia Shirley's funeral would be small, and it was. Five people attended. I don't suppose she or her friend would mind in the least. Privacy had always been their wish and their way.

We always try to make a funeral as the deceased would wish it to be and when people say "It was just what she would have wanted …" we feel we have done well. Others say "I reckon she enjoyed that …" which poses the question of whether the dead are really alive and in some way viewing things from 'above'. Is this a foolish question? It is one which people ask and which stirs up passions. Some people don't believe the 'after life' has that form at all; others say the dead 'sleep' or 'rest' until a future day of resurrection, in which case they presumably see nothing at present; others say that the dead "reign in glory and are at the Lord's right hand", in which case they presumably know and see everything. On the other hand, an increasing number doubt that there is any form of future life at all. It is a ticklish question to be answered at a super-sensitive time. People want to be reassured. People want the priest to make clear and emphatic statements which affirm their hopes. And a great many priests respond with the platitudes that please. "He is at peace with Jesus," or another platitude which never fails to comfort, "she and Charlie (or whoever the husband was) are together again." And everyone says "How nice." In my opinion, we are dabbling in the unknown, playing with people's emotions, and claiming for ourselves knowledge which belongs to God alone. We should be more honest.

We do not know what lies beyond the grave and we should say so. People may want emotional security at the time but in the long run that does not come from kidology but from integrity. I can say with complete integrity that I believe God is good and that whatever is in store will be better than we can either dream or deserve. But what that is, it is not ours to know. The variety of preaching on the subject is bewildering. Some say "They are together again," others "They are with Jesus" or

"They are at rest," "They are gathered to glory", "They sleep in peace." It is no wonder the people are confused. A little honest agnosticism is overdue and will be a blessing.

Back at home, the office was deserted, and at peace. The waste paper filled two black sacks. Relief all round! My advice to any up-and-coming clergy is – don't ever have the office in your house. You find yourself at the centre of every dispute and every anxiety, even ones not of your own making. There are enough disputes and anxieties in parish life without inviting them to take up residence in the house.

The phone was ringing as I came in and the message brought an unexpected twist to the day. It was Sue Collard, head of the comprehensive school. She wanted me to help start regular worship time in school. I was surprised. I thought the regular school assemblies required by law were the worship time. She explained that this would be additional, preferably on Mondays. As the parish priest, I felt I should be positive and encouraging, so I have agreed to meet the head of R.E., Mark Williams, to discuss it further. I will have some questions to ask. Why, when schools have complained for years that the worship required by law is too much, do they suddenly want more? Why do any children need to worship in school on Monday when we have provided worship in every village on Sunday? Does this new initiative come from the children, or is it something which enthusiastic adults have decided would be good for reluctant children? There is a great difference. The service, I was told, would have to fit in between 8.50 and the start of school-proper at 9.05. That sounds like an assembly slot to me. But it will be entirely voluntary. I will help if the plan is soundly based and has a real purpose, not otherwise.

It was Toller's Church Council tonight. We met in Dinah Austin's living room and we were all on Christian-name terms, as at Melplash last night. There the resemblance ended! Whereas Melplash had done all the business in one hour and in full agreement, Toller took two hours and didn't agree on much. Even the date of the Spring Plant Sale became a conflict between those whose plants would be ready by a certain date and those whose plants wouldn't be ready. The letter which it was proposed to send to every house, telling the village of the Millennium window, seemed good to me – but some wanted one correction made and others another. Letters by committee are a bad idea! The accounts also seemed good to me, the figures were favourable and should have been cheered; but no, some wanted them typed, some wanted them audited before they could be accepted for the annual report. There was even a little fracas over the appointment of the school governor – everyone agreed that the choice was good, but not the manner of the choosing. The name had not been brought to the full council.

All these nagging little nuisances are my fault, in one way. Because I have vacated the chair and because the decisions are no longer made by the vicar in the time-honoured way, there is a leadership vacuum. Then people rise up to fill the vacuum. But what happens if two people rise up for one vacuum? This could be an issue in any of the twelve councils, not just in Toller. It is all much easier if the vicar takes the chair and runs the show, but then, how will the people own it?

Friday, 5th February

Today was a pleasant change from parish pump. Local things are always interesting because the play of personalities is as fascinating as my childhood kaleidoscope. In those days, every time I looked into it, the pattern changed, even at the slightest touch. Local life is like that. Anyone who thinks it is a predictable routine, doesn't understand parish life. The slightest change in the personnel and the whole dynamic makes a new pattern. The slightest jolt and it all changes again. As a child, I couldn't believe the variety of patterns; no two alike. As an adult, I find the kaleidoscope of people-patterns just as varied and just as intriguing. However, a change is as good as a rest, and today was a change. I went to Keynsham, near Bath, to interview a Sudanese man from the Zande tribe, Dr. Tabu Paul. It was necessary in order to complete the next issue of the Sudan Church Review.

Dr. Tabu lives with his wife and four children in a small Council house on the edge of Keynsham where he is a Reader at the parish church. He is a cousin of Daniel Zindo, who was killed in the car crash in October. Had Bishop Daniel lived and become the Archbishop, Dr. Tabu would have become his Commissary (i.e. spokesman) in the U.K. In short, the death of the bishop had also meant a fall in his influence. I expected this tragedy, and all the others which have plagued the Sudanese church and people, to have left Tabu dejected, if not demoralised. Not a bit of it! He smiled broadly, boasting as his sparkling teeth flashed that he had never been to a dentist in his life. He laughed loudly, especially when I photographed him and his wife together. He is built like Captain Mainwaring, she like Boadicea. "You can see who is boss here," he laughed. In fact, she made the tea and kept discreetly out of sight while we men talked.

When we mentioned the late Daniel Zindo, he simply said, "The Lord knew what he was doing; his time had come." I asked him to explain what he meant, because it seemed to me that Zindo's death was most untimely and quite tragically wrong. "We cannot argue with the Lord," he said. "We had one plan, the Lord had another." I decided, as a guest, not to enter into a doctrinal dispute, so I continued to listen. "The Lord gave," he said, "and the Lord hath taken away. Blessed be the name of the Lord." I asked how the accident happened and was told every detail. Zindo had tried to get his own driver for the journey, but the driver's wife was sick so he didn't come. Zindo had tried to get a second driver but something delayed him. In the end, he accepted a young driver with very little experience. Zindo's elder son had pleaded with him not to go but to wait for one of the regular drivers. However, the bishop refused to be delayed further and had set out with the inexperienced driver. To me, this was a clear case of human error but to Dr. Tabu it was an equally clear case of divine will. I said, quietly and with deference, that human weakness was the cause. "We must not question the reasons of the Almighty," he said. "We must accept, accept, accept." I was on the edge of the great theological and cultural chasm which divides African and Western Christianity. To me, this African Christianity is offering the sort of fatalism which belongs to Islam. It also seems to come from an hierarchical world-view, which explains why Africans are so often subjected to despotic tyrants who rule, in the image of the all-powerful God. Divine rights entitle Him to be the most despotic ruler of all, whose cunning plan to delay the real drivers so that he could kill off Daniel Zindo had to be accepted, accepted, accepted. To my Western mind this is a devilish theology which I cannot accept at all. It would be entirely agreeable to a certain type of Biblical conservative, easily backed by scriptural quotations, but it made me very wary indeed of the increasingly popular demand that Africans should lead 'Revival Missions' in England, at the Millennium.

The real purpose of the interview was not theological, it was to seek his opinion on the successor to Zindo. He fears, as we all do, a split between the Civil War factions resulting in Northern leadership under the Islamic government and a Southern leadership in exile. He doesn't see how the constitution can be kept because there is no way the Electoral College can cross the war zones to meet. And if the constitution is not kept, the new leader will not be accepted by the 'losers'. He fears the bishops will meet – it is planned for Feb. 15-17 in Nairobi – and will disagree and each faction will go its own way with its own leader. We all fear the same. This was the special value of Zindo. He had the respect of both sides, had lived on both sides and was undoubtedly the senior figure in every respect. But God had plotted his downfall and we mustn't ask why. When the Bishops meet, there will be 'flies on the wall'. The Bishops of Bradford and Salisbury and the Chairman-elect of Sudan Church Association, Michael Paget-Wilkes, will be observers. Officially they will not be allowed to speak but unofficially, if things are getting sticky, they may be able to encourage or advise. This will be strongly resisted and bitterly opposed by Bishop Gabriel Roric on the grounds that it is colonial interference in the affairs of an autonomous Province. In fact, his protests will be nothing to do with their independence. It will be to do with the fact that he is in league with the Islamists and has personal ambitions. Oh, what tangled webs we weave!

Dr. Tabu was charm itself, and I said my farewell with great respect for his courage in exile and his courtesy toward me. The problems he

177

and his people face are so complex and so overwhelming that I quite understand the temptation to say "God knows what he is doing," and leave it to Him. Some call that faith – I call it escapism.

It had been sunny all the way to Bath but by the time I was making my way home the sun was setting and throwing the most amazing colours over the hills and across the fields. And the radio was issuing bulletins every half hour on the condition of King Hussein. His life is ending. He is back in the country he has ruled for 47 years, but only to die in his homeland. I am gripped by the story of his life. I feel involved, though I am not involved in any way. I feel as if he is one of the great landmark figures who embraces us all. I feel as if I want to belong to such a man. I felt it when I travelled in Jordan; I was proud when I was sailing in the Gulf of Aqaba and two police launches came alongside and asked me to go ashore for security reasons. "His Majesty is going to ski on water," they said. I went ashore readily, thinking that he had been walking on water most of his life. From the shore, I had watched him water skiing, and very good he was. I was proud, just to have seen him. How he has kept his people together, I do not know. The flood of Palestinians who crossed the Jordan after the 6-day war defeat and the loss of Jerusalem amounted to an invasion of refugees, greater than the population. Imagine fifty million refugees flooding into U.K.! Yet Jordan has survived and has grown from nothing to become the most respected and influential power for peace. It is the moral authority of their dying king which has done it. I never saw Gandhi, the 'Great Soul'; I haven't seen the Dalai Lama, that other peacemaker, but I have seen Hussein-el-Talal, King of the Hashemites. What a trio; I am proud to have lived in their time. How odd that one is a Hindu, one a Buddhist, one a Moslem. But if they are not sons of our heavenly Father, I don't want to be either.

Saturday, 6th February

King Hussein remains alive, but only on a life-support system, which could be turned off at any time. But who will dare to switch off the life of the King? Surely, no one. After he has survived twelve or more assassination attempts, five Middle East wars and endless civil strife, it would be wrong to end the struggles of such a man at the press of a switch. He must be allowed to die naturally. Fortunately, Islamic law also requires it. Meanwhile his chosen successor, the first-born son, Abdullah, has been sworn in as Regent. Even he should not press the switch. How could he become King is such a way? It would be the worst possible way to start, the people might never forgive him, and he might not forgive himself.

I called on Rose Bullock before lunchtime. Her parents are staying a few days and they are transforming the garden, front and back. It is a tiny pocket handkerchief plot which hasn't had any attention for years. In a garden-conscious area, it has been a bit of a let-down. This is a good move. As bonfires are not permitted there, I came away with a load of garden refuse for a bonfire here.

Rose has had many tests and all seem clear, which is the main thing. She has not a long-term health problem but she certainly has a short-term problem. She has to lie low and let the skin graft 'take', which just means waiting and waiting. She doesn't want visitors. A lot of people have offered to call but privacy is preferred. We none of us know how we would react in the same situation, but I think I would want visitors, and enjoy them. And I would be writing letters and enjoying that. And I would be phoning people up to check on what's going on, and enjoying that. Thank you, Lord, for making us all so different. It's like my kaleidoscope again, the variety is absolutely endless. No two alike, which is a breathtaking thought.

I had sermon trouble today, quite bad sermon trouble. I just could not get anything out of the given texts. I have preached on the creation often enough but this time I was completely thrown by the new version which leaves out the well-known phrase "firmament of the heavens" and substitutes "dome in the sky." The 'dome' turns up seven times in the text. There will be more heads in hands tomorrow and more hollow laughter. I can see that the words 'dome' and 'sky' are shorter but are the words 'firmament of the heavens' so difficult? It is a puzzle to know

179

why the change is made. And if this 'dumbing down' is also happening in family services and in preaching, we will end up with nothing distinctive at all. I've seen some absurd own goals in football, but this self-destruct can match any of them. We are in danger of going tabloid. The tabloids make a profit, but nobody respects them, or even believes them.

King Hussein solved my sermon problem, but not until about midnight. His life hangs by a thread and in such circumstances I felt justified in abandoning the given texts (domes and all) and substituting the texts and collects "For the Peace of the World". I will invite the people's prayers and the address will be one of my own meditations from the Holy Land, the one written in Jordan, looking across the river to the Holy City. It may not mean so much to people who do not know the Middle East and have not travelled there, but it will mean a lot to me and sometimes that is a good thing. And surely it must be right to focus attention on a world event such as this, rather than continue in the routine way as if nothing is happening in the world. Also, the text for Peace in the World is entirely suitable ... "*I say love your enemies and pray for those who despitefully use you, so that you may be sons of your heavenly Father ...*" Has any man alive lived up to Jesus' teaching better than this Moslem? My sermon ideas went into full flood and wouldn't stop flowing. I hope sleep will dam them up. I must get up in time for the 7.00 a.m. news so that I know whether I am preaching about the living or the dead. I will have to be careful in the prayers, too. The old Prayer Book prays only for "*Christian Kings, Princes and Governors* ... He will have to find another spot. And if he has died, the Prayer Book prays only for "thy servants who have departed this life in *thy faith* and fear." Some people wouldn't allow him to be included. Yet they would include themselves! Religious bigotry! Forgive our foolish ways, dear Lord and Father of mankind.

Sunday, 7th February

I rose before the crows to tune into the News. King Hussein was still alive. I would stick to the "love your enemies" theme and to the healing he has brought to the Holy Lands. It may not be well received; I know I have more experience of that part of the world and more interest in Islam than anyone who will be in the congregations, but both my head and my heart tell me that I must do it, whether it is popular or not.

The Beaminster congregation at 8.00 a.m. didn't give a flicker of an expression when I announced the change in the readings. I doubt whether the average worshipper is the least concerned what is read, but they do like it to be well read. They might have been more appreciative if they had known the change saved them from the "dome in the sky" experience.

The Netherbury congregation was completely different, which isn't surprising because 9.30 is a much more sociable hour than 8.00 a.m. The sun has risen, for one thing. And coffee is served, which is another thing. No one left before the coffee and everyone chatted a long while. And one of the congregation told me she had taught King Hussein's daughters (by Noor) horsemanship. And another of the congregation reminded me that the late Vera Watkins had bred Salukis in Netherbury for the Arabian princes! And everyone seemed to appreciate the opportunity to reflect on the Holy Lands, the search for peace and the complexity of it all.

I appreciated something else. Netherbury Church is coming out of a dark night, and it will be to a very bright dawn. Since I was last there they have suffered a trauma. The floor under the organ sank. It was rotten right through. The whole organ, tons of it, has been dismantled and is laid out in a thousand pieces, filling one third of the church. The foundations were revealed, and shaken, I shouldn't wonder. The new floor is now in place. How can *any* floor possibly sustain the weight of that ugly colossus? So there was no organ music this morning. And what happened? Undaunted and unabashed, the choir led the whole thing unaccompanied, including an anthem during the communion, and very good it was. I wonder how many thousands of pounds the repairs will cost. Judging by the way we managed without the organ, I doubt it will be worth it. Then we could use the space for a choir vestry and we could introduce instrumentalists ... but such ideas give rise to disputes and hostilities which know no bounds and then I become the cause of division instead of reconciliation. So it is safer to say nothing. But how will progress be made?

The encouraging thing is that the new golden lighting and the new limewash on the walls has transformed the church. There is a new atmosphere of light and warmth as soon as you enter, with hot coffee and good chat before you leave, and bright music in between. Even one year ago none of these things seemed likely. Netherbury has long been our sleeping giant. Now it is stirring.

King Hussein's death was announced as I drove from Netherbury to have lunch with Joan in Sherborne. It was expected, yet I felt a cold shiver go right through me and goose pimples came all down my back. Foreboding. What will happen next in the Holy Lands? Intrigue and bloodshed to an unprecedented degree, is the worst scenario. All the world leaders will gather for the funeral tomorrow. Yet they are the people who have failed to respond to his lead. Some of them hold to power by pandering to the political extremes in their own land, which is what causes all the trouble. Compared with him, they are wimps.

In Sherborne, Kilele was trying to understand the fuss. He heard me telephone requests to Beaminster, Stoke Abbott and Broadwindsor that the flags should be lowered to half-mast. "Why are you doing that, Uncle?" he queried. "I thought we were trying to kill Hussein." He was confused, not surprisingly, between King Hussein of Jordan and Saddam Hussein of Iraq. It was a mercy that lunch arrived and I didn't have to start explaining Middle East politics to an eight-year-old. Instead, he and Timothy sang a grace which their father had taught them. Then their grandmother sang a grace in Arabic and then they waited for me to sing another grace. For some reason, I intoned the versicle "O Lord, open thou our lips" and taught them the response

"And our mouths shall show forth thy praise," which they sang very well. However, Kilele didn't think much of it. He said "That wasn't a proper grace, Uncle; it didn't bless the food or the cook." Timothy came to my rescue. "Of course it's a good grace," he said. "You've got to open your lips before you can put the food in your mouth." He is still only four. I wish I had kept a collection of his remarks, and Kilele's. It's sad that they fly forgotten as a dream. I hope and pray, most heartily, that will not be the fate of the late King's dreams.

Nine days later ...

Ash Wednesday, 17th February

This is the only Wednesday in the year without a morning communion – it is in the evening for Ash Wednesday – which meant that the Team meeting came forward an hour to 10.00 a.m. What a blessing, because I had to be at Peggy French's funeral in Stoke Abbott before 11.30.

Peggy French had been a pillar of the village church ever since she came to the village in 1946. And Godfrey had been church warden and 'godfather' to half the village up until his death ten years ago. It is impossible to estimate their contribution to the church and the village for over fifty years. Captain French used to summon me whenever he wanted to make his views known, which was quite often, and I would sit in his study, a little awe-struck by the huge pictures of the ships he had served. And I would listen to the wisdom of the great sailors he had known. He was devout, but commanding. The clergy called him "God," for short, and it suited him. Peggy, who had looked after him so wonderfully in his old age, had raised a family of four and all of them had been at her bedside when she died. They had rung me and asked me to join them. They could see she was dying, and it was obvious that a priest should be called, to pray. But they only got Ansaphone; I wasn't there. By the time I heard the message, it was midnight and she had died. I was angry with myself but the very next Ansaphone message was from Keith Yates, priest, supposedly in retirement. They had called him and he had said the prayers for the dying and commended her soul to God. The Team principle had covered the crisis. The church she had served all her life served her at her death. My anger turned to gratitude to Keith, though I was disappointed to have let the family down.

They requested a private 'family only' funeral. I knew that would be difficult because she was a public figure, some sort of a village 'icon'. It would be difficult to keep people away; they would all want to say their farewells. For them, there would be a thanksgiving service, in a month's time, which would be a celebration. I thought the balance was fair and wise. The family could mourn privately and immediately; everyone else could give their thanks publicly, later. It isn't often I telephone people and ask them *not* to come to church, and it isn't often that they are so keen to come to church. When I explained things, they understood but I was impressed by the common feeling "Oh! Well, if *you're* there, it's all right." This was deep. It shows the sense in which the priest is thought of as more than an ordinary person. At times he becomes the representative person. The villagers couldn't be present but the priest would be, and so they felt represented. The interesting thing is that every Sunday when I stand at the altar, time and time again, I believe that is what I am doing – representing the people, not only those present, but also those absent. I doubt many people think that is what I am doing on a Sunday, but today at Peggy's funeral they were glad to think of the priest in that way. Flashes of theology come shooting in, all unconsciously, when events sharpen our senses. Peggy's death and burial did that for me, and for a good many more.

Back at home, the Team meeting was over and not one of my colleagues could come to tonight's Ash Wednesday evening service, which left me to get the ash which would be put on everyone's forehead. I was expecting to preach and I was expecting to preside and I was ready to launch the Lent Course, but I had not expected to make the ash. For some reason, this duty had escaped me for thirty and more years. I went to the fireplace and dug some out of the grate. Joan said I couldn't possibly use that, it was wood ash and it wouldn't stick. I tried, but she was right, it didn't. As she fires kilns, she tends to know more about these things than most people, certainly more than I do. I telephoned David Shearlock; he had been Dean of Truro and he knew about such things. "Ah! Yes, dear boy," he said. "Get last year's palm crosses, burn them up and use the ash, that is the tradition." Sounded simple, but I couldn't find a single palm cross, though we searched the house from top to bottom. I burnt some paper but that was utterly useless, as Joan said it would be. It didn't make ash at all. I was beginning to panic because I had to be the far side of Dorchester at the Archdeacon's house by 2.30, and it was already 2.00 p.m. "Leave it to me," said Joan, and she promised to deliver the ash to the former Dean so that he could check its quality. This was a great relief, so I shot off to the Archdeacon, and left her to it. When the service came at 7.00 p.m., Dean David said there was enough ash to mark the whole of Dorset. "We only need a few grains," he said. Joan had taken him two boxes. "Wherever did she get it?" I asked him. "Oh," he said, "she told me she had forgotten to have the chimney swept and so she put her hand up the chimney and filled two boxes with soot." While I was wondering what to say, he added "She's rolled it all out with a rolling pin; it's very good stuff." So we used it, and everyone was well and truly ashed.

The Archdeacon had been helpful in the afternoon. I am convinced Archdeacons have the worst job in the Church of England. They doubtless want to be preachers and pastors but they have become bureaucrats and administrators. They stand between the bishop and the rest of the clergy, trying to make each understand the other. They are usually called when there is a problem no one else can deal with, and there are hundreds of those. They are

185

always in the front line when there is a dispute over parishes losing a priest or a vicarage – and they always have to know the details of every priest's domestic and household business. I would find it hateful, every minute of it. All the things I dislike most about the maintenance of the institution, they have to do, God bless them. So I approached Paul Wheatley with sympathy for his unhappy lot, and I was determined not to add to his woes and worries. In fact he was remarkably calm and cheerful, as though he actually liked the work and hadn't anything else on his mind at all.

He knew about Rose's illness and he had called to see her and he knew about David's illness, and he wondered how I was managing. I explained that we were committed to fourteen services each Sunday but that David's two and my four only made six and left eight each Sunday to be covered by priests who were meant to be retired, and by Readers.

The paper I presented explained why I am reluctant to use the retired priests for more than they are doing already. They are *retired* and they are *volunteers*. They shouldn't be expected to cover the stipendiary clergy, neither should they be expected to give up their family weekends and their time away; and the parishes should not depend upon them. There can't be any other profession where retired people are expected to step in and do the work of the paid people, for nothing! But it's not a matter of money; there is a principle. Retirement should be respected; one service on a Sunday, when they are available, is a bonus and a blessing – not a demand we can make. And then there is the question of the Readers; the paper raised a big issue which the Bishop should consider, and so should the whole Church of England. The expectation in the parishes is mostly for sacramental services, which the Readers are not authorised to offer. Should permission be granted for them to take extended communion in the parishes? And, if not, should they be ordained so that they can administer the sacraments? Otherwise they are ready and willing, but useless as eunuchs. So the paper reached the conclusion that the short-term solution lies with the church wardens. They are the locally elected leaders, they have the local respect and the local knowledge that neither the Readers nor the retired priests can ever possess. They should offer the traditional morning or evening prayer when the clergy Team cannot fill the gap. The Archdeacon accepted the paper (Oh dear! I had given him one more problem!) but he smiled and seemed quite unfussed, and promised to respond.

But the real trouble isn't Sunday. People think it is, but it isn't. The real trouble is the "care of all the churches, that comes upon me daily."

Thursday, 18th February

I came down for my usual quiet hour at 6.30, believing that all would be at peace – but the fax was already running. It was sure to be Andrew from Kampala where the time would be 9.30 a.m. It was. And the news was good. The long-awaited House of Bishops' meeting had ended in Nairobi and the Sudanese Church had chosen its new leaders. Bishop Joseph Marona, the senior bishop, had been elected Dean of the Province and Bishop Daniel Deng had been elected Secretary to the Bishops' Council. Andrew's fax said "We are rejoicing in Kampala" and added that Joseph Marona had said "When God calls, it is difficult to dodge" and also "My brother bishops have been very supportive." The second comment may prove more significant than the first. And Daniel Deng had said he would go "straight to Khartoum to prepare the way for the Dean to visit." The appointment of an archbishop was delayed until all the synod members necessary for a constitutional election could be gathered together in one place. At a time of desperate war, with roads blocked and mines laid and many areas isolated, nobody could tell when that would be.

This was indeed good news. It meant that the dreaded division of the province into two factions, along the north:south lines of the civil war had been avoided. The church would remain together, a symbol of unity at a time of division. What a mercy! It also meant that Joseph Marona from the area held by the 'Liberation' army would return to the government-controlled area and it would be up to the Islamic regime to grant freedom of movement and protection. Joseph would need courage and the government's claims for freedom of religion would be challenged. Both would be put to the test.

The decision also meant that the bishops had turned their back on the temptation to move into Bishop Gabriel Roric's government camp. Many Sudan-watchers had feared that, as a minister in the government, he would use his influence, and the promise of greater security and comfort, to lure bishops to follow the political stance he had taken. Not so. The chosen leader was from the anti-government area, and the chosen secretary was an outspoken critic of the government, although within the government area. Brave men. How soft is our Christian ministry in this country, by comparison! We don't know what hardship is. We have a house provided, a pension assured and a stipend which goes straight into the bank. The Sudanese bishops have none of these things; instead they are pushed from pillar to post avoiding minefields and ever watchful for the stab in the back.

Andrew's news meant I could now write the last page of the Sudan Church Review and get it to the printers. It would have been foolish to have published the Review on time but without the news. It would now be a couple of days late but would have the news. As soon as it was daylight, I telephoned the late Daniel Zindo's cousin who had been his commissary in U.K. I told him the news and asked his opinion. "This is great news." "This is tactful and diplomatic." "These men will hold the Church together" was his verdict. The call lasted half an hour because he was expansive in his praise and pleasure. The hope and optimism that keeps the Sudanese people alive was overflowing. I didn't want to put the phone down – parish life is very pedestrian by comparison. Yesterday's visit to the Archdeacon with my 'paper' was suddenly put in a new perspective. The Sudanese Church has been kept going by lay people, sometimes for years and years, and they don't need bishop's licence to do it. The two cultures are so far apart, but we are One Church with One Lord. But can there be greater extremes than the security and well being of West Dorset and the dangers and traumas of Sudan? And I have the privilege of a foot in both camps.

It was the first of the Lent Lunches today and it happened to be at Broadwindsor and it happened to be for The Sudan. I would have gone to it, whatever the charity, because these Lent Lunches are a priest's delight! The midday soup and cheese is good value at a couple of pounds, and no time is wasted in getting my own lunch, which is another bonus, but the real boon is neither of those things. It is the sheer pleasure of sitting down for an hour or more and listening to the chatter, the questions and the things people are saying. Even complaints become more agreeable over the lunch table than they are over the telephone. The prospect of a Lent Lunch for almost all the forty days of Lent is very attractive indeed. I hope to go to them all! I would recommend them to any priest and to any parish. A more pleasant way for the priest to meet lots of people, and for the parish to raise lots of money, week in week out, has not yet been devised.

Before the ending of the day, our little weekly 'Pew News' was written by me, typed by Myrtle, printed by Barbara and all three hundred were folded while I watched the 10 o'clock news; meanwhile I had written 'The Last Word' for the Sudan Review, delivered it to Kathy at Creeds the Printers, who faxed it back for proof-reading while the 10 o'clock news was on. So they work all hours on our behalf, as well. A very good way to end the day.

Friday, 19th February

This was my first Friday for years and years without Mary in the office. She has given her time and her effort to our office, excessively. It has exhausted her, and me too. She helped in many ways and her good intentions were boundless but the time has come for her to live her own life, and look after her failing health. I have asked her not to come any more. Saying 'enough is enough' to a volunteer is a problem and when it is one as loyal as Mary it is an acute problem. But my judgement is that her daily duties were ceasing to do her any good, had ceased to do me any good and had become a strain all round. Let's hope she will be forgiving.

Now that the office will only be open for limited hours and limited purpose, it will do *more* good, not less. It will become what it was meant to be – a duplicating and printing service for the parishes, and no more. That function is enough. And that can be done on one or two mornings a week.

An office can easily become more important than it should be. We don't want centralised power. An office, especially one in the central place, Beaminster Rectory, can easily become a power base. That is death to Team work. If this Team has a distinctive claim to fame, it is that the power has been diffused, spread around, shared out. The last thing we want is to have the power brought back into hands at the centre. This is always likely to happen if the central office becomes too big or too important. So it will do everyone good to phase the office down, and even phase it out. It has brought blessings. It has been no charge on anyone. In fact, it has saved the parishes money. It has provided a service, cheaper than any commercial place. It has brought a lot of people together and Mary has given every hour (thousands of them) for love. It has done well, but it is time for a rest. If the office closed permanently, it would not be a bad thing. It would be a good reminder that there is no central authority. Village autonomy and centralisation can never marry.

My worst nightmare for the Team is an office-led bureaucracy. A central power-house sending out orders to the villages – targets to be achieved, audits to be returned, achievements to be assessed, evaluations to be made. This is the current jargon. A lot of people would have it that way. The office would become Big Brother, the villagers would be its subjects, the machinery of management would take over. This sort of thinking is all the fashion. It is a bigger threat to the Gospel than Islam, Hinduism and Buddhism put together, because they are at least seeking holiness which is more than I can say for the business world.

We had the second of the Lent Lunches today and it was Beaminster's turn, with John and Mary Whettem. The way they have coped with retirement stands as a model to me. They help with everything, interfere in nothing and are open to everybody. John does a Sunday service whenever he is available but he hasn't become a slave to it; they counsel, they travel and they sit in the congregation when John hasn't a duty. Not every clergyman is willing to do that! As a breed, we like to be in charge. And when we are not in charge, we are inclined to abstain altogether, as if being in charge is more important than worshipping. John is the complete opposite, and when my retirement comes, that is how I would like to be. Joan must feel something very similar about them both or she wouldn't have bothered to drive over from Sherborne between lessons, to be there. She had to get back in a bit of a hurry because her new headmistress-elect was about to be introduced to the staff, and a lot hangs on that. So the Lent Lunch chat was very much about private education and the problems it faces. The rapidity of closures is alarming for those involved and no-one can point to the reason. Some say it's financial, but I doubt that. In many circles, there is more money flowing around than there used to be, not less. I think the reason is heads and governors in public schools find it harder to adapt to changing times because of the strong traditions which resist change. These traditions which have been their strength, could become their downfall. The new headmistress at Sherborne is from South Africa, which is most unexpected. At least she won't be tied to the Sherborne tradition, but it's hard to imagine she will be in touch with modern Europe either. She takes over in September. Interesting days lie ahead. I hope they won't be too painful.

Stoke Abbott Church Council met tonight, and very enjoyable it was. A magnificent fire with logs a few feet long greeted us when we arrived at Chartknolle and a glass of wine cheered us. How different from the days when we met in the freezing cold hall and the lights used to go out until we put 10p in, and the wooden chairs and the floor creaked. The Chartknolle atmosphere tonight lent itself to bonhomie and positive decisions, just as the village hall atmosphere had led to petty differences and pessimism. We were all in expansive mood when it came to planning the dedication of the Millennium window. The Bishop of Sherborne has accepted the invitation, all the Team church wardens should be invited, with their banners, the Beaminster choir with their organist and it should all be followed by an old-fashioned feast. I doubt we would have made those decisions in the village hall. Environment does matter and this evening's was so pleasant that, even when the meeting ended, nobody was in a hurry to go.

This was partly because it was the first time Stoke people had gathered together since Peggy French's death, and everyone wanted to chat about the plans for the thanksgiving service. They hadn't intruded into the family funeral and so they had been deprived of the chance to mourn. Mourning is important. We need to do it and that is the purpose of these 'Rites of Passage'. Every culture has them, human nature needs them, they provide both a therapy and a safety net for our emotions. I needed it too. And that was why we all stayed, chatting. I noticed that the minutes of the last meeting ended with the words "the meeting closed with thanks to Mrs. French." How apt, how true, yet it seemed so painfully sad as well. I was pleased to have been at the meeting – not just for the fire, the wine and the business but because it helped the village mourning process.

Phyllis Mudford, Peggy's constant companion and carer, hadn't come to the meeting, so on the way home I called on her. She still has oversight of the French family home and the awful news was that burglars had broken in during the night. The alarm had rung and frightened them off before they did much damage but she must feel very vulnerable and insecure. It was really awful that she had to face that ordeal within 48 hours of the funeral. She was bearing up with the sort of fortitude which made her such a strength to Peggy. We managed a few laughs before I left and she said she felt much better, which I believe. My visit had made her open the door at night and we had talked about Peggy, cheerfully. Simple things, but very necessary.

Saturday, 20th February

I do not like going out on Saturday evenings. It's the big social night for most people, but not for me, and I don't regret it. Saturday night is the perfect time to tidy the week up and polish the Sunday sermon. And if I have to go out, the neat and tidy wrapping up of the week doesn't happen and the sermon polishing has to be brought forward. Saturday night is the last chance to write the letters I have put off, to read the reports and papers I have shelved, to phone people I have not visited so that Sunday arrives with my desk clean and my mind clear. Sounds boring, and probably is, to most people. To me, it is more relaxing than a night out and more cheering than any number of beers. I don't like Sunday to arrive with unfinished business on my mind, so Saturday is the clearing-up day.

However, there have to be exceptions, and tonight was one of them. It was the long-awaited "Wand of Youth" performance by Alastair Bannerman and his sons in Beaminster Church. Ever since Elisabeth became ill, nearly two years ago, Alastair has been without his natural theatre partner as well as without his marriage partner of nearly sixty years. So it was a great effort, at the age of 84, to gather the remainder of his family for one more theatrical evening. For weeks he has been saying "I will never do it." "I'm as nervous as a kitten." "This is my last, definitely my last." I don't believe it, and I don't think anybody else believes it either. The love of theatre, the need to be centre stage, the lust to have an audience in your hand waiting on every word is in his blood. It drives the adrenalin, it (and a drop of whisky) keeps him going. He won't be able to stop, tonight or any night. He will stop when he drops, and not before. He says he could drop at any time. Of course that is true of any of us but, at the age of 84 and holding centre stage, it would be just the sort of spectacular exit he would wish.

So I brought the Sunday sermon forward and tried to polish it in the morning, instead of the evening. It didn't feel right! It was the wrong time of day and I couldn't settle to it. Stupid. But my adrenalin was not running. I need to get right into a sermon, right inside it, so that it becomes a part of me, not something outside of me. And I couldn't do that on a Saturday morning with people calling, shopping not done, the morning mail to answer, the sports pages un-read and Sunny waiting for his walk. There is a difference between a sermon which comes from inside and one which hasn't got that far into the system. I know the difference and I bet the congregation does, too.

All these musings on sermons were strangely paralleled by Alastair's show in the evening. It was evident that for him and his two sons, Andrew and Tim, the whole performance came from inside so that, to me and I think to others, it was no longer a performance, we were swept into the midst of it. That is the joy of good theatre, we take on another persona for a while. This is exactly what we hope for in an act of worship. The worshippers should be raised to a new and higher vision of themselves and others. Theatre and liturgy are closely related, if not twins. And both can fall terribly short, if the part the leaders play does not come from the inside. It did tonight. But what about tomorrow?

Sunday, 21st February

I was very happy with the Beaminster service this morning. The numbers were not exceptional, about 90, but the music was good and the choir looked and sounded splendid; the scriptures were read clearly and had evidently been practised carefully; the intercessions were thoughtful but not lengthy, as I would expect from Robin Musson; there were two assistants with the chalice which meant the communion was orderly and completed in under five minutes; and the family atmosphere was completed when the Sunday Club children came in at the communion to present their work. These young ones also saw the presentation we made to Len Dawe who had kept the keys of the church for more years than anyone could remember. The young ones joined in the applause which we all offered for Len, a faithful 'Elder', if ever there was one. This Beaminster liturgy is a very fine example of mainstream Anglicanism – traditional and dignified. And all the family was there.

This good experience poses an awkward problem. I can not for the life of me see why it is necessary, with such a service, to add into the programme rota 'family services'. We had just attended one, and a very good one. The whole family were there – the older ones all through, the younger ones joining after receiving teaching suited to their age. Ideal. Next week they will come to their own form of 'family service'. There will not be 90 adults, there will not be a robed choir, or any choir, there will not be a great traditional liturgy, there will not even be a priest. The children will not enter a world of mystery and wonder, surrounded by believing adults. They will be deprived of all that. They will have a simple little service "which they can understand." No mystery. Very dull. Opinions differ about how children learn to worship, and it is more than a local difference. It divides the church up and down the country. I am in no doubt that today was the right way. But a good many think the opposite, so next Sunday there will be a family service, especially for them. How will they ever learn the great tradition? We are scoring own goals, all over the place!

The winds howled around Toller tonight and the rains came in horizontally. I went to Evensong instead of David, who wasn't well. I doubted anyone would be there. Toller on a foul night is bleak indeed. And twenty-five people turned up! The music was a bit mournful, the Lenten penance in Victorian hymnody can be morbid. I did my best to raise a smile but, whether it was the weather or the Lenten season I do not know, nothing would bring a flicker of an expression. If the English take their pleasures seriously, you should see the way some churches take their religion! Church going can be so depressing. After wading through that rain and battling with those gales in the pitch dark of a winter's night, they deserved better. But probably that is what church is expected to be. Depressing.

When the service had begun, the great West Door began to rattle. I thought it was the wind, and carried on. But the rattling carried on as well, so the two church wardens went to fix the handle. In fact the door flew open and in blew Mary Moorhead. She must have driven from Beaminster through those storms, although she says her eyes are failing! She had been to the 8 a.m. service in Beaminster and again at 9.30 and here she was again, at 6.30. It must mean she has forgiven me for ending her office hours, which is very charitable of her. At the end, I asked why she had come all the way from Beaminster on such a night. "I've always

195

been to Evensong," she said. "And I don't intend to stop now." Saintliness and insanity are close neighbours.

Monday, 22nd February

I would have welcomed a break this morning. Yesterday was demanding. Apart from the four services, I had to put Team News into its final form. It was one of those awkward months when it just did not fit. One whole page was blank, and lots of empty spaces all over the place. And that wasn't the only problem. I had somehow forgotten to commission a cover. At this late stage, there was only one thing to do – find a suitable photograph symbolising the spring. I rang John and Marjorie Aird and they brought a selection to the house, within thirty minutes. I knew they were the right people and they produced the goods without any fuss. We have the most marvellous resources in these parishes. One of the blessings of being in a parish a long while is that I know where to find them. The modern fashion of moving a priest on as soon as he is settled and knows who is who, seems madness to me – another of our 'own goals'. But the cover wasn't the last of the problems. I had to write 'fillers' and hope that they would fit into the flow of things and that readers would not recognise that they were fillers. It also meant writing a full-page 'Tailpiece'. David had written a substantial page about his M.E./C.F.S. symptoms and I had hoped that would act as Tailpiece, but a whole page about illness would have been a depressing way to end the issue. So I wrote about the woman at Synod who was a gardener and thought if bishops were pruned the rest of the branches might grow. There is a lot in that! I used to call it 'perimeter theology' – putting the strength on the edges. No one took any notice. The church have always thought a strong centre is necessary, and so has business. I don't. I am true to the Reformation, which was about de-centralisation. Bishops and others have conveniently forgotten that. Anyway, I enjoyed the chance to write such a full page 'space filler', but I didn't finish it until 2 a.m. It had taken six attempts, all written longhand, before I got it the way I wanted it. How much quicker the computer keyboard would have been. But I get the feel of the words with a pen in my hand and not with a keyboard at my fingertips. So it took till 2.

It was all worthwhile when I arrived at Creeds this morning with all the text ready for printing. They must have thought I looked in need because they brought me a coffee.

It was the first of the Lent Course groups tonight, and thereby hangs a tale or three.

It is quite amazing that things which should be devotional become a matter of dispute. The way we worship is the most obvious example. The aggressive words and the bitter feuding which has surrounded the use of the old 1662 Book of Common Prayer and the new Alternative Service Book has shortened my life. Thank goodness I value and enjoy them both. What would have happened in these parishes if I had also been prejudiced and belonged to one side and opposed the other? Would we ever have reached the fine balance we have achieved? And now the 'powers that be' are going to inflict another round of arguments upon us, with another new prayer book which will replace the one we have just got used to! Do these people have the slightest idea of the pain and conflict they cause in the parishes – not to mention the expense. I have yet to find one parishioner anywhere in these parishes who wants yet another set of services and another set of books. The best letter I ever read in the "Church Times" was only two lines long – it suggested the Liturgical Commission should be given a rest and invited to meet again in twenty years' time! It is an embarrassment that our own bishop is the chairman of the Commission and the driving force behind the new forms of worship. He is probably the nicest of men with the best of intentions but he would be more of a bishop if he was a pastor to stressed clergy instead of the head of the Commission that causes so much of the stress. I faced the hostility caused by the first new book in full measure; it went on for years and years and still reverberates. Now, just as we have found a modus vivendi, we are being made to face it all over again. More division, more disputes, more rancour and more expense will all cause more introspection, while those outside will remain outside, only too thankful to be able to get on with their own lives without adding church disputes to their problems. It seems sad, if not cruel, that having weathered one set of storms which damaged so much of my early ministry, I am heading into another which will disturb the end of my ministry. It all seems so far from anything to do with the Kingdom of God, just another way of scoring own goals.

Now even the Lent course is a cause of dispute! The diocese has given us a course called 'Vision 2000', the bishop has urged us to use it, the Archbishop's 'Springboard' Team say it is an essential part of the preparation for the millennium and I, out of loyalty, think we should do as we are bidden. To reject the diocesan course and the bishop's personal request would be unreasoned rebellion. That's my view. And David T's as well. In fact, he had been in most pulpits urging whole Church Councils to do the course together, as a Church Council. But others are saying it is simplistic, that the book is not worth the £2.50 it costs, that the presentation is 'naff' and that the whole thing is a part of the 'dumbing down' process which is turning us tabloid.

So when Beaminster Church Council gathered to begin the course tonight, not everyone thought it was the best place to be. In fact, I would gladly have swopped with Jane Rose who was in Peru, or Harry Livingstone who was in Australia. Roger Peers was giving one of his lecture tours, David Hile's deafness means he is leaving the Council, Bert Osborne had been at work which, at the age of 78, is enough for one day, Chris Longridge was at an education meeting in Dorchester, Richard and Margaret Satchell didn't come, which left twelve of us, the apostolic number.

To my surprise and relief, we had a lovely evening. This course is going to be as good as the people choose to make it. Yes, it could be a little juvenile but where there are a number of people at the beginning of their journey of faith, that may be what is needed. Tonight it became quite profound as each of the twelve recounted how their faith began, how it was nurtured and some of the moments which became life-changing. We all revealed things about ourselves – enormously interesting and very effective in building trust and binding together – which was exactly the aim of the first week. I think this course is going to be multi-adaptable and that is very clever. It needs to be highly adaptable because we have ninety people doing the course in nine groups and they all look very different to me. I shall be going to four of the groups most weeks, so I am pleased I feel comfortable with it. The one thing I am not comfortable with would apply to any course – it is all talk, talk, talk. If we could talk our way into the Kingdom of Heaven, we would all have been there, years ago.

One month later ...

Wednesday, 24th March

This Lent has not gone according to plan – but what does go according to plan? Very little in my life! A business man has to keep his plans, that is his job; a parish priest has to respond to others' needs, that is his job. And no one can plan for that. All those efficient people who want to make the church more like business don't understand this.

I had planned to attend four Lent courses a week. I should have known that was over-optimistic; I have managed two a week. On the other hand, I had not realised the value Lent Lunches would be. I've been to twenty-two of those. They've turned the lunch time into a good social hour; I am sorry they are at an end. Also they have raised more than £2,000 for different charities. Who says village churches are in decline?

The good news is that Rose has now been cleared by the doctor as fit for work. She can drive again, but favours only short distances and one Sunday service at the moment. She needs time to get into the full swing of a seven-day ministry.

The bad news is that David is worse. His doctor was willing to sign him off as unfit for work but he felt he should carry on while Rose was out. Very kind of him, but not necessarily very wise. I won't be surprised if, in the long term, his illness turns out to be the more serious of the two.

The worst news wasn't about health at all. I went to the worst clergy meeting of my life and learnt things I would rather not know. The meeting was called to discuss the diocesan plan to reduce the number of full-time clergy to eight in the Deanery by 2005. As the long-established Beaminster Team has three priests and the newly-established Golden Cap Team has also been given three, this will leave only two for the remaining Team when it is formed. And at present they have six! The question is, can Powerstock, Loders and Askerswell who have Gregory Page-Turner; Bradpole and Walditch who have Maureen Allchin; Burton Bradstock and the Bride Valley villages who have John Atkinson and Anthony Ashwell; Bridport with Trevor Stubbs and Allington with Roger Shambrook, all join together while reducing to two priests? None of us thought that was realistic. What were the alternatives? Someone suggested the Golden Cap and the Beaminster Teams should both manage with two instead of three so that the new 'Bridport' set could have four. Another view, which is supposed to be the present Diocesan policy, was to make the whole deanery into one Team with the Rural Dean as rector and villages being cared for by locally ordained volunteers. I thought that nonsense. All it does is show that the 'centre' neither values nor understands the 'perimeter'. Such a Team would have no natural ties, it would be a Team in name only. It would be no more than a device for the administrative convenience of the diocese, not for the health and strength of the local church.

My solution was to persuade the diocese to allow nine priests, three for each Team, and that the six years before the 2005 deadline should be used to select, train and ordain our own non-stipendiaries to supplement each Team. No-one disputed that. It was my next comment which stirred up trouble. I said that 'natural wastage' (i.e. retirements) would help the planning and could begin with the departure of Allington's vicar when he leaves. I didn't know I was lighting a fire. He quickly pointed out that he was a special case and that he had to be replaced. Then my unwanted learning curve began. It turned out that the Allington people had opted out of our Bishop of Salisbury's care and they now belonged to the 'flying' Bishop of Ebbsfleet. So they now belong to the 'other' or 'second' integrity which the Church of England, in its lack of wisdom, brought in to retain those people whose conscience didn't allow them to accept the ordination of women. When the Bishop of Salibury passed the pastoral care to the Bishop of Ebbsfleet, he was obliged to guarantee them a priest of that integrity. So the Beaminster Team might have to lose a priest, so that the eclectic gathering at Allington could have one to themselves. And none of us could go there to share our ministry because we, like the Bishop of Salisbury himself, were not recognised. We were 'tainted' by association with women; they wouldn't accept us! What mad aberration in the church had brought such crazy legislation into being? Before Allington's vicar left the meeting I managed to tell him that I didn't think his people belonged to a 'second' integrity, I thought they had no integrity at all and the only honest thing to do was to leave the Church of England. I often disagree with the Church but I don't expect special arrangements to be made in my favour. I have to accept the decision. I also found it outrageous that all the priests of the deanery were 'tainted' in the eyes of the Allington minority and that our sacramental ministry was unacceptable. If they belong to a diocese, why do they need another bishop? They have become a law unto themselves, a state within the state. If they want this special sort of priest, why should he count as one of the limited number we are allowed? As it is, we are encouraging their narrow-minded prejudice.

We are feeding the rebellion, stoking it. We must be mad. I had no idea we would pay such a price for the ordination of women. And if the end of the matter locally is that our Team loses one of its three priests so that Allington can have its own, then injustice will be added to madness. Imagine this farce being repeated all over the country. It's a nightmare! Own goals! Own goals! More own goals.

I have always supported the ordination of women, and I don't regret it. But I have learnt that its supporters came from different angles and had different motives. I supported it because I believed Jesus was a radical liberaliser who was overcoming the prejudices of his time and opening the door for women. His theological discourse with the Samaritan woman at the well was a sign of this, though it annoyed his disciples. The way Jesus valued Mary of Magdala when the Pharisaic Philip invited him to supper was another sign, though that also annoyed all the guests. The fact that she became the first person to proclaim the Resurrection makes the same point, though the disciples doubted her. It has taken too long to complete Jesus' work – twenty centuries! And that was my motivation, at the time of the vote, and it still is. However, I now realise that there was another campaigning group with an entirely different agenda.

The 'equal rights' and the 'women libbers' were coming from another angle. They saw it as part of the power struggle between the genders. These people were less bothered with theology, little concerned about the Church of England and just wanted to be ordained as a statement. I hadn't realised that the Church would be saddled with some people who, once they were ordained, would be very little interested in the work, having achieved their status. For these women, the next thing will not be a devotion to Our Lord and love for his work, but another campaign for the next status – women bishops. God save us from the sort of women who have that ambition! God save us from that sort of men, too!

I am not looking forward to the next ten days. There will be too many services and too much preaching. This morning I preached about

Oscar Romero because it is the 19th anniversary of his death today and his statue is now installed above the West Door of Westminster Abbey. Tomorrow it is the Feast of the Annunciation and I am the preacher at the Deanery M.U. Festival. Next day I must give the address at Ernie Wildern's funeral in the morning and pay a tribute to Dick Colborne in the afternoon, and I will be preaching four times on Sunday, that is eight times in four days – and all before Holy Week starts! It is unreasonable. Bishops and politicians have speech writers. Thank God I do my own research – imagine having to preach someone else's stuff! No, thank you.

Thursday, 25th March
Feast of the Annunciation

I knew there would be a big crowd (of women) at the M.U. Festival in Broadwindsor, and there was. I had planned to stay in Broadwindsor after their Lent Lunch, until the service, an hour or so later, but it didn't work out that way. The morning had been so confused, it threw the plans completely.

I met Tony Betchley at 10.00 to discuss his mother's funeral on the Tuesday of Holy Week. It will be big. She was popular, had lived all her seventy-six years in Beaminster and her sudden death had shocked everyone. Tony was full of memories of 'old Beaminster' and these stories fascinate me. The number of people with such stories to tell, and the ability to tell them is reducing. With Ernie and Dick to bury tomorrow and Mollie on Tuesday, we will have lost three in a week. So I chatted to Tony longer than I should. Back at home, Barbara Harris had printed Pew News but it needed folding, three hundred copies, with a Christian Aid leaflet in each one. I reckoned I could do that in half an hour. It usually fits exactly into News at Ten. But the news is not at ten any more and I wanted to hand them out at the M.U. Festival so, after the Lent Lunch, I returned and finished the job. There were also four hundred copies of the clergy report to be signed. I knew that would take more than half an hour. People tell me it is a waste of time and quite unnecessary to sign each one. Once is enough, let the photocopier do the rest, they say. I know that is common sense but I don't feel comfortable with it. I wrote the report. I am answerable for it and so I want everyone to see my signature on it, so that they know who to write to if they don't like it. It took an hour and a half to sign them all and, even if nobody notices, it is worth it to me. Besides, while I was signing them I could polish the M.U. Festival sermon in my mind, which I did.

These M.U. events always leave me with mixed feelings. There were a dozen or more banners around the altar and at least two hundred people in church, and the hymns were well known and well sung. So far, so good. And different members of the M.U. did the readings, led the prayers, and administered the chalice. So far, even better. Why was I not satisfied? It is because when a multitude of mothers gather, I always feel we fail them. Looking down on them from the pulpit, I imagined their reservoir of experience bursting the banks and flooding every church in the area with the pains, problems and cost of love. They know all about it. But the Church doesn't know how to tap into the great resource and let it out. The M.U. is potentially such a power for good, yet somehow it fails to unleash the creativity of mother-love. Anyway, I did my best to articulate some of the pains and problems which go hand-in-hand with loving. Simeon's words to Mary "and a sword shall pierce your own heart ..." gave the clue and I felt sure some of the mothers recognised themselves in the pictures I painted. Then we adjourned to the hall and the cakes were served, all cream and chocolate, and trays of sandwiches came round and the Mothers' Union was doing what it is famous for – though I believe it could do bigger and better things. And everyone was very nice and polite and said "Lovely service, Vicar" when I left. Yes, it was very nice. But the Church had managed to keep the genie in the bottle, yet again.

The comprehensive school governors' meeting in the evening was another two and a half hour marathon. I tried to concentrate but my mind was turning to Ernie Wildern's funeral in the morning and the back of the agenda was useful for making sermon notes. It was obvious I wouldn't be home before 10 p.m. and so it would be a late night session to complete it. Fortunately, by the time the governors' meeting ended, the sermon was half prepared. I felt a little like a naughty school boy as I remembered the way I used to pretend to listen to the geography lesson while secretly picking the best football team beginning with 'B', or something like that. Now I was pretending to follow the governors' debate while preparing Ernie's funeral. Anyway, by midnight it was done and I knew every word was true, and worth saying.

The day had begun at 7.00 a.m. and ended 17 hours later. How much longer can I keep this up? I have eaten a Lent Lunch and a Kit Kat. The strange thing is, I enjoy it.

So I made a midnight coffee, put some brandy in it and settled to have half an hour with Wisden Obituaries. I read up Reverend J. R. Bridger. He used to play cricket for Hampshire in the post-war years, taking July and August off to do it. Clergy life must have been different in those days.

Friday, 26th March

Ernie Wildern's funeral went off well enough, though I told Wakelys they would need a hundred service sheets printed and in fact only thirty or so people turned up. I was surprised. There were a few family, mostly from 'away', and a few neighbours, and not many more. Considering he was the oldest Beaminster-born man, I thought there would be more. I suppose at the age of 97 he had outlived all the people who had known him in the days of his health. He was one of nine children and he had outlived them all, by some years.

There were two good things about it. One was that his nephew 'John' Cox, who has done so much for him in the later years, was brought in a wheelchair from his hospital bed. It would have been very sad if he had not been there after all the care he gave Ernie, until overtaken by illness himself. The second good thing was that I knew the things I said about Ernie were true and that they revealed an age of simple faith, now gone for ever. I made sure we said the old prayers which were indelibly etched in his mind. He used to say the whole prayer book service, with his eyes shut. This is what we are losing. I hope the priests of the future will not be so taken up with variety as the spice of life that the people can no longer put down deep roots, in the way that Ernie did.

After the Yeovil cremation, I took the chance to dash into Yeovil Hospital to see John Wright and Daphne Oliver. Not a lot of luck. John Wright was 'being seen to' which meant he couldn't be seen by me and, just as I arrived to see Daphne in the women's hospital, the fire alarm sounded, emergency lights flashed and visitors were not allowed. It turned out to be a false alarm but, by the time I reached her ward, lunch was being served and it wasn't very convenient. The cancer has gone deep but she remains as gracious as ever, preparing for another chemotherapy ordeal at Bristol, soon. When I got back to the car it had a ticket; thirty pounds down the drain. Yeovil Hospital has the worst of all the many parking problems. Sometimes I have gone there, not found anywhere to park and have driven away again. Perhaps I should have done that today.

Immediately, I was due back at the crematorium for Dick Colborne's funeral. This saddened me. Dick was a hugely popular Beaminster figure. He was also the last (but one) of the Beaminster people who went over on 'D Day', now fifty-four years ago. And he had shown similar courage in facing his long degenerative illness. Beaminster Church would have been filled, for Dick. Dozens of people had asked when the funeral would be, and they had all been disappointed that it was to be private. Dick had been made an 'honorary citizen' of Beaminster last summer and that was a popular occasion but he never sought publicity and he had asked for a private funeral. And so it was. A dozen family. No hymns. No address, though I managed a tiny tribute within the prayers. I would have wanted the trumpets to sound for Dick, but it was not to be. At least, not 'here'. But I hope they sounded 'on the other side', loud and clear, to make up for it.

Back at home, the good news on Ansaphone was that the April edition of 'Team News' was ready to collect at Creeds the Printers. They had produced it on time, in spite of all their other commitments. They are marvellous, at least to me. I went straight over to collect them but by then it was after 5.00 p.m. and all the staff had left and I had to load the seventeen boxes into the car myself. The axles sank lower and lower, and so did I. They filled every square inch of space around Sunny, whose ears and dewlaps drooped lower. He hates this chore each month, and I don't blame him. But he likes it even less if he is left at home. I drove home gently, lest the car break in two under the weight.

Back in Beaminster, I unloaded them all and within a few minutes the distributors were arriving from each village to claim their quota. They don't waste any time, the system is highly efficient but, as most of the distributors are older than I am, I felt obliged to do the loading for them which meant that, within the hour, I had carried all 1700 magazines three times! When they had all gone, I made a Bovril for strength and followed it with a brandy for the spirit to prepare the Holy Week services.

The Holy Week services, I reckon, will keep me in church for seventeen hours, if I include Palm Sunday. In addition, there will be Mollie Betchley's funeral on Tuesday and the bishop's service in the cathedral on Maundy Thursday, which is sure to be a long affair. I shall be in church for twenty hours! Those hours need preparation, they won't just happen, so I settled to it. Half-way through the evening, I thought the photocopier was in danger of burn out, so I gave it a rest. By then, Joan was home after visiting her mother in Parkstone. "Are you going to finish all that tonight?" she asked. "I doubt it," I said. She wanted to know when I would be free. "Monday week," I said, half as a joke. But she didn't think it was funny. She was in a lot of pain from a long-standing tooth problem. She had seen six specialists and none of them knew what to do about it. The infection, it seems, has passed into the bone and she is worried. "I have to make appointments, appointments, appointments," she said, "and wait a week each time – now I have to make an appointment and wait a week to see my own husband" – and she went to bed. Oh, Holy Week, Holy Week, what do you do to clergy marriages! So I worked on into the night, hoping to have some time to take her out tomorrow. Better to have a broken photocopier than a broken marriage.

Saturday, 27th March

Joan went back to Sherborne quite early, saying she had a kiln to fire at the school, some planting to do in the garden and that it wasn't much use staying with me because I wouldn't have any time for her, even if she did stay. The trouble is, she is right. I had to do the two visits for tomorrow's Christenings, I had to duplicate the Good Friday leaflets for the parishes and plan the programme for Broadwindsor's Meditation on Monday. By then it was well into the afternoon.

Even so, I drove over to Sherborne to see how she was. When I opened the door, she said "What did you have for lunch?" Of course I hadn't had anything. "You look nearly dead," she said. "You're not looking after yourself," and she announced she had bought my favourite pork chops for supper. So I took Sunny, and the two Godsons out in the car and we went to the Hilfield Friary where the Brothers gave us tea and Kilele said to one of the brothers who was wearing sandals "Don't your toes get cold?" and Timothy laughed and laughed and said "Can we tickle them?" and the Brother didn't mind, so Timothy tickled his toes with a stick and everyone laughed. On the way back, we gathered wood for the fire and by the time we were home both boys were asleep and supper was ready.

"You look completely different," said Joan, after supper. I felt it too. It might have been the boys' good cheer. It might have been the fresh air. It might have been that Keegan's England had beaten Poland 3-1. Whatever it was, I convinced Joan it was her cooking and the pork chops, and it might well have been.

Palm Sunday, 28th March

Two things disturbed me today. They didn't spoil the services, which went very much as people expected, but they spoilt my enjoyment of them.

The first thing was petty, but aggravating. The new lectionary which the Church has given us did not have the entry to Jerusalem as the Gospel – neither did it have the Zechariah prophecy "Rejoice, rejoice Jerusalem, behold thy king cometh unto thee, meek and riding upon a donkey ..." for the Old Testament. I restored them, so that the people heard them, as they would expect to do on Palm Sunday. If I had kept to the readings given, we would have had passages from Isaiah and Paul and five full pages of the Matthew Passion, which we will hear on Good Friday anyway. The familiar Palm Sunday readings now form a new "Liturgy of the Palms". It all seemed too clever by half. It is a million miles from the expectations and wishes of parishioners and one more trap for clergy to fall into. However, it was a petty point compared with the second disturbance.

The real problem was that, while we were celebrating Jesus' peaceful entry into Jerusalem and holding palms to honour the "Prince of Peace", we were bombing the Serbs and creating greater cruelty and chaos in Kosovo than already existed. This poses the preacher a big problem. The easy thing is to ignore what is going on in the world and pretend it is not happening. And that is why the Church is becoming an irrelevance to many – it sidesteps the awkward issues by escaping into the spiritualities of yesteryear. The preaching problem for me was acute. It was evident that all three political parties backed the bombing which was also supported by nineteen NATO countries. That is a very powerful bloc. But I wondered if certain questions had been asked and answered. Don't the gung-ho politicians realise the effect it will have? For one thing it will unite the opposition. It will make Milosevic into their hero. A more effective approach would be to divide his supporters. Also, the bombing will immediately increase the tempo of the ethnic cleansing of Albanians because they will take the full force of Serbian anger and revenge. The bombing will be counter-productive. If the real motive is to stop the ethnic cleansing, it will fail. It will increase it. And there is another issue. To 'neutrals' in other parts of the world, we will be seen as the big bully boys having another bash at the little people. In the past nine months, we have bombed Afghanistan and Khartoum and we are still bombing Iraq, all without the desired effect. And it has all been done independently of the U.N., while we bomb Iraq for not obeying the U.N.

All these things I believed and wanted to say, but I didn't and that made me feel a wimp and a weed. I didn't say it because it would be thought disloyal by some and arrogant by others and because all of them would think it was politicising the pulpit. Also, I don't want to appear to support the scandalous Milosevic, and a lot of people might interpret it that way. So I kept quiet on the matter, and hated myself for doing so, on the day that Jesus entered the occupied city of Jerusalem, in peace. This is how we fail Our Lord and make the Church irrelevant.

However, my silence had one good effect. The main Beaminster service had two Baptisms which drew a huge number of people who don't normally come to church. A sermon of any sort would have been difficult and a sermon on the issues of the day would have been completely out of place. Besides, Our Lord didn't preach once in Holy Week. I wish we followed that example. He acted great visual parables like riding a donkey into Jerusalem, taking a whip in the temple, washing feet in the Upper Room and Breaking Bread at the Last Supper. They were memorable acted parables, but with very few words. No preaching! Wise man, thank you. So as soon as the huge congregation was settled, I asked them to unsettle themselves and go out of the church into the spring sunshine and stand on the grassy bank, taking a palm cross with them. They made a wonderful sight, such as I imagine might have gathered on the hillside in Galilee to hear the teacher. Local workers and passers-by would have heard him. And that is how it was this morning. They had a goodly number of exotic tattoos with rings in odd places but, without exception, they held up their palm crosses for a blessing. And they listened to the Palm Sunday Gospel which I declaimed in my loudest voice, before we processed into church singing the great Palm Sunday hymns unaccompanied. I was impressed. A sermon would have been out of place and forgotten as soon as it was finished. But I am sure these images will stay in the mind a long while. It's the old adage, all over again: "What I hear, I forget; what I see, I remember; what I do, I believe." Jesus would never have heard that saying, but that is how he became the great teacher, and never more so than in the week of his Passion.

Monday in Holy Week

I should have been chairing the Strode Room managers this morning but I asked Jane Rose, the vice chair, to take over because there was no other time I could meet Mollie Betchley's daughter before tomorrow's funeral. I don't doubt Jane did it efficiently and without any fuss, as she always does. She is utterly reliable, which is why she is called on so much and by so many. She keeps trying to shed one responsibility or another in order to have a less complicated life but the reverse seems to happen; she gathers more responsibilities as a squirrel gathers nuts. And she seems to draw people's problems, like a magnet. She is easy to talk to and has some sort of sensitivity which people recognise. I can't put my finger on what it is and I don't suppose others can either. It's the sort of thing people look for in a priest and don't often find. At least they find it here in the church warden, which is the next best thing. The danger with someone like Jane is that she will be overloaded and will reach breaking point. We all know it was one extra straw that broke the camel's back. Anyway, she handled the Strode managers this morning and she was at the Eucharist this evening, so she survived that straw.

The afternoon in Broadwindsor Church was unusual. Several people among the ninety who had been attending the Lent course felt the need to stop the talking and start the silence. I thought that was long overdue and deserved encouragement, so I found myself leading it. Silence isn't a matter of just sitting there, doing nothing. It needs guiding and it needs a focus, especially if it is to last two hours, as planned. So Arthur

Bowbeer had made a rough cross and laid it in the sanctuary and others had surrounded it with night lights. Anne Ward arranged some Taizé music to play in the background, quietly, for two minutes in each twenty. Dorothy Shiner had arranged for the five Bible readings used in the five sections of the course to be read, one every twenty minutes and I had agreed to introduce each theme, and close it prayerfully. It takes a lot more preparation to speak for one minute than it does to speak for ten minutes. But it is a very good discipline which we should practise more. We forget that the longest of Our Lord's parables can be read in two minutes, yet we are still re-telling them and finding new thoughts in them, two thousand years later! So a good sermon does not have to be a long one. On the contrary, it is almost certain to be a short one. Most sermons I have heard would have been a lot better with half the words and half the time. We don't want to fall into the modern trap of "soundbite theology" but neither do we need to prolong the agony. We have been spoilt by the fact that we have a captive audience who, according to convention, neither question us nor challenge us. It hasn't done much for our own sharpness. And it makes it difficult to know whether we are communicating or not. It wasn't like that when I cut my teeth at St. Francis School. With those boys, I knew within thirty seconds whether there was rapport or not. And I learnt how to shut up quickly when the rapport was not there. Those addresses, twice a week for seven years, probably helped me more than them. Anyway, the call at Broadwindsor was for brevity today. And the surprise was that the two hours passed in a flash. I thought it a good and reflective way to start Holy Week and I hope it becomes a regular feature, year on year; and that the temptation to fill it with words is resisted.

The evening Eucharist at Beaminster was a refreshment. Dean David presided and read the first part of the great Passion narrative and I was able to sit in the congregation and drink it all in. How seldom can clergy do this! Tonight I could, and I did, and loved every minute. One of the troubles with clergy is that we are so used to doing things our own way that it isn't easy to sit and hear somebody else doing it their way. We criticise it and correct it, inwardly, instead of accepting it as refreshment.

A musician once told me that he couldn't bear going to other musicians' concerts because he spent the whole time spotting imperfections and by the end he was utterly depressed and frustrated. It was the reverse tonight. Hearing Dean David was a refreshment and left me with the hope that I am as clear, calm and recollected as he is, when I preside. And the other refreshment was that I could sit, cross-legged on the floor, to pray and to listen. That posture helps me. That is how I always pray in my room. At the altar, I can't do that. So the first day of Holy Week has been refreshing. But it won't be so pleasant tomorrow. Mollie's funeral, followed by cremation and interment of ashes will dominate the day and I will try again to see John Wright in Yeovil Hospital, without getting another parking ticket. Joan will be the loser – again. She is due into Dorchester Hospital for another check under anaesthetic, and there is no way I can take her. She will have to ask friends from work.

Tuesday in Holy Week

A lot of people came to Mollie Betchley's funeral, as I expected. This was guaranteed by her own large family, but there were also old Beaminsterians who had known her from childhood and the many friends she had made in 76 years in one place. She had chosen all the hymns and had left various notes and markings in her prayer books, including a prayer she had written herself. Sometimes we do not realise how deeply rooted the faith is. She seldom came to church but she held fast to the faith. There are those who think that is not possible. I know it is. If the Kingdom is only for church-goers, it will be very dull. Many of the signs of the Kingdom which I see are outside the Church and that doesn't surprise me because most of the signs of the Kingdom that Jesus saw were outside the Jewish 'church' of his day.

After the cremation, I went on to Yeovil Hospital, found a parking place and tracked down John Wright at last. He was still trying to make light of a sorry story, but there isn't much light to make of it. He has been in and out of hospitals (mostly in) for more than three years, during which time he has had both legs amputated and various other operations. Now he has bed sores, allegedly because Dorchester

Hospital gave him the wrong sort of mattress. The doctor called while I was there and said he wanted a second opinion and he was consulting another doctor – whose name I missed. "Oh no," said John, "not him again." "Why? Do you know him?" asked the first doctor. "Know him! Every time he sees me, he cuts another bit of me off," said John. The first doctor crept away rather sheepishly and I was surprised he didn't have all the medical records at hand in such a complicated case. I stayed a while and heard that Gwen still came in to see him every day but that she had damaged the car on the way in yesterday and it was being taken away for repair today. The church car service would come to the rescue, I hoped. "They're marvellous," said John. "Gwen has never been without someone." That is a tribute to Colin Cuff's organisation and it was good to think we are doing something positive, useful and effective especially for John who played the organ in so many of our churches and for Gwen who has masterminded Beaminster's flowers for every wedding and every festival for the last ten years! If we can't do something for them, we should pack up shop. I could see John was still trying to smile, in spite of everything. Some people's resilience leaves me filled with admiration and always wondering 'How would I cope?' I daren't even think about that.

Joan had driven from Beaminster to Yeovil and on to Sherborne so that I could take her to Dorchester for her latest tests. We arrived at the hospital at the required time but there was no way I could wait three or four hours and no way she could drive home after anaesthetic. Jenny, her head of department at school, offered to do it, which was a sign of grace but it meant Joan would be returned to Sherborne and not to me. As I would be in church, that didn't make much difference. While at the hospital, I tried to visit Dorothy Storey but the receptionist insisted she had gone home. I didn't believe it because the same receptionist had been wrong on my last two visits, but I decided not to make an issue of it and thanked her for her help. When I returned home, I phoned Edward Storey to find out the truth and, surprise surprise, she was home. Just as well I didn't make an issue of it. Even so, I was only just back in time to inter Mollie's ashes. A couple of dozen family came, staying with her right to the end.

In the evenings of Holy Week, Hooke always has the late night service of Compline. It is a very short service of prayers and psalms, with an evening hymn. It takes about 15 minutes and it amazes me that so many people come, some travelling to get there for more time than the service lasts. Tonight I thought I would make their journey more worthwhile by adding the Gospel of the day, which was a short passage from Saint John about some Greeks who wanted to see Jesus. Afterwards, two or three people asked me why that Gospel had been chosen for Holy Week. "Why not a part of the Passion?" they asked. Why indeed? I thought. No doubt the compilers of this new lectionary are profound thinkers who have their reasons. Perhaps one day it will become clear to us lesser mortals.

It was a relief at the Beaminster service which followed to hear the Passion narrative and there is no doubt that is what the people expect to hear in Holy Week. If Beaminster had obeyed the new lectionary, they wouldn't have had it at all. God may move in a mysterious way, but He ain't got nothing on the people who produced this book.

Anyway, Joan is back in Sherborne and O.K., but she has to go in again on Thursday. Oh, no! That is when I have to be in Salisbury at the cathedral service, so I won't be able to take her then either.

Wednesday in Holy Week

Two worries afflict me, every time I start to prepare Holy Week addresses, Good Friday devotions or Easter celebrations. I don't know if other clergy suffer the same afflictions. I hope they do.

The first affliction centres on the awful theology that surrounds Good Friday and Our Lord on the Cross. Are we going to tell the world that God the Father needed, or desired, a sacrifice – and a human one at that? That he demanded blood to be spilled to pay the price of sin? Did God the Father really need to be placated, and have his anger appeased? Is this what we will tell the world about God and about his fatherhood?

This is primitive in the extreme.

If I thought God was like that, I might fear him but I wouldn't love him; I might recognise his power but I wouldn't want to spend eternity (or even a few hours) with him. It will be sad if in the Holy season we again show the world a primitive God with tendencies to tyranny and sadism, a despot to dread.

The language of sacrifice, ransom, paying the price of sin and appeasing God's wrath – which must have meant something once – will now only serve to align our God with medieval notions of punishment and terror, or the violence of divine retribution more usually associated with corrupted forms of Islam.

When the cross is lifted high, isn't it enough to thank God that our at-one-ment with him – begun with the loving gift of creation, confirmed by his loving presence among us, and completed by his return to the Father – was revealed on the first Good Friday, for all the world to see? Yet blood sacrifice and ransom theology will be all the rage in some places this week. Ugh!

The second affliction centres on the tradition of associating the Resurrection of Christ with the Exodus from Egypt, as if both revealed the ways of God. I hope not. The Exodus from Egypt, which we are expected to read at such length on Easter Eve, reveals God as the most violent sort of racist who would be put in prison today for incitement, and rightly so. Yet people hear it (or do they switch off?) and don't seem to see the horrific sort of God it reveals. Yet it makes my stomach churn. When Moses leads the Hebrews out of Egypt and God divides the waters of the Red Sea so that his favourites can pass over on dry land while all the others sink to the bottom, what sort of a God is revealed? Some say it shows the Lord "strong and mighty in battle". Others think it reveals God as a racist nationalist whose philosophy of extermination as the final answer aligns him with Adolf Hitler more than with Jesus Christ. And worse is to come when Joshua enters the Promised Land and the massacres begin in earnest with God cheering him on. This portrayal of God as militarist, violent, ruthless and tyrannical makes both Saddam Hussein and Slobodan Milosevic look like very modest gentlemen.

I have two hopes as we read these Easter texts yet again. One is that the people who hear them are wise enough to let the readings drift over them like a passing cloud. The second hope is that they disturb and afflict other clergy as much as they disturb and afflict me. If they do, we may achieve a third hope which is that the Church will eventually refute these texts as revealing anything about God. What they do reveal is something horrific about racism, nationalism and the nature of man.

With these things in mind, I prepared all eight 'Stations of the Cross' for Good Friday. I am only expecting to do the first station but I always live in fear of someone not turning up or being taken ill at the last minute so, for peace of mind, I prepare all eight. It is particularly necessary this year because the new Catholic priest hasn't said 'yes' to attending, and he hasn't said 'no'. For the past fifteen years, the Catholics have come and have covered four of the stations. It has been good to be together but I can't take it for granted under a new regime. I have 'phoned him and delivered the full texts, but no reply so far. He is so charming when we do speak that I find it hard to believe he won't come and do his full part. Perhaps he will have a better office system by next year. I will 'phone him again first thing in the morning, before I take off to Salisbury, because I must know one way or the other.

Maundy Thursday

I wonder if the Bishop knows the amount of effort which is required of his clergy to join him in the cathedral in the midst of Holy Week? I can understand his wish for us to attend. It gives every priest the chance to focus beyond the parochial which might otherwise become all-absorbing, and that is good. It brings us all together, as priests, once in the year to worship with our Bishop, and that is good. Incidentally, it must make quite an impact on anyone who chanced to be around the Close. The procession of clergy was so long it took ten minutes to get into the cathedral! But these things happen at a cost. I had to leave home before the post came, to catch the 8.35 a.m. from Crewkerne, and the return train wouldn't get me back home until 4 p.m. Then there would be the post waiting to be answered before our own Evening service. I would have preferred not to go but, with both David and Rose unfit, the Beaminster absence would look as if we were disloyal, which we are not. So I went. At least I could read on the train, one hour each way.

We robed in the Chapter House, seemingly hundreds of us, and several impressions struck me. First, we are incredibly fat; a solemn promise to diet might have been more to the point than renewing our ministry vows for the umpteenth time. This excess of weight must say something about our lifestyle, and it can't be good. Second, the number of women seemed to have multiplied since we last met. I had the strong feeling that before long women vicars will be the norm and men the exception. The roles will have been reversed within a generation. This may be exactly what the Church needs, but it may not. The third thing that struck me was the generally doleful and down-beat atmosphere we created. Perhaps the others shared my misgivings and wondered whether the journey was really necessary. Jeremy Davies, the precentor, tried to lighten the mood with a briefing about the music and that lifted things a little, but not a lot.

The service sheet revealed what we were in for. Not only communion but also the renewal of vows, the blessing of the oils for the sick, the

Chrism, and for something else. Why three different oils? And why must the Bishop bless them? Has he a secret power denied the rest of us? There are dangers down that path. As I turned the pages, I wondered about catching my return train. "This could take two hours," I said to my neighbour in the procession. "No," he replied. "George Carey has said he wants shorter, sharper services. It will be over in an hour, you see." In the event, I was nearer the mark than he was, by a long way.

I was pleased to see a nave altar with the bishop on a raised dais for all to see. The Bishop of Sherborne was also there, mitred, but on a lower level and he didn't appear to speak at any point. That was not a message about Collegiate Episcopate; it looked more like an Episcopal curacy. I expected the singing to be superb, but it wasn't. Several of the hymns were new to me and I wasn't helped by the priest next to me whose voice was more raucous than tuneful. He bellowed so strongly that I went completely silent and noticed that others nearby were not singing either. I may not lead my Sunday congregations well in music, but at least I don't mislead them like that. I was looking forward to the bishop's sermon. It was unnecessarily delayed by having three readings instead of two but eventually the bishop's opportunity to address all his clergy arrived. He told a very good story from De Mello. I knew it, but that didn't matter at all. It was memorable, funny and profound and took two minutes to tell. Just like our Lord. I was pleased, very pleased, to have such a bishop. Then I realised to my dismay that was not the end, but the beginning. He stood up and started ... and continued and continued and continued. I couldn't follow the thread, no matter how hard I tried. I suppose there was a thread, possibly about music. Certainly it ended with an appeal to sing his Rimsky Korsakov setting of the Lord's Prayer, in every part of the diocese. In fact when we reached that point, an hour later, it wasn't well sung at all. The only good thing was that the fellow next to me didn't even try to sing it, which was a relief. I made my little effort but had the feeling that this tune won't set the diocese alight, or do much for the Kingdom.

My conclusion is that it was good to be there, the choreography was excellent. But I had the uncomfortable feeling that in a changing Church of England I am now on the margins.

Our own Maundy Thursday effort in the evening was a little simpler, but we kept to the idea of all the ministerial Team robed and together round the altar. David was missing, suffering his wretched illness at home, but the rest of us were there. Rose made a welcome return and read the Gospel, Lilian read the Pauline version of the Last Supper, Ros and Richard administered the chalice, Fred served the altar and David Shearlock preached in a clear, sharp style and prayed similarly. We ended with the lights dimmed, my colleagues stripping all three altars, while I read the 22nd psalm, and the people left the dark church in silence. It was over in 50 minutes and I hope and believe it was a quietly acted parable which prepared us properly for tomorrow.

Good Friday

The country tradition on Good Friday is to put the potatoes in, not to go to church. I learnt that in my first year when all the village churches were locked on Good Friday and resisted the invitation to pray. "Friday?" said Harry Hardwill, who was a farmer and also the Blackdown 'chapel warden'. "A service on Good Friday? You'll be wanting to bring us beds down next," he said, and so there was no Good Friday service. And twenty years later there are still only six of the fourteen churches which have a Good Friday congregation.

There had been just as much surprise in Beaminster when a Maundy Thursday service was introduced. "What for?" asked Bob Travers, the church warden. "To commemorate the Last Supper," said I. "Don't we do that every Sunday?" he said, and that was the end of the matter for him, and he never did come. But a dozen or so did, and it has grown to a regular seventy or so. It was a similar story on Good Friday. Beaminster had a single hour, Evensong, and the Church Council thought the introduction of the Three Hours was excessive. Yet the Stations of the Cross in the first hour always brings more than a hundred people, and today it was nearer two hundred. But the people who come are not the older country folk. They are putting the potatoes in, or cutting the grass. The growth in Holy Week congregations reflects the changing population in the countryside, more than a growth in devotion. It still puzzles me that so many devout country folk who seldom miss a Sunday service never appear on Good Friday. Perhaps I shouldn't be so surprised because the old Book of Common Prayer didn't provide an Order for Good Friday and those traditions have roots, even deeper than the potatoes.

So it wasn't a great surprise that the Mosterton congregation at the 10 a.m. Devotional Hour was only a dozen. I read the Passion from the Authorised Version and the Litany from the Book of Common Prayer and offered a four minute thought on the criminal's prayer from his cross "Jesus, remember me ..." I've never heard an address on that theme. Those other crosses seem to have been completely ignored. Anyway, his words have become my favourite prayer. In all the confusions and complexities, I can at least manage that. It is only three words. "Jesus, remember me ..." No need for any more than that. I like the idea that it was first offered by a convict. It makes me feel that, whatever I have done, it can be my prayer. So I valued the hour and, with Joan's hot cross buns in between, I was nicely prepared for The Three Hours.

The Catholics came and the priest brought a chaplain with him, who carried the cross while we moved around the eight stations. This year the crowd was so big that none of us could move very much. Thank goodness I moved a hundred chairs to the side yesterday or there would have been no space at all today. I never quite understand the appeal of the stations, but it is hugely successful. Is it because the eight paintings make a visual aid? Is it because the standing and walking make a small identification with Our Lord's last journey? Is it because we do it only once a year? I don't know.

In the past, the second hour has always been the thinnest of the three. Not today. At least seventy people attended the presentation of readings by Celia Smith and Alastair Bannerman which accompanied the music of Gillian Ashwood and the singing of Colin Smith. It was the best hour I have attended on any of the Good Fridays. Its portrayal of slavery and man's longing for freedom, related with the Passion of Christ, the universal man, was brilliant. Colin Smith's voice filled the church as he sang the old Negro Spirituals; his wife, Celia, quiet by contrast, articulated every word of her gruesome readings; Alastair declaimed the scriptural passages and Gillian played the piano, both with the sensitivity of the true professionals they are. We are lucky that such talent has come to Beaminster, and at least seventy or so people appreciated it. Not so long ago, the church would have been locked at that hour!

I missed the third hour at which David sang the whole Litany at Evensong. He said the number of people was very small. A few years ago, it was far the strongest of the Three Hours. The change might be the growing popularity of the other hours but I have my own theory. A couple of years ago, Richard Legg introduced the Good Friday Liturgy from the new Services for Holy Week authorised by the Liturgical Commission. We were invited to venerate the cross and to receive the sacrament at Holy Communion, a clear break with long-standing custom. The people didn't expect it and, although very few complained, they have voted with their feet ever since at that hour, even though we restored Evensong the following year. The reformers don't always consider the strength or the value of local custom. Liturgical reformers in particular seem so convinced that they know best and so scornful of all others. Richard had been adamant that the Mass must be celebrated on Good Friday and that Evensong had had its day. It has now.

Easter Eve, or Holy Saturday

This is my panic day. It is impossible to think about Easter Day until Good Friday is over and that gives one day for all the preparations, including the sermons.

I did my best to visit every church but only reached eight of them. In some, the flower ladies were still at work; in others it was all done and the peacefulness was sweet-smelling.

I telephoned all the retired priests to make sure they were fit and well and ready for action. It was meant to encourage them but, as always, they encouraged me.

No one else seemed to be in a panic, only me. The churches were extremely well organised and ready for action. I wasn't. The way the systems click into operation is impressive. No one appears to give orders, but it all gets done. Everyone appears to know their role. Any army commander would be proud. If the military analogy is pressed, I would probably rank as the General, but I am entirely redundant, at least in the preparations. I suppose I come into my own tomorrow. And I am not ready. The General should be ready, and I am not. The General should know what all the troops are doing, and I haven't a clue. I think I had better abandon the military analogy.

One thing I do know – no matter how good or bad the General, the work will all be done by morning, and not by me. They are wonderful, one and all. And it is all done for love, no one gets a penny reward. They are models for this greedy rapacious modern world. Even if there were no services tomorrow, something excellent would have happened.

For the priest, the greatest bonus will not be in the flowers, no matter how they please the congregation. The greatest blessing for me is that all I need to do is arrive and take the service. Margaret Grant, the sacristan always arrives one hour before the service and leaves one hour after (that means thirty hours this week) and we know all will be in order. Every book will be in the right place, opened at the right page. Every chalice will be polished, every wafer will be counted, every candle will be lit, every chair will be in place, every vestment and book marker will be in the colour of the season, every leaflet will be distributed, the registers will be open, the pen will be ready and if I was in a cathedral I would not be better cared for. Margaret learnt all these things at a great Croydon church and she has kept up-to-date; she knows every ceremony – and its requirements – far better than I do. She never has to ask me what should be done, though I often have to ask her, and she always knows. All these things are good, but the best is yet to come. She does it all without a moment's fuss. The priest may arrive in a rush and a panic but within a minute the urgency will be gone because he will realise everything is under calm control and he can concentrate on his part with nothing else to worry about. It is one gift to have all the know-how but it is another gift to use it wisely. Margaret has both gifts and uses them unfailingly every day of the year. A church needs a good many background workers. It is a help to have an efficient secretary, a diligent church warden, a wise treasurer but the gift of grace above all the others is to have a sacristan who knows her stuff and is devout with it.

Easter Day, 4th April

If numbers mattered to me, I would be a happy man tonight. The stories coming in from all the parishes are of bigger Easter congregations than ever. They do not tally with the media view repeated all year round like a mantra that the Church of England is in terminal decline. Not here. The tiny church at Burstock is typical. The minutes of its meetings show that at the Annual Vestry in 1957 the vicar rebuked both church wardens for failing to attend the Easter Day service when the congregation had been nil. The story today is of sixty people in Burstock Church. This is not the sort of story the press bother with. At least I shall record it, because it is true.

If numbers were my game, I would sleep well tonight. But they aren't, and I won't sleep well because two things have irked me, even in the midst of the Alleluias.

The first thing is – we have stretched our resources beyond the limit in order to provide a priest in every church so that Holy Communion can be celebrated. Fifteen churches and fifteen services of Holy Communion. Canon Law has been met and the faithful have received their Easter Communion. We've used two priests in their nineties and two other retired priests have doubled their services, and we've managed to do it. But we haven't provided anything else. Holy Communion, fifteen times, and that's all. If you were confirmed, there was something for you. If you were not confirmed, there was nothing for you. This can not be right if we still want to be called the church of the nation. We have made ourselves an exclusive sect of communicants. We are meant to be the inclusive church of the nation. We have turned confirmation into the password. It isn't. Baptism is the mark of membership. A quick calculation estimates that 30% of our villagers are confirmed. This means that 70% are excluded. Of our 600 school children, about 30 will be confirmed, which means 95% will be excluded in the future. This cannot continue! There is a fundamental flaw. And the fundamental flaw is placing the extra hurdle of confirmation in the way. Baptism is the sign of membership, and the communion table should be open to the baptised. We would then become again the inclusive church of the nation instead of the exclusive sect of the confirmed.

The second thing which irks me is this – the resurrection is too easily treated in a simplistic way, almost as if it is the happy ending to a fairy story. In fact Godson Kilele, when he was five, said "and did he live happily ever after?" when I told him the Easter story. The hymns also encourage the simplistic. At all my services today, I had to endure my un-favourite hymn "The strife is o'er, the battle done." The churches were full and the people sang most lustily but the day after tomorrow, we will be burying 38 year old Bernadette, a mother of two, and her children will be in the front row, aged 4 and 8. How dare we sing "The strife is o'er"; it is an insult to that family. In my mind are the pilots bombing the Serbs and the Kosovans fleeing their homeland. How dare we sing "the battle is done." It's an insult to every refugee and every victim of injustice in the world. These 'Alleluias' are all very well in the golden spring of secure West Dorset, but what do they mean in most of the suffering world? Besides, this resurrection is no simple matter. When the former Bishop of Durham (Dr. Jenkins) asked what sort of resurrection body Jesus had, the faithful felt threatened and didn't answer. But the question should be faced. What sort of body passes through walls when the door is locked (as in the Upper Room), is not recognised by his followers (on the Emmaus Road), or even by his closest admirer (Mary Magdalene at the tomb)? What sort of body is it that "disappeared from their sight" at Emmaus and was not recognised at Galilee? Did the body de-materialise at Emmaus; was it a phantom in the Upper Room? The Easter congregations should be challenged with these questions because the world needs an answer. My faith lies in the fact that the risen body still carried the scars of the crucifixion. Thomas felt them. They were real. So are the scars we carry. Bernadette's children next Tuesday will bear those scars all life long. Those Kosovans, and all other refugees, will not be cured by Alleluias, however loudly they are sung. They will continue to carry their scars, all life long. John Bunyan got it right in Pilgrim's Progress when Mr. Valiant-for-Truth declares as he is about to die "My marks and scars I carry with me, these are my trophies ..." This is a richer message than any number of Alleluias. The resurrection is not to be reduced to the magic of a fairy story, the nonsense of a "conjuring trick with bones." The resurrection proclaims that God will bring good out of ill. That is His way and that is good news for us all. Man may bring ill out of good, hence the crucifixion, but God will bring good out of ill, hence the resurrection. That's what it's all about.

In the afternoon, we dashed over to Sherborne with Easter eggs for our Godsons. Kilele wanted to go to the Youth Centre and play football on the tarmac. There were a few other teenagers there booting a ball about and after a while three of them came up and said "Give you a game..." So Kilele aged 8, Timothy aged 4, and I, aged 64, lined up against three youths aged about 16. We were soon a goal down and Timothy wandered off to "look at the daffodils." I don't blame him because, at the age of 4, the sight of these sixteen-year-olds bearing down on him at full speed must have been a bit off-putting. Soon Kilele and I were two down, and then three down. We had agreed to play 'first to five', so it didn't look as though it would last long, which was a relief because my hamstrings were seizing up and my calves seemed to have locked solid, at which point Kilele scored. "Come on, Uncle," he said. "We can win this." So I felt I had to do my best and, within a minute, Kilele had scored again. My lungs and most other parts were failing when the score reached four all. Kilele called his brother back from the daffodils. "Go in goal," he said, "and don't let the ball go past you." The game restarted and the youthful three stormed down on our goal, defended by Timothy, all alone. The trouble was, he was lying down, with his feet in the air and the ball went straight in the goal. We had lost. "Why did you lie down?" asked Kilele. "I ran out of petrol," said Timothy.

On the walk home, Timothy said

"Uncle, why are all the daffodils yellow?"

I passed the question to Kilele.

"Because God painted them all yellow," he said.

A little later on, Timothy enquired again

"Why don't we ever see God painting them all yellow?"

I passed the question to Kilele again.

"That's because he paints them at night," he said.

We walked on a little further, until Timothy said

"If God paints them at night, how can he see them?"

There was a long silence, and I was thankful Kilele was dealing with the matter. Eventually, Kilele turned to me.

"Uncle," he said, *"why are all the daffodils yellow?"*

Oh mysteries! They fire the imagination, they are the food of poets and the stuff of romance. Oh! Soul-less day when we solve the mysteries and look up the answers on the Internet.

So I will sleep well tonight, after all. Not because the churches were full but because why the daffodils are yellow, like the resurrection, remains a mystery.